Splicing the light

To Nancy

One of the great

human beings in my life!

John Stewart

J. D. Stewart

Note for Librarians: A cataloguing record for this book is available from Library and Archives Canada at www.collectionscanada.ca/amicus/index-e.html

Printed in Victoria, BC, Canada.

ISBN: 978-1-4251-2546-2

10 9 8 7 6 5 4 3 2

Chapter One
A Conversation with God

He was just a North American, a fucked up garden-variety neurotic with dreams of glory, swimming in cliché. But oh the sadness, the chestheavy weight of it, the laboured breath and the sweet, sweet righteousness of the moment, as free of bullshit as his life was crammed to capacity with it. In an odd sort of way, it was almost restful.

"So, I'm going to do this God, just in case you give a shit." He put the stopper in the tub of the bathroom he shared with ten others in the rooming house and turned on the taps. The sound was like a kind of small rumbling thunder. Perfect. "Knock and it shall be opened. Isn't that what you promised, you bastard? You fucking liar." The tub was an old porcelain thing on claw legs. He released a stream of strawberry bubblebath gel into the torrent, foam swirling in the backwash and bubbles, spreading out deep and dense. "I will not ask more of you than you can bear. Well I guess this kind of indicates that you've been asking more than that for a long time now doesn't it? More than what? More than we can endure and not go crazy? Bull fucking shit! Are you getting this? Oh brother, what a fool I've been. A loving god would not do this. You have given me an unlivable life." His voice was cold and hard with a strange sense of distance to it. The voice of one embarked on a journey to which he had already surrendered the best way he knew how.

He had a sense for surrender. Playing cowboys with his friends as a child, he was always the one to die. He died well, fell from trees and porches, hills and stairways with great abandon. He was good at it, and often ended up in racking sobs over his own imagined dilemmas. Poignancy was a thing he understood well from an early age. He spoke its language, understood its timing and nuance. Sadness made him feel less alone among the others. *"Maybe this time, on my twenty-second birthday,"* he thought, *"I can do it right."* He went down the dark hall to his flat and

returned with the sacraments of his final farewell. A tape deck
with old Chopin nocturnes. Two bottles of red Hungarian wine.
A Rosenthal glass with a narrow stem flaring to a wide base. A
rigging knife of the kind used by sailors to cut lines of various
kinds. Locking blade on one side and a marlin spike on the other.
It was a mean looking thing, pitted with nicks in the once sharp
edge. He could not use a razor. Too neat and functional. It would
not make the statement he needed to make. Anyway, he was
squeamish about the sharpness of razors. He could get his mind
around the notion of dying but not around the impersonality of a
blade that sharp. No one would bother him. The Greek black belt
down the hall would be at his karate studio for hours yet. The
young programmer for the University of Toronto's radio station
would be dishing up Stockhausen or some other
incomprehensible atonal shit into the wee hours and the squeeze
trumpet player had disappeared.

For two weeks, mail had been piling up for him on the
radiator downstairs. Only Mr. Bender, the absentee landlord,
dropping in unannounced to check on things, might get in the
way. But Jackie didn't care about anything anymore. He was sure
of that. Not anymore. Not for other people, not for himself. Not
even for the thoughts in his own mind or the feelings in his own
heart. They were as unworkable and unlivable as anything could
be. That much he knew. So, he turned on the tape, poured himself
a glass, locked the door, put the white painted chair beside the
tub and delicately, almost reverently, placed the knife, glass,
bottles, candles and tape deck on it. Still the water came crashing
down. He could feel the tumult of it through the soles of his feet.
Something was missing. He could afford to forget now. What
good had any remembering of any kind, ever done him? He
locked the door, dropped his clothes in a heap on the floor and
stepped into the hot water. He had heard that if the water was hot
enough and the cut made underwater, a person would feel
nothing.

The tub was almost full now and as he sank to the bottom, he
remembered the matches. "Shit" he said and struggled to his feet,
turning off the taps. "I will lift mine eyes unto the hills from
whence cometh my help" he muttered to the empty room. His
mind in a quickening downward spiral, he unlocked the door,
walked buck-naked down the hall to his room again. It had

grown dark outside and he had left the lights on. To his mind, the light spilling out beneath the door shone like teeth through a smile. Just like teeth through a smile. Just for a second, he thought about getting his writing book and recording the image, but said simply "bullshit," entered and retrieved a pack of matches from the kitchen counter.

On his way out, the phone rang. "You'll have to do better than that" he said to the empty room, "no proxies, no stand-ins, no symbols, no fucking metaphors. You show me how this is fucking possible" and the tears started to flow as a choking lump rose in his throat. Again and again the phone rang. "No, no more" he said and walked back to the bathroom leaving the door to all of his earthly possessions wide open behind him. He would allow himself no last minute savior, no cavalry coming over any hill. He wanted the word of God, clear and unequivocal there and then in a shitty run down rooming house, on a planet turning in the immensity of His doing. For Jakie felt God's presence everywhere and the indisputable fact that not once had his creator ever acknowledged him, was driving him, literally, insane. Either his perception of the divine was wrong, or for reasons of his own, God just wasn't talking, and if God would show him no mercy, he would have no mercy on himself.

Locking the door behind him, he lit the candle, turned off the lights and ran the water again, sliding under the frosting of bubbles. He was unprepared for the silence that took shape in the room as he turned off the water. It was as soft, still and there as a breath held. The drops that fell from the faucet echoed incongruously bright and light amid the reckoning. "We are made in the image and likeness of God, it says" he droned, and the reproach in his voice was unmistakable, "ya, ya, ya." He poured himself another glass and this time drank it all straight down, pouring another immediately and swallowing that, too, as fast as he could. The thick candle was stuck to the bottom of a cheap glass ashtray, ornate drippings piled layer on layer spreading out to the edges. How many heartfelt conversations with his fellow university students had passed over its flame he wondered as he leaned over and turned on the tape deck. Number one in C sharp Minor, Rubinstein's touch so supple, so impossibly young and tender. The notes falling to the last slow drops from the faucet. Jackie looked at the cover photo. He had gray hair, his face wrinkled and the posture stiff. Where did he find the brilliance to balance the power and the gentleness?

Jackie poured another glass, spilling a little in the process. The wine, deep red in the bottle, taking on a sinister rusty hue as it swirled into a small area free of bubbles, the swirls staying together as though unwilling to mix with the water. "For we are fearfully and wonderfully made" he sighed picking up the knife and examining its scarred and weathered exterior, opening the blade until it locked into place with a loud snap that resonated a moment in the room and was gone. Then he worked his fingers under the marlinespike and pried it open until it too snapped open to the other end. How many seemingly impossible knots had he induced to give and then let go with its help? If only God would enter his life with a vision or a word as penetrating as this shining piece of pointed steel and work the knots of his being out. But Jackie knew that you only take the knots out of things you care about. Things you intend to keep. Things you intend to use. He knew he had been abandoned and to make things worse, almost laughable, he suspected God had abandoned him for being himself. Conundrum. Catch 22.

He drained the glass and poured another, this time pouring wine into the water. It wasn't like the movies. Still, when they found him, it would be grizzly enough. He hoped he could get drunk enough to do it. Drunk enough to stop thinking, drunk enough to do what he really wanted to do. He held up his arm and turned it over, bringing the blade to his wrist. He had heard somewhere that people who were serious didn't slash across, cutting tendons and God knows what else as they went. No, better to enter the veins and cut up the forearm for a few inches along a vein. He pressed down slowly with the blade, surprised at how far down the skin went without yielding. The pain was as clear as any music. Clearer. Much, much clearer. In his present condition, he would never be able to do it. He could not even draw blood, and pulling the blade up his forearm, left behind only a searing white trail like a paper cut.

And then it was some moments later and he had been somewhere with the music. And the music was so beautiful. Jackie wondered how anyone could contain it or even be a conduit for it. He did not want it to be beautiful. Beauty was a reason to live. Perhaps if he was drunker.

By the time the first bottle was finished the sun had come out from behind the clouds. It found the mirror over the sink and began to stream directly onto the bath and the formations of bubbles. As it did, each bubble became a fleeting prism, a tiny rainbow of exquisite colour. More beauty. There and gone, there and gone. There and gone. Jackie held his hands out and eclipsed a portion of the rainbow show. Anger was welling up within him and rage. It seemed to him that he did not even have as much chance of truly being as a bubble in a rooming house bubble bath. Soon, he was sitting there guzzling straight from the bottle, pathetically slashing at the tiny pretty bubbles and sobbing and the more he slashed, the more bubbles there were to slash.

When old man Bender found him after looking in through the keyhole, he was sure he was dead. Red in the tub. Knife on the floor. Head tilted off to one side and the water ice cold. One bottle of wine on the floor and another nearly empty one floating in the clear water.

"Jeesus Christ you scare me" he said as Jackie came around "I am thinking here is everything blood and dead body. For Chrissakes what are you doing anyway? The whole place stink of wine and you stupid drunk. What are you doing with a knife in here anyway?" Jackie mumbled something about trying to fix something, but the old man was not convinced. "I got a good mind to kick you out of here. This is a shared bathroom. Shared. What is everyone else supposed to do?" As he spoke, Jackie pulled himself to his feet and stumbled toward the door. "Are you crazy or something?" the old man bellowed "You can't walk around the hallway like that. What has gotten into you?" With that, he picked up Jackie's jeans from the floor and threw them at him. Jackie leaned against the wall, a sardonic smile on his face and started to put them on.

"Backwards, you idiot. You are putting them backwards on." By now his Germanic sense of order and propriety was strained to the limit. "Verdammt, other way, other way."

"Oh ya" Jackie squeaked with a giggle. With his right leg in, he spun the jeans to the left to where there was no leg.

"Oh shit" shouted Bender, throwing him a towel. "Here." Jackie wrapped it around his waist over the jeans which fell to the floor and headed for the door, dragging them. On the way through, he turned to the old man.

"We are fearfully and wonderfully made" he said lifting his arms into the air, rolling his wrists and sweeping the fingers of both hands in a fanned arc in toward each other until the backs of the hands almost touched and out again. A kind of slow motion starburst of the flesh that completely disarmed the old man, a movement as full of grace as his voice was of despair and acceptance. The old man didn't know whether to hit him or laugh.

"Shut up and go to your room!" was the best he could manage. "Try not to break anything. I will deal with you tomorrow."

The next week passed and the old man never said a thing. Not a word. Passing in the hall, the two continued to exchange pleasantries as though nothing had happened. From the beginning of the second week, however, Jackie began checking the mail as soon as the postman had delivered it. One day, there was a large, thick gray and green envelope there addressed to him. The Carlyle Institute of Psychiatry's stylized flourish like Zen brush work trailing down to the right from the name and then slightly, but undeniably upward. Nervously, he stared at it for a moment before picking it up. Anxious and elated, he fumbled up the stairs to his room, tearing at the paper. There were several pages. A green sheet titled simply Gender Identity Clinic, a letter addressed to him with a bold faced sentence in the first paragraph requesting him to fill out the enclosed questionnaire, write his "life history", and provide two photographs, one cross-dressed if possible. The last pages constituted the questionnaire itself.

Chapter Two
The Carlyle

Jackie couldn't figure out if he was a success or a failure as the sliding doors of the Carlyle opened to a mechanical hum before him. He thought of "One Flew Over the Cuckoo's Nest," newspaper articles on crazy people, a first year psych course he had taken, myriad thoughts and images about madness. The Gender Identity Clinic was on the third floor.

"May I help you?" the middle-aged receptionist asked as she slid back the glass pane. Jackie told her he was there for the gender assessment interviews. "Yes, Mr. Northam" she continued "Please take a seat here and fill out these forms." She ushered him into a small room with a table and one chair. "Someone will be with you shortly." There it was again. At the sound of his own name, his heart had sunk like a rock. Not at Northam, at Mister.

"It's an identity clinic, and they have already made decisions about me" he thought to himself. *"What's the point then?"* There were several pages of questions. As he read yet another in the hot stuffiness, "Have you ever had the urge to have sex with animals?" From somewhere above, he distinctly heard screaming, rhythmic, terrified screaming. Then it faded away. For a moment, he wondered if they still used electro shock therapy. He wouldn't allow them to do that. "Have you ever wanted to have sex with small children?" He continued to tick off the "no" boxes impatiently. "Have you ever thought of hurting yourself?" He answered "yes."

"Come on, come on" he thought. *"Ask me, get to it."*

"Have you ever tried to commit suicide?" He ticked "yes" and the pencil went through the page. A lump was rising in his throat. More screams filtered in from somewhere.

"Just like a fucking movie" he thought. *"Figures. Come on, come on."*

"Have you ever thought you were a female?" Jackie leaned back in his chair, smiled grimly and inhaled long and slowly.

"Finally" he thought and a sweet warm feeling of joy filled him as he ticked "yes." For pages the questions came about his

sexual preferences, masturbation practices, clothing tastes, how he perceived himself and how he thought others perceived him. The last page asked him to complete some pictures that had only just been started. Two X's became the tail of an exotic angelfish, a straight line—the diameter line of a circle, a graceful, rising arch became a broken rainbow from which jagged pieces fell in tortured shapes into nothingness.

The hours and days that followed were a dizzying maelstrom for Jackie as he struggled to give the best answers he could to endocrinologists, psychologists and psychiatrists of various kinds. Some of it was humiliating as photographs were taken of his bra and panties placed in a neat pile on the floor. He almost walked out when a glass tube with wires attached was placed over his penis and he was presented with a stream of projected images from mincing males to voluptuous women to calm mountain scenes.

"Oh please" he thought as the pictures passed, *"get to it"* but they never did. They never did find the short circuit that his life had become. The uninvited thoughts and feelings firing off according to some agenda not of his making. The pictures were sexual or pastoral with nothing in between. So he sat there and endured and did not respond at all. The thing on his dick found nothing.

"So what exactly are you looking for?" Jackie asked.

"Please don't move around and just concentrate on the slides" the technician in the white coat replied sharply.

"Wait a minute" Jackie said, irritated, "I'm cooperating with all this, and you won't even tell me what's going on? This is pretty personal stuff you know."

"The doctors will explain everything after a while," was the only response.

In the cafeteria between appointments, Jackie watched the expressionless gazes of a collage of victims. The avoidance of eyes, the mutterings, the too loud voices, and the silent faces, the frightened, the confused, the hopeless patients bordered by the lineup of doctors at the cash. With certainty in their eyes and confidence in their words they seemed to Jackie to glisten like a vein of gold in a mass of something, somehow, less.

"I know nothing" he thought. *"At least I don't trust what I think I know. One moment I know from male, the next I know from female,*

mostly I know from somewhere in between. Oh fuck, leave me alone."
And he thought of how tired he had been from his earliest
memories. From sitting in his grade four class at Cranbrook
Elementary School staring wistfully to the private girl's school
across the street, Miss Tottingham's and wishing he was there.
Amazed at the power of the desire, how it tugged at every part of
his heart and how the feeling felt so oddly—old. There was no
other word for it. Old and panicky because it was a kind of
knowing, like he knew something he shouldn't. Mary Janes, navy
tights, a neatly pleated kilt, crisp white blouse and smart blazer.
The girls played with such abandon, so little holding on, so much
lightness, so little investment in outcome, so much joy in the
playing itself.

He saw himself arriving there in all his fraudulent maleness
and being welcomed, received and redeemed in their midst like a
long lost playmate and sister come home. And every minute that
he did not go, there was another minute of not being himself, a
precious moment that even at that age he knew could never be
reclaimed. How many nights had that part of him which lay
buried but conscious like a zombie in a coffin cried itself awake
into this his present? And so he sat there as the teacher tried to
improve his penmanship and the letters always started so
smoothly and always finished ugly.

He started wearing his sister's clothes. The first time he
looked at himself in the mirror wearing a black bikini top and
bottom, he just stood there astounded as though seeing himself
for the first time.

The last appointment at the clinic did not go well. Jackie
arrived at the reception window twenty minutes early. The glass
slid open. The glass slid closed. Half a minute passed. The glass
slid open.

"Doctor Yau cannot see you. The next appointment is in an
hour and a half. You can wait in reception or the cafeteria."

"What do you mean she can't see me? This appointment has
been booked for a long time. What's the reason?"

"No reason given. She just can't see you."

"That's outrageous. Is that the way you treat people around
here? You can't just refuse to see a person and not even say why.
If I don't get an explanation, I'm out of here." There was no
answer. Sometimes it was silence that bothered Jackie more than

anything. It was so...depowering...so...final. There was almost no defense against the good old silent treatment. "Okay" he said "could you please arrange for me to register a complaint with someone before I leave." He struggled to remain polite.

"You can talk to the main reception you passed on the way in." The glass slid shut.

Jackie waited a moment before walking over to the other side of the building. A nervous, tight looking woman with long dark hair and pinched features sat with slumped shoulders behind a counter marked "information."

"Hello" said Jackie. The woman's eyes narrowed as she looked up. In the warmest tones possible, he said "A doctor has just failed to keep an appointment with me and refused to give a reason, so I'm really upset. I'd like to speak to someone in charge to register a complaint before I leave. Can you tell me who I should speak to?" The answer surprised him.

"There really is no one and you don't have to get angry with me."

"I'm not angry with you and I'm speaking very calmly. There must be someone in the building who can register a complaint. No one should be treated this way. I can give my complaint here and be on my way, or I can send a letter to the department of health." With that, the woman sighed hugely and started thumbing through the Carlyle Directory. She picked up the phone, told someone that Jackie wanted to register a complaint, silently wrote Doctor Jonas, Aggression and Anxiety Clinic, 11th floor, room 111 on a piece of paper and thrust it at him.

"Thank you" Jackie responded and headed upstairs. As the elevator doors opened on the eleventh floor, he could see two women in ordinary business dress conferring at the end of a long hallway. Passing room 111, he could see that it was in darkness and no one was there. "Okay" he sighed and walked over to the women.

"Hi, they sent me up from downstairs. They just called up. Can you tell me where I can find Doctor Jonas?"

"I'm his secretary, but he's not here now. He's lecturing over at the university."

"Unbelievable, why would they send me up here?"

"I don't know."

"Look, all I want to do is register a complaint with someone in authority around here before I leave. Do you have any idea who I could talk to? There has to be someone."

"Sorry, I really don't know anyone."

"Well, who is the Director of the institute?"

"Doctor Pennington, but he will be tied up in a meeting for some time yet."

"Of course he will."

"I'm sorry?"

"Forget it. Thank you for your time. You know, if you people were out there in the business world, and couldn't perform this simple customer service function, you'd be out of business in a month."

"I'm sorry there just really isn't anyone you can talk to."

"What else is new?"

His heart pounding with anger, Jackie returned to the gender clinic's receptionist. The glass slid open.

"I would like to speak with Ms. Warner, the clinic secretary who set my appointments please. You sent me downstairs. Downstairs sent me upstairs, and the doctor who was supposed to be there, wasn't. You cannot treat people this way. I am not leaving until I have my scheduled appointment, a reason for cancelling it, or an apology. The dour receptionist disappeared for thirty seconds and reappeared with Dr. Yau who was all smiles and apology.

"Oh, come in, come in Mr. Northam. There has been a terrible confusion. I understood your appointment was cancelled. If you need an apology, I can apologize, someone certainly made a mistake."

"The appointment was with you, Dr. Yau. I accept your apology, but it is an extremely unprofessional way to treat a client." The meeting itself was actually quite uneventful, but was followed by four more with various psychologists. The last appointment was with Doctor Pennington, himself. He ushered Jackie into his office where a neatly dressed secretary in her sixties sat poised, pen in hand.

"Come in. Take a seat" he said with a grand sweeping gesture, showing the way to a chair placed between himself and the woman. "My name is Doctor Pennington, and I am the

Director of this facility" he said, but there was something very odd, almost surreal about the way he spoke. With each word, his anger rose, his words lengthening grotesquely. "I understand…" he said, staring not at Jackie but straight out the window, "that you feel that you have been…inconvenienced…this…morning." He spoke as one speaking to a complete idiot.

"*Oh my God*" thought Jackie, "*what's this?*"

"Well, I will have you know that this institution is considered to be one of the largest…" He was very loud now and an unexplainable passion was building, "…best known…" He began to turn in his chair "…psychiatric facilities of its …kind…in the world…and…" The cadence, articulation and stress in the doctor's speech were all so bizarre and unnatural that Jackie wondered, just for a moment if the whole thing was a stress test of some kind. See what the patient does when faced with a threatening situation. It was either that or…Suddenly the doctor, a full four feet away from Jackie, thrust hard with one of his legs propelling his wheeled office chair directly at Jackie with him in it matching the forcefulness of the charge with an intensifying of volume and anger and a bulging at the eyes "…and so I am VERY SORRY THAT THIS HAS NOT GONE AS YOU WOULD HAVE WISHED MR. NORTHAM BUT…"

"Back off" Jackie ordered looking him in the eye less than two feet away. "You are in my space and you are not going to bring that kind of aggression and that tone of voice into my space. Back off!" His eyes still bulging but without missing a beat, Doctor Pennington accordioned back to his former tone and posture, floating this time in wheeled effortlessness back to his desk.

"…we are doing the very best we can under very trying circumstances. Our budget has been reduced and yet the need for our services continues to increase, so I hope you will bear with us." The whole thing semed so freakish that Jackie turned to the secretary expecting to see a surprised expression. Instead, her face showed no emotion at all.

"*Well*" Jackie thought "*It's either a stress test or this guy is a flaming lunatic.*" Jackie was a very good judge of character, but this guy…he just didn't know. Either he was a really terrific actor or he really was a surrealistic dick head. Jackie tried just for a moment to imagine receiving any kind of guidance from the man. Whether he was faking it or not, could such a man have anything to say about the sensitive side of life or intuition or vulnerability? Jackie knew he could not. No, the good doctor had just joined the ranks of the living dead with which Jackie had littered his world. People like the eight so-called friends he had cut out of his life one sunny afternoon after realizing that not once had any of them called him on the phone or come to visit. He had always been the one to make contact and one day that just wasn't good enough anymore. Not one of them, when confronted with the question as to why they never called, could or would explain. And so Jackie cut them out of his life, all but three.

On the next day, Jackie was scheduled to attend the final meeting to get the test results. All of the psychologists, psychiatrists and administrators were present, seated around a large rectangular table. Doctor Pennington called the meeting to order. He did most of the talking, describing in technical terms, Jackie's physiology, from his "heavy" bone structure to his "square" face. But the language was oddly vague. It did not go into the key moments of assessment where Jackie had felt the breakthroughs. Like when one doctor asked him, "Have you ever felt like a lesbian?"

"Yes, exactly, wow, yes" Jackie had blurted out before he could restrain himself. "Ya, like, I know and feel things I shouldn't feel."

That wasn't in the report.

"Wait, wait, this isn't right" he said during a pause in Doctor Pennington's summary. "You're not giving me anything I don't already know and you're not giving me the results of each appointment I had."

"In our experience" the doctor interrupted, "it is not in the best interest of people in the assessment process to disclose all of the various findings."

"Why not?" asked Jackie in disbelief.

"Because they don't have the background or training to correlate the various diagnoses."

"Oh please," said Jackie sarcastically, "who is more aware of what I think and feel than I am? This is ridiculous. What have I been doing here for two weeks going through all of this for if you aren't even going to give me detailed feedback?"

Doctor Pennington leaned over to the administrator on his right and then to the one on his left and whispered. Shoulders were shrugged and then, irritated, and impatient, tossing his pencil onto the table where it fell with the sound of dead wood, he turned to Jackie.

"Alright Mr. Northam, we can do this." To the doctors around the table, he said "Just the essentials please." There was a momentary widening of eyes and nervous stretching as they all digested the instruction. For the next half-hour, they gave their findings.

"Okay, Mr. Northam, I hope this has been helpful. If you have any questions or need to see a counsellor, please feel free to make an appointment at any time. Ladies and gentlemen, thank you" he said, and the meeting was over.

The glass and steel doors of the Carlyle opened. There was no epiphany, only a small displacement of the wish to kill himself. The doctors had given their pronouncements and if they were all right and Jackie had heard correctly, he was gay, straight, bisexual, transsexual, transvestite, repressed, neurotic, normal, healthy, had no problem whatsoever, was in need of long term psychotherapy. No wonder the Director had not wanted them to put their cards on the table. Each, skilled in his own area and up to date on the latest research had seen him differently. How was he to see himself then? He valued the opinions of others.

"They don't have a fucking clue" Jackie thought. *"Okay, so they're the best and they don't know. Great. What does that mean? I'm all alone with this."* Bright yellow fuchsia bushes blurred by as he walked quickly up the sidewalk to nowhere in particular. Trees were bedecked with the tiny perfect leaf clusters of spring, soft, pliant and pale in their newness. The sun on his face felt all the warmer for the cool air.

"You have a square face and a heavy bone structure." Why did Pennington have to go and say that? Jackie's heart had fallen then. No matter what he felt or knew to be true, he had a square face and heavy bone structure. Unmistakably male. A sometime woman in a male body. A cosmic short-circuit. Clear signals...sparks...clear signals...smoke...clear signals...silence. Part of something...all of nothing.

"Fearfully and wonderfully made" thought Jackie *"by the same Creator that from one self drew forth both male and female."* Alone. "Fuck, fuck, fuck, fuck, fuck" he muttered, "What the hell do you want me to do?" Ahead of him was a small parkette with a vacant

bench surrounded by blue crocuses and lilies of the valley. Mangy squirrels bounded through the fresh emerald grass. His heart was racing as he sat down and he tried a Zen breath technique to calm himself. A redwing blackbird landed singing its odd watersong on a branch overhead.

"What am I supposed to do?" Jackie asked aloud through his gathering tears and the bird flapped three times then flew away to the east. Jackie watched it intently and drew in a sharp breath as a look of recognition spread over his face. "Okay" he said slowly. "I can't get a fix on who I am. Psychiatrists can't agree and God doesn't answer. I'm afraid of who I may be, and I'm afraid to be alone. The answer suddenly seemed so obvious to him. He had a few thousand dollars in the bank from supply teaching. Fear had to go. Confusion likewise. Come what may. He would go to Europe. Alone. There in a sea of strangers he would find his way free of crushing North American judgment. If he was a man, he would find that, if a woman, he would embrace that, if gay, he would learn to live it, and if straight, he would, he hoped, learn to be at peace with it. There was something he was not being, and the lament his life had become would have to end.

Chapter Three
HYDRA

He was more than he thought he was. Less than he knew he could be. Like a wave come to life in the midst of a measureless sea. Midnight on the Greek island of Hydra found him across the table from seriously creative friends. There was a good chance he would be making love to the Swedish girl later. His belly was full. There was still plenty of cold Retsina, the resinous, pine flavored wine they washed the dust down with after a hot Mediterranean day. Dressed in a long, hooded cotton djalaba from north Africa, he was not the person he had been in Toronto. That was, after all, the point, to leave it all behind, the oppressive Canadian sameness, the safety, the streets void of passion, the clichés, the sexism, the fear of being alone.

He let his wrist fall to a natural angle. Back home, he wouldn't have done that, would have caught it in mid flight. It would have seemed somehow unmanly…people would make decisions about you, decisions affecting your future.

Here he had no future, no past, no judges that mattered, just a coterie of friends who had drifted together from far parts of the planet and would dissolve again into the four directions as easily as a Buddhist chant through an open window.

There were two American military police from a base in Germany who just wanted to smoke their dope in peace; Spacedemon, a paranoid nuclear missile silo weapons expert and cartoonist; Babs, the Irish barmaid; Con, her penny whistle playing brother; Rosanna, the Ethiopian jazz musician, and Hiro from Japan who had been on the road for ten years. Others came and went as the days passed but basically that was the group. They traveled for a few weeks together. It seemed like years.

"My name is Spiro. Are you the one who wants to know about the sailing yacht?" The voice came from a young man who helped himself to a chair beside Jackie. There was a beautiful two-masted ketch moored a short distance away in the harbor. It had occurred to Jackie that a few months spent crewing on it would be an exciting way to get some adventure. So, he had put out some feelers.

"That's me," he answered.

"Well, the captain wants to talk to you," the young Greek growled.

"When?"

"Of course, now, but you better change."

Jackie hadn't played a role since leaving Canada three months before. The thought of doing it again made him hesitate.

"Are you serious or not?" Spiro demanded.

"Ya, ya I'm coming" Jackie told him "but how did you find me?"

Crossing his legs in his polyester pants and tugging at the sleeves of his wrinkled silk shirt Spiro said with some distaste, "That was not very difficult." With that he got up, crossed the cafe and ordered a glass of premium scotch in a loud voice at the bar.

The yacht was a hundred and twenty feet long. A beauty from before the days of plastic boats, her wooden hull fair but starting to peel, her deckline a graceful arc rising to a sharp clipper bow. With her narrow beam she would be fast on the open ocean but wet.

As Jackie walked closer, the toll the Mediterranean had taken on her teak became apparent. He imagined spray landing on the bleached wood turning it a rich brown.

"Below" said a voice from behind. It was Spiro making sure the tourist had found his way. It bothered Jackie the way the young man had been able to get so close without detection. "The captain is below. He is waiting for you. I told him about you. Do what he says and you get a job for sure, and then you don't forget Spiro, okay?" With that he turned and walked off down the crumbling concrete pier toward the cafe lights that ringed the small harbor.

"*Okay kid,*" Jackie thought to himself "*this is what you've been looking for. Adventure, the unknown, travel, new things, interesting people, exotic experiences, a chance to find the real you.*" Then it happened, what always happens in the face of adventure. Surface tension. Those forces that cause the surface of any liquid to take its minimal shape. Suddenly he was thinking of his comfortable cot outside on the balcony of Grigorio's Taverna not a hundred yards away. He could see it across the harbour. Rosanna the

Ethiopian jazz musician who had a cot at the other end of the balcony was leaning on the railing smoking. The green shutters downstairs had been opened against the faded yellow plaster walls. Grigorio was moving slowly between tables, setting things up. In an hour, bazoukia music would mix with the kitchen smells of garlic and grilled meats wafting up to his bed. How important they seemed just now. It was surprising and irritating. He had not learned about surface tension. It would soon snap him back. It existed, as he was to find out, to keep the faint of heart in this existence in line.

The ornately carved name on the transom was "Mir".

"Aboard the Mir!" he called in his best Great Lakes Yacht Club manner, "permission to come aboard?" No answer. He waited. "Hello...anybody there" he tried. No answer. The companionway was open and the main cabin hatch had been slid forward. A harsh light below revealed part of a dark mahogany interior. The boarding ladder creaked as he stepped off the gangplank past the large spoked wheel with its worn handholds and started below.

Seated at a stained mahogany table was a thin, wiry man of indeterminate age with deep-set shifty eyes like black holes.

"Ja, ja sit" he commanded, "you are the...the one who is looking for a crew position."

"That's..."

"I tell you some things" the man continued in a severe German accent. A couple of small scars on his chin were visible through a stubble of gray hair. His moist eyes darting left and right, stopped on Jackie an instant and then continued their restless movement. Jackie thought it strange since there was nothing that he could see of interest below. Just the usual yachty things—barometer, oil lamp, chart table. That and a curious smell of engine oil, mildew and something else he couldn't identify.

"You are looking for work, yes?" the man asked staring down at the table.

"Well, ya, I guess so" Jackie stuttered. Not a good beginning. Everything was getting real too fast, and there was something faintly alarming about the man.

"Well, you are or you aren't. Look, junge, I don't have time to screw around."

"Careful boy," Jackie thought to himself. "this guy's weird."

"Ya, well, that depends." he answered.

"Ja, ja on the conditions. I know I know. Look, I tell you straight okay? If you stay, you stay, if you go you go. To begin with, you like to know maybe where is the crew." The thought hadn't occurred to Jackie. He nodded. "They jumped ship last week, every one of the bastards, captain too."

"Oh, so you're not..."

"The regular captain? No, I was flown in from Germany today by the owners. They want this vessel underway within forty-eight hours." Jackie wondered what the rush was. The man looked tired and worried.

"You will find out soon enough there is a problem with the engines, but we don't need them anyway for where we go. This vessel sails very well. Anyway what is already broken cannot break any more," he said looking down into his bony hands. The point escaped Jackie. He faked it.

"Ummhmm" he answered. He was beginning to feel way out of his middle class depth. There was a momentary silence as the new captain sized him up.

"So where does the boat go and what does...I mean is it for passenger charter or what?" Jackie asked.

"Where we go is back and forth between North Africa and Piraeus, the port of Athens, once in a while trans Atlantic to the Caribbean or United States. What do we carry, I don't want to know. Just we do what the owners want. If you want to sign on, you will do the same. There is a lot of night sailing. Anyway, I get off the point.

"This is going great," Jackie thought. "Man, this is the real stuff. Danger. This is dangerous shit! Finally, I've got a life!"

Getting a life was truly important to him. He really didn't think he had one when he lived in Canada. And yes, one day he would think he was the biggest ingrate on the planet, the next, a visionary who saw things as they were. Dad was a General Manager for a project management firm. He was seldom home when it mattered, due to the workload. When he did return, it was always with rules inviolate. Real communication was not high on the list of topics at the dinner table.Mom was a devout fundamentalist Christian. Jackie attended Oakville Heights High School along with the sons and daughters of other financially comfortable executives. His neighborhood was white and prosperous. The neighbors included the designer of a famous military aircraft, a chemical executive whose company invented the hula hoop, the owner of a transport company, an airline pilot whose son became a world famous magician, and an advertising sales executive. His son, Jules Boyer, was Jackie's best friend. In the deep, dark recesses of the basement of the Boyer's historic house, the two had carved out "the pit". That was when they were in grade six or seven.

The pit was an old storage room behind the massive, antiquated furnace that reached out and up with arms of rough ducting like some great fire breathing octopus. You had to walk down rickety old stairs into the rich, damp smell through the dark to a string and pull it to get the single light bulb to turn on.

The boys got along well. They were in grade six at the same time though in different classes. So they never saw each other during class time. Garbage day, Wednesday would find them zooming down The Eighth Line on bikes, on their lunch run home—a two mile stretch of smooth, down-sloped asphalt. The long driveways of Oakville's upper middle class stretching back from it on both sides to large houses tucked far back among the willows and pines. Where the driveways met the road, large empty metal garbage cans stood glistening in neat formations of two's and three's , both sides for the full two miles, like silver armored knights.

Despite the principal's threats every Wednesday morning on the P.A. system to make the juvenile delinquents responsible pay, the temptation was always too much to resist and by 12:15 not a single can stood upright or undented as far as the eye could see. The boys exchanged leads in squadron formation pumping pedals furiously, looking for that sweet aiming spot that would send the cans flying without ripping rider from bike. By the time they got home, they could hardly walk.

At Jules' home, Jackie was introduced to Tchaikovsky. When Tilley, the maid, had given them permission to lie on the ornate Persian living room carpet which she had just finished vacuuming, the boys had stretched out , put on headphones and cranked up the volume. Jules had read the liner notes and in the quieter sections, filled in with a knowing commentary.

"This is where Napoleon's army is riding across the countryside...this is back in Paris and someone is in love with someone...this is the cavalry charging...those are REAL canons going off...those are REAL Russian church bells...listen...listen.

And Jackie did listen. After a while he was there riding among the soldiers amidst the thunderous jangling of hooves and metal ornaments, a blinding passing of piercing reflections through the pastel countryside, on his way to glory or death with his brothers in arms. Strange that he should have come to hate men so completely.

"You will have to cut your hair and beard. The owners don't like long hairs. You will sleep and eat on board. Two hundred dollars U.S. per month and you will have to sign ship's articles for one year. That means you belong to me, to this vessel, for one year. Are you listening? Do you agree to these terms?"

Now surface tension and intuition can absolutely stop you cold and that's what happened. Something was wrong and it was impossible to pinpoint—not so much what the man across the table said or didn't say, not so much the way things looked. It was more a feeling of something missing in the flow and turn of events, a sense of time suddenly grating upon itself and something in the moment made Jackie afraid. Of what, he didn't know. And so he played for time, although his mind was already made up.

Heart pounding with excitement he said, "I'll think about it," slowly getting to his feet. A large part of him did not want to leave. "*Toronto boy*" a voice called out accusingly from somewhere in his uncertainty. Maybe he would always find reasons not to do something dramatic. Maybe he was a Toronto boy in a world of Toronto boys, petrifying in amber day after day, crying his frustration to the gods with no real intention at all to break free from the silent mediocrity of his life, but intensely aware of it.

"Suit yourself" the captain said, "there are always young men looking for adventure. If you meet any, send them over. I will make it worth your while." The words cut deep.

"*Phony bastard*" Jackie thought to himself stepping onto the gangplank, his heart pounding. "*You were right there. Right there. And you blew it. Give it up, go home. Be a teacher. Sit in a staff room and bitch about the little bastards in ten general. Admit it, you're a fraud. You've learned something painful about yourself and you just can't take it.*" There was no moon in the sky. Lights did not reflect in the strange Harbour. The air was empty and there was silence or no silence. The flavor had gone out of everything...the color drained. Nothing mattered. Everything suddenly fell into some kind of focus and he couldn't look at it. He couldn't live with the self he knew and he couldn't live with the fantasy. For the first time in his life, nowhere was home. He felt allergic to the present and his own skin. The night and everything in it, strange and malicious.

Next morning, awakened as usual by the hot new sun, he rolled over on the cot and looked through the wrought iron balcony rail to the yacht. It was gone. Full of regret, he got up and went down to a cafe for breakfast.

"Impounded by the navy in the middle of the night for smuggling heroin from Morocco" Spiro said matter of factly, appearing from nowhere and pointing to the empty slip, "captain and a couple of poor slobs who signed on after you left, pffft, gone to prison." With his hands he mimed something disappearing. "Lucky you didn't stay around."

Since Papadopoulos and his junta had come into power, many people had gone pfffft. Apparently they had been watching the boat for months. Trembling, Jackie grasped his coffee with two hands. Of the many voices speaking to us, he learned right then, some are to be listened to and some are not. What had it been? He struggled to remember. Then it came back. The grating of time on itself...something like that. He didn't even know what that meant. Sometimes we are given things before we are ready for them and almost always before we are ready to be grateful. Now he was grateful. To what, he did not know, but he felt embraced...and when he looked around, there were cats playing on the cobblestones, gulls crying in the azure sky and whitecaps breaking free in numbers beyond knowing from the indigo Aegean. Suddenly everywhere was home. He felt dizzy and started to let go of something.

"*Herman Hesse was right in Siddharta,*" he thought to himself. "*The Maharishi was right. Wicca was right about a lot of things. Life responds if you trust it. Things happen. Good things. Walk through life with the Michelin Guide in your hands and wonder shuns you. Venture forth into the wide world believing it a sentient thing with your best interests at heart and it will reward you with all kinds of unlooked for wonders. Wonders like kindred spirits.*" Rosanna was a kindred spirit. Jackie had met him in Athens three weeks earlier, before they set out for the Island of Hydra where the incident with the yacht took place. This will take some explaining.

Chapter Four
A Rooftop In Athens

To understand the Outside Inn, to really understand it, you need to be a certain kind of person. Fed up is good. Cynical is better. Hungry is best of all, hungry for any kind of life, hungry for the exotic. This kind of hunger is not hard to come by when you grow up in the grey stonelands of urban North America, where the floors are all even, the people insured, and the streets devoid of passion. When, what seemed liked years later, Jackie returned to his city's airport, he was struck dumb by the expressionless faces of the people covered, to call it dressed would be to dignify it, in shades of grey. And why not? What centuries old bridge would any one of them cross on the way home? What famous building would they pass? What historic avenue would they walk? North America is too new, too shallow. We thirst amid vats of wine too young to drink. We are impatient with our own wine. Our impatience brands us immature. A country is its spirits. North America is a perpetual purple Jesus party of the soul. Put the stopper in the residence bathtub and every student of life pours his booze in on the way to the party. Triple X and Beaujolais, single malts and Old Sailor.

So when Jackie got off the bus that had taken him around the edge of what seemed like every hairpin in the Peloponnesus mountains all the way to Athens, he felt like he had skipped two grades in the Academy of Wonder. Someone, somewhere along the line, maybe it was Hiro in Madrid, had told him that he should check out the Outside Inn in the Plaka area of Athens. That's the neighborhood where the artisans who built the Acropolis lived in narrow winding, cobblestone alleys.

Heaving his overloaded backpack down from his shoulders onto the stone steps, Jackie knocked on the heavy wooden door. No answer. There was no sign on the building, but the street number was right and a torn piece of cardboard wedged into the mail slot said in faded nail polish, "That's right! You're here! C'mon in!"

"Cool" Jackie thought and pushed the door open. After the intense mid day heat and light, the relief was immediate. He took a long deep breath. It had never ceased to amaze him how scent conjures up emotion and imagination. The air was cool in his nostrils. There was a rich blend of old wood, musty carpet, stale wine, marijuana and things that could not be placed. His eyes were having trouble adjusting to the dark and he called out, "Hello...hello". There was no answer, no reception desk, nothing that indicated this place was a hotel at all. "Anybody here?" he called. "Anyone around?" His eyes were slowly getting used to the low light and he could make out a stairway with worn carpeting going up to the right. "Anybody up there?" Nothing. Maybe a floor creaked somewhere. He wasn't sure.

"Ohhh what time is it?" a voice moaned from the next floor in a strange accent.

"You talking to me?"

"Yes of course I talk to you. What time is it?" The creaking got closer. Jackie told the high pitched male voice that he didn't know because he didn't have a watch.

"No watch?" the voice snorted, "typical". Dark bare feet came down below the ceiling which cut the head of the stairs off from Jackie's view, then what looked like loose white pajamas gathered at the ankles. There was a pause while coughing and hacking actually lifted the heel of the stranger's left foot off the ground, then the rest of him came down...belly button, lithe dark torso, skinny arms and indistinct head with long black hair and mustache. The man picked his way carefully down each step. Jackie put about even odds on him making it all the way to the bottom.

"What day is it?" he demanded.

"Idiot" Jackie thought to himself, "It's ..." and then he realized he didn't know. "I don't know" he said, "My watch was..."

"That's good" the man cut in groggily, "I don't trust people who know the time. Who needs to know what time it is in a place like this?"

"What a strange thing" Jackie thought, "not to need to know the time." He couldn't give an answer and he wasn't expecting one. "Is this the Outside Inn?" he asked. The man seemed to ignore the question..

"Got a smoke?" he asked scratching his bum with one hand and running the other over his stubbly chin. He was close now and Jackie could see that his eyes were very bloodshot. "What's your name mister early bird?" he asked in a not unkind tone. "And can you play that guitar?" He grabbed the small Spanish six string that Jackie had bought from an American girl on a train in France and sighted down the neck.

"I'm Jackie" he said. As usual, it was hard to speak his name and it sounded oddly artificial and unconvincing. For some reason he could not explain, last names seemed as meaningless as watches in this place.

"Jackie" The man repeated, accepting the French cigarette and matches Jackie handed to him. There was doubt in his voice. "Gouloise...excellent" he said lighting up and inhaling deeply. "Jackie, the American with the French cigarettes."

Jackie tried to tell him that Canadians are not Americans. "Well, you live in America don't you?" he countered. "Americans live in the U.S." Jackie said. "I'm Canadian."

"Good for you" the man said with disdain. "Let's see where we have been" he mumbled turning Jackie's backpack around. "France, Spain, Italy, Corfu...very nice...and Greece goes here" he said pointing to the place where the young Canadian had already measured but not attached a small Greek emblem. "Oh yes, this is the Outside Inn" he said with a wistful smile followed by a sudden loud fart that shook the stillness. "God...ouzo and french fries. Do you want to sit down on something?" Jackie said he did and moved to open the door thinking they would sit on the front steps.

"No, no" the man gasped moving quickly to push it closed, "the light, the light. Sorry but nobody even gets out of bed around here till after noon. You see...we party a lot here and it is" he fumbled for a word "customary for people to be quiet and just sort of...recover in the mornings. How did you find out about us anyway" he asked motioning Jackie into the next room. There were a couple of old chairs and a dilapidated sofa all with throw covers draped over them. He put Jackie's backpack and guitar gently up against the wall and they both sat down. "We are not exactly in the Michelin Guide. How did you choose us?" Jackie told him that Hiro had passed the name along to him in Madrid.

"Are you staying here?" Jackie asked. It was obvious that he was. "I mean do you work here or what?"

"Yes and yes" he said. "Oh, my manners are very rude. I am" he said getting to his feet and extending his hand, "MorocCO"

"Morocco" Jackie repeated.

"No. MorocCO. You have to accent the end. MorocCO."

Jackie tried again, "MorocCO."

"Tres bien monsieur. Just so. MorocCo." He paused to think for a moment. "What city are you from?"

"Toronto" Jackie said reluctantly.

"Excellent" came the instant reply, "ToronTO and MorocCO. I think you are home, ToronTO" he said expansively taking a last drag on the cigarette. "Come, I show you around. If you have anything expensive in your pack, bring it with you."

The first stop was a back room. Except for the attached kitchen and a tiny bar without liquor, it could have been a recreation room from back home. The floor was tiled and the walls were paneled in a low grade veneer. Ashtrays were everywhere, and there were orange crates with candles in various shapes of wine bottles on top. "This is where we mostly eat. I do most of the cooking. Sandwiches, soup, stews, that kind of thing" said MorocCO. "Through there," he went on, pointing down a small hallway off the end of the room, you can get outside into a small courtyard. Some people go there for quiet or to hang out laundry to dry. You have to do it yourself. We don't do that kind of thing except for the bed linens. We do that every day. That is if you want a room. Rooms are five dollars U.S. per night." Jackie asked him what the rooms were like. "I show you." he said and headed for the stairs. Coming down was a scruffy, heavyset, bald man in his twenties or thirties. He looked Arabic. "I be back around four o'clock" he said gruffly to MorocCO and stomped off out the front door, leaving it open. "That was Mufti" he said closing it, "stay away from him. He is not really very okay. It's a long story. We are trying to look after him, but you never know. He has good days and he has bad days. When he talks to himself, stay away."

"Okay" Jackie said and began to wonder what the hell Hiro had been talking about. "Just to go" he had said in the bar just off the Plaza de Toros, the bull fight arena in Madrid. "Just to go.

They say it not possible to explain this place, so please just to go and then you know."

"How long have you been here, MorocCO?" Jackie asked as they reached the second floor.

"Who knows, maybe two years. Could it be two years? No, impossible. Anyway here is what the rooms are like. They are all the same." With that, he quietly opened the door but it soon started to grate on its hinges.

"Mother of God!" a strong female voice howled from inside. The door continued to open revealing a pale, Rubinesque figure of a woman, her back to the two men, blonde hair down to her waist, kneeling astride two stout, hairy, male legs whose toes were pointed out in the throes of ecstasy. "Don't go anywhere darlin'" she commanded in a sultry voice. With that, she swung herself off the bed in one fluid motion and drew up to Jackie's guide, her glistening breasts swinging to a standstill. The Canadian steeled himself for the blast to come, but she didn't say a word, just stood there as a pained moan issued from the sheets where an American military M.P. with whom Jackie had gotten drunk with some weeks earlier in Corfu, propped himself up on his elbows to get a fix on the cause of his fall from heaven.

"Fucking unbelievable" he growled and pulled the blanket over his head.

"Sergeant" Jackie answered with a laugh.

"You shut up" the woman snapped, "I'll deal with you later." Her voice had a rich, resonant Irish lilt to it. She looked Jackie briefly in the eyes, then turned to MorocCO who was now fidgeting for cigarettes he didn't have.

"Please" Jackie said invitingly.

"We'll see about that" she half whispered without taking her eyes off the Moroccan who had by this time broken into a sweat. He was struggling so hard not to let his gaze fall to the mammary magnificence before him that Jackie thought he was going to internally hemorrhage. "As for you, you dirty little bastard, the very thought of it, sneakin' around peepholes and bringin' your friends with you. Are you not able to find a decent outlet for it these days?" She was grinning broadly now and MorocCO's stare left the horizontal. "Don't you even think about it, you twisted little man" she warned lifting his chin with the little finger of her right hand. "Now if you don't mind" she said drawing closer until she was flush up against his bare chest and lowering her voice to a whisper, "I was in the middle of something that I would very much like to get back to, that is if you don't mind. Of course if you'd like to join us, I could ask the Captain" she said correcting Jackie, "if he has any interests in that area."

"No, no no" stuttered MorocCO, "I go… I go … it was an accident."

"And what are you looking at might I ask?" she said turning quickly toward Jackie.

"Oh, nothing" he blurted, transfixed by the power and beauty of the woman. It was a real effort to look up.

"Nothing? Is that you think. Well to be sure, I think I've been insulted. Captain, did you hear that? One of your smug countrymen standin' here lookin' at me says he's lookin' at nothin'. I demand you defend my honor."

"Honor?" MorocCO repeated and laughed out loud grabbing Jackie by the sleeve and ushering him out through the door.

"Oh you go to hell!" the woman shouted, "and take the innocent one with you, and close the damn door!"

"Then there is always the roof" said MorocCO, leading Jackie down the hallway. As they climbed another set of stairs, behind them came the muffled sounds of someone yelping in pain and the woman yelling "Captain, my bloody ass!"

"That was Babs," said MorocCO, "She has some other name, but I forget. Do you like her? She loves me, only she doesn't know it yet. One day…one day I will…" He pushed open a metal fire door at the top of the stairs, and the intensity of the light made them both wince. "If you don't like the rooms, you can stay here for only a few drachmas, about fifty cents per night." Jackie walked out onto the slate tiled roof and looked around. "Amazing", he said spotting the Acropolis high on its hill, proud and shimmering in the full blaze of the Athenian sun.

"Yes" said MorocCO, "At night it is all lit up with floodlights and if you sleep up here it is even more amazing.

"People actually sleep up here?" Jackie asked. "Oh yes" he answered, "You get a straw mat to roll out, and if you need a blanket, you can rent or use a sleeping bag if you have one." Like a lot of North Americans on the road trying to find themselves, Jackie had brought along a lightweight sleeping bag. There was no knowing what you might have to call home and snuggling down into something familiar at the end of a day of adventure seemed like a good idea. His carried the very best grime of Paris, Madrid and Barcelona as well as a rough beach in Corfu. On the first night on the sand there, he and a travelling companion, Ulrich, a chef from the German army, had almost been swept out to sea in the middle of the night. Seems they nodded off just as the tide was coming in. Dumb move. Getting soaked goose down dry again, he discovered, is one of the truly tedious things a person can do in this life. Anyway the thing couldn't get much dirtier on the roof so he decided to call the place home.

"You can lock up your passport and anything else in the office downstairs," MorocCO said walking to the low brick wall that ran a foot high around the perimeter. Jackie asked if anyone had ever fallen off but he only laughed. There was an oddly shaped storage room like a pie slice turned on its edge at one end. It was dark inside. It sounded for a moment like laughter was coming from it.

"What's going on over there?" Jackie asked.

"Who knows" replied MorocCO "but you should always knock before you go in there. Most people leave a brick just outside because there is no door.

"What's it for?" Jackie asked, but his guide just shrugged and smiled mischievously. "Whatever you like. It's dark and later it gets hot." It sounded like the place got used a lot.

"Okay" Jackie said, "I'll stay up here." He thought he had died and gone to heaven. A straw mat on a rooftop in Athens with a view of the Acropolis and who knows what kind of other people. "Fifty cents?" he asked. "Fifty cents" MorocCo said.

That was how Jackie came to a rooftop in the Plaka in Athens. After the strange overdose he was feeling from running around art galleries in Paris, Madrid and Barcelona, this would be just right. North America and all things middle class, safe and predictable seemed so far away. It seemed that with each moment, he breathed easier, like his life was being replaced by big, beautiful question marks in myriad forms—faces, temples, streetsounds, foreign sunrises. For the first time, though, he began to be a little afraid of who he might be and what he might never have found out if he hadn't gone to Europe. Something was moving somewhere in a life he had not yet claimed as his.

Chapter Five
SANGA

The little courtyard wasn't much to look at. A square, fifteen feet by fifteen feet, bordered on all sides by weathered brick walls with rusted plumbing sticking out all over the place. A sun bleached Cinzano umbrella over a white plastic table and chairs. In the shade, off to one side, a wooden bench with initials and names carved into it from one end to the other. A history of the passing of strangers. He traced the gouges with his finger... Dieter... Ryutaro... Eva... Celeste...a pastiche of names, real and improbable, and one that had not yet yielded to the encouragements of sun and rain and smog...Rosanna.

Jackie climbed on the bench, faced the wall and sat down on his heels Zen seiza style. This was the way of Soto Zen, always facing the wall, hands folded in his lap, right palm over left, thumbs lightly touching, back straight, tongue resting lightly on the roof of his mouth. The silence was deep and rich. Wisps of cirrus cloud racing before the sun in the azure sky above made the wall seem to pulse with light. With the first breath, he met the tightness in his back and shoulders like old friends. From the tips of his toes to his head and face, one by one, he relaxed each muscle group from the tiniest to the largest. There was no need to hurry. No need at all. He inhaled deeply and noticed the bricks and mortar that made the wall before him. Following his breath naturally, for that was the practise the Zen master had given him, he focussed his entire being on his breathing. To be conscious of breath in a manner so detached as not to interfere with its natural rhythm was not easy. He could not tell if he was deciding when to breathe or if each breath occurred on its own terms. In the first few breaths, it always seemed as though he was controlling it. And yet, when he thought about it, each breath in, each breath out, seemed impossibly long. Sometimes there was even a curious sense of panic.

It was helpful, at such useless moments, for him to be struck without warning by the Monjutor with the kiyosaku stick suddenly, from behind...whack, whack...whack...whack. Two times on the left shoulder, two on the right. Useless questions disappeared, distractions vanished. Odd how the Monjutor always seemed to appear at just the right unspoken moment. But that was back home. This was half way across the world. Slowly, a single brick in the wall before him, became his universe, its rough surface oddly fascinating...breath in...and then the single grains of sand that made up the brick...breath out...and then one grain that glistened a moment in tiny spectacular rainbow of colour and was gone...breath...why was that...breath..."*Ah yes, I moved*" Jackie thought to himself. "*My breath, it moved me and the moving changed the angle of the light on the sand grains and...*"*Stop analyzing*" another part of his consciousness countered as he returned to the following of his breath. The tiny shining appearing and vanishing in time to him. He knew what his master would say. "Do not resist distraction and do not hold on to it. Let it be what it will be, and when you are again mindful, follow your breath.

And so Jackie, followed his breath until the shining was no shining and the wall no wall and there was no breathing and no Jackie until the present and all that seems real came back like a joker, sneaking back some time later when his breath was imperceptible and his pulse very slow..."Every grain of sand knows..." The words whispered poignantly in his mind. Whose words they were Jackie did not know. It was sometime later. The courtyard was in deep shadow and the wall before him had not appeared for what seemed both an instant and an eternity. Suddenly there it was again. The drab brick wall...but the words were somehow important. Jackie felt a pang of urgency. "Whose words are these?" he thought to himself. Again the voice presented itself "Every grain of sand knows..." "Knows, knows what?" he demanded, of whom, of himself? He did not know. He did not recognize the voice. Strangely, it did not sound like the voice of his own thought. He was not sure what it was. This had not happened before. Yielding to the conundrum, Jackie made the gassho, the bow with hands together as though in prayer and bent down in gratitude and respect toward the wall. From the knees down, his legs had gone completely numb. It took some effort to turn around and get them over the side of the bench. There stood Mufti. Square and solid in the doorway, his face in mid change from smile to scowl.

"Ummmmmh?" he growled questioningly.

"Hello" Jackie responded, the blood racing back into his legs so he couldn't decide whether to laugh or cry as the pins and needles set in. It put him into an ambiguous smiling grimace which Mufti seemed not to notice.

"Ummmmmmh?" he growled again, taking a hesitant step forward. In the shadows, dressed in black and dark as he was, he moved like an amorphous mass.

"Hello" Jackie tried again. There was no response, but the man's head inclined in an effort of intense listening.

"Why are you here?" the man demanded venomously.

"What do you mean..."

"I don't know YOU!" he thundered, moving closer. Jackie still could not see his eyes. A hood of some kind cast a deep shadow over the face. Jackie tried to move his legs. It would take a few more seconds before he had full control. Once, a Zen friend had broken his ankles trying to run while his feet were still numb. The man was broad at the shoulders and moved heavily on the small stones that made the floor of the courtyard.

"This is not good" Jackie thought to himself, *"but at least he is talking to me. What was it MorocCO had said? Watch out for him when he was talking to himself. That was it."* Suddenly, a huge hand, scarred and rough reached out from beneath the cape or cloak or whatever it was and gestured menacingly as he drew to within a few feet.

"YOU do not know me!" he roared, but this time there was an edge of pleading and fear in the voice.

"I never said I..." Jackie started.

"YOU can not know me. I am not afraid of YOU!" he screamed, faking a punch in Jackie's direction.

"Ah shit" Jackie thought *"here we go. I do not fucking need this."* Now he was frightened. He had only been in a couple of fights in his young life and had wakened up on the floor both times. Still it had made a deep impression on him and he had vowed never to be a victim again. On the other hand, the intellectual fibre of his being told him that only losers fought and the surest way for an artist to fuck up evolution was to stoop to meet neanderthal threats on their own level. He did consider himself an artist. He tried words.

"Okay...okay...I don't know you. Okay? I..." With the next step forward, Mufti moved into the best part of the remaining light in the courtyard barely an arm's length away from Jackie and the wall when Jackie finally saw the eyes...the wide, wide pupils and the skin drawn all tight and furrowed in fear around the whites and the eyes were riveted beyond Jackie and the words had been for someone else and Jackie turned to look at the empty wall and thought, *"Oh my God."*

He thought about lunging to the left and running out through the door, if he could get that far. There was no telling what this crazy son of a bitch was going to do, and Jackie wasn't about to stick around to find out. Just then Mufti's closed right fist hammered into the stucco which covered the brick in places. There was a sickening thud and large chunks of the white material fell away inches from Jackie's head.

"Ha!" the big man shouted in triumph, "Ha! YOU don't know ME. Devil!" and with that he let go with another straight right that would have floored an ox. This time the chunks that fell were speckled with blood. With that, Jackie did a quick side step and wheeled for the door, careful to keep Mufti in his peripheral vision.

"Never take your eyes off your opponent, Jackie's karate teacher had said when Jackie, in bowing to the sensei, had let his eyes shift to the ground in respect. The sensei had then duly kneed him in the face."

"Too fucking right" Jackie thought *"Never take your eyes off"* but Mufti, flailing with great vigour now and shouting in Arabic, had not budged. In fact, he seemed not to have noticed him at all. As Jackie realized this, he was sent sprawling into the door frame by MorocCO who ran past him into the courtyard. He stopped a yard away from the great man who was starting to tire.

"Mufti, Mufti" he called in a surprisingly tender voice, but before he could call again, the man stood bolt upright, covered his ears and let out a hideous scream. Suddenly, he began to back away from the wall horrified at whatever form his demons had taken. Feeling his way, he backed up until he was near the door, then wheeled around and ran screaming for two steps, stopped, removed his hands for an instant, looked up and back at the sky, listened intensely, then covered his ears again, howling and running flat out through the hotel into the street.

"I told you" said MorocCO "everything is not really so okay with him, but he does not hurt the people, only..." he said turning again to the wall on which there had grown a large patch of red, "only himself. He hears things. People say that he was a holy man somewhere in the Middle East and that he has been chased half way along the Mediterranean by his voices. Please, I ask you again. Don't be near him when he is talking like that."

"But" Jackie replied, "I thought he was talking to me. I thought he was angry at me for something."

"No" MorocCO said, "Mufti now talks only to Allah, may his name be kept holy, and his demons. Believe me, for him, you do not exist, but just to be safe, do not speak with him and do not call his name. Okay?"

"Okay."

"So, you are frightened, yes? And you have not eaten. I make you some nice houmous with pita bread. You have some good, fresh feta too, yes? Nice tomato, olives, some Retsina? It sound so good, I think I join you and..."

"Yes" said Jackie, his voice odd and distant. "Yes I was, am frightened. I was fucking scared out of my mind, man." He had come to Europe to get, in his own words, "real." He had never admitted to being afraid of anything to anyone before, and he had never imagined admitting such a thing to a male. Strangely, the longer he stayed in Europe, the less he gave a shit about what anyone thought of him. He had already changed so much. Letting go of pretense and facade in all their forms, like pretending to be strong when he wasn't, could get him into all kinds of trouble, but he had to admit it, doing and saying what felt right at the moment, regardless of the consequences was beginning to feel oddly satisfying, and curiously stimulating. "Yes, I was afraid" he said.

"You are not as afraid as you think" said MorocCO with calm assurance, and facing him directly. "Your eyes do not say afraid. I wish they did."

"No?" replied Jackie, guilt coursing through him, "Then what do they say?" MorocCO appeared to struggle with himself and for a moment said nothing. For a moment, the two looked away in different directions.

"Please. I meant nothing" he offered.

"Come on MorocCO. I can take it" Jackie pressed, good
naturedly, but determined to find out what this curious little man
thought he had seen in him. "Come on. Are you psychic or
something? If you saw something important. I want to know
what it was. I respect this kind of thing. I'm a bit psychic myself."
And it was true. He was psychic in a haphazard sort of a way. It
had seemed to come and go over the years, increasing in the last
few years since he had finished with university. He had seen
things move without apparent explanation in a very small room.
His grandmother had appeared to him at the time of her passing.
Right there on some New York interstate at eleven o' five at night,
she had appeared in his mind, almost as a thought but also as an
image and had said that it was okay, she had passed on and very
simply he should know that and be glad for her and not to worry.
Later, he found out that that had been the exact moment of her
passing in a Toronto hospital.

So he did believe in those types of things and he knew that
genuine knowing creates its own kind of atmosphere. In the
presence of those who had genuine understanding of things, he
could read a kind of aura of authenticity. MorocCO had that aura
at this moment. Whatever he thought he knew about Jackie, was
fact. It was as though he had a piece of him in his possession.
Jackie felt somehow violated and his curiosity was turning to
anger. And yet, somewhere in the deepest recesses of his own
psyche, Jackie felt that he already knew what the little man had
seen or sensed but he couldn't bring it into the light of his own
understanding. It was way down there, whatever it was. Still,
someone else having a part of you, there, in their knowing—it
was outrageous, but who was he to complain. Had he not done
hundreds of tarot readings for people without once thinking
about what now appeared so obviously to be an awesome
responsibility? He wondered, if he was now MorocCO, what he
would say.

"The journey is your guide, not me." MorocCO sighed with a
shrug of his shoulders. Impasse. Jackie decided to let it go. For the
moment.

"Good enough for me" he said, and the two went back into
the musty darkness of the Outside Inn. It was not good enough,
not nearly, but the full bodied wine washed down the rich, salty
feta in a cold, slow motion explosion of flavour. MorocCO was

busy in the kitchen, so Jackie ate alone. By the third plastic cup full, he felt the events of the last month since his arrival in Europe welling up around him like the wake of a speedboat that suddenly slows. He was lifted, exultant and feeling positively enraptured in the unfamiliarity that now made up his moments.

"MorocCO, do you have a pen and some paper around here?" he called out.

"What you need?" the chef answered, appearing from behind the refrigerator with his hair tied back in a bright red bandana and crisp white apron.

"Paper, I want to do some writing, and a pen if you have one."

"No paper, but you can use this." He threw him and pencil and Jackie found an old cigarette package in the garbage. "More Retsina?"

"Ya, what the hell." The cup was filled again. Jackie slumped back in a tattered sofa that had been stained and patched many times. But they were just that, stains, the thing itself was as clean as it could be, looking around, Jackie noticed that despite the low lighting of the place, the broken floor tiles with their cigarette burns, the cheesy decorations and the general creekyness of the place, it was actually very clean, nearly spotless. "Hey MorocCO, how come this place is so clean?" he shouted.

"What the matter, you don't like clean?"

"No, man, I just mean I haven't seen any maids since I got here and you could almost eat off the floors."

"Then I take this as a compliment. I cook and I clean as much as I have time. Some people who stay here, if sometimes they don't have money right away, then we let them clean to pay for one or two nights, but we make them clean very good."

"Who's we?"

"The manager and the owner and me. You don't see either of them. They don't like to come in here...too busy making money."

"So basically you run the place?"

"I say yes, but if you ask Babs, she will tell you that she is the boss" MorocCO said with a laugh. "Yes she loves me very much, that one" he mused wistfully and ducked back into the kitchen.

"By the way" Jackie continued, "I meant to ask you, what is this I hear about selling your blood in Athens?"

"Selling what?" MorocCO yelled over the sound of something delicious frying, maybe it was onions, but there was some spice Jackie had never smelled before.

"Blood. Selling blood. Somebody told me that if you were hard up you could sell your blood here."

"Why you want to do that? You don't need money. You have enough money."

"No, not me, I'm just curious." MorocCO appeared again around the refrigerator.

"Some guys who are desperate sell their blood to the hospitals or clinics for ten dollars American for one pint. They sell again and again, but there is some waiting period. You can tell them. They are all pale and have no energy. Most of them are heavy drug users. It is not something you should get involved in. Take it from MorocCO, ToronTO. I don't say don't use drugs, just our life is precious. It is a gift from God. To sell one's own blood. It is a kind of crime against nature. Do you understand me?"

"Ya, I do" Jackie answered. "I agree with you."

"Do not give away too much, ToronTO" he said looking him straight in the face the way he had earlier.

"Again" Jackie thought to himself, "There it is again, that same look, the same ominous kind of words." But before he could say anything, the chef had spoken.

"Okay, I shut up now. Soon you learn MorocCO talks too much about nothing, just one big mouth, talk, talk, talk, talk, talk, all day talking. Maybe it is because you are a good listener. Yes, you are to blame ToronTO. Next time I say something stupid, just tell me to shut up okay?"

"Okay" Jackie laughed, "Shut up!"

"Oh yes, you are my good friend. I shut up now. Thank you very much." With that, he slapped his own face and returned once again to his pots and pans.

"Every grain of sand..." Jackie wrote on the cigarette package, stopping to look at the words, to sound them out to himself "...knows." Then he took another long swallow and slumped back into the soft sofa. He wondered how a grain of sand could know anything. Probably it was a metaphor. Jackie was pretty good with metaphors. And symbols...things that represented other things...things that weren't themselves. He was comfortable with this because it resonated with the sad fact of his own life. Not once since he had been born had he ever spoken or acted spontaneously. Well, so he felt, but he was as given to exaggeration as anyone. He lived much more in a world of feeling than thinking, or if he lived in a world of both, the feeling always came first. It was the currency with which he traded, the coin of his own psychological realm. He trusted it, when he was young, very, very young, before things started to happen to erode his faith even in his own emotions.

Walking into the grade seven English class at Linhurst Public School in Oakville, Ontario, he took his seat one fine April day high as a kite with the scent of spring that filled the air from the softening, muddy earth. It was that one day when spring happens it all its fulness. It was overwhelming, that smell, transporting him to a rich world of sensation and excitement. He could sit and close his eyes, inhaling the fragrance and feeling the brave spring sun on his face for hours. It was in just such a state that he entered the the English class of Mr. Swinson. Jackie thought the two of them had been getting along pretty well. He liked the subject or had liked it until one day Mr. Swinson had taken him aside and told him to stop reading The Rise and Fall of the Third Reich. Too adult, too serious for a boy of Jackie's age. His parents should know better than to encourage such a thing. Jackie protested that he was already at page eight hundred, that he understood most of what he had read, had selected the book himself and wanted to finish it. Swinson was unconvinced, but relented. Jackie wondered what he had done wrong. This April day was to be different, however.

"Okay, knock it off. Get out your workbooks and a pen. You're going to do some creative writing" he had barked." Yesterday, you all recited your lines of poetry. Today I want you to write a poem. You pick the subject. And try to make it rhyme. You get this period and tomorrow as well to work on it. Get going!"

Thirty minutes later, Jackie had finished his first poem. Worse yet, he told someone.

"Oh you've finished have you Mr. Northam?" the teacher asked cynically, striding over to the boy's seat.

"Yes sir" Jackie said with pride, hoping the teacher would enjoy reading it as much as he had writing it. The whole thing had just come to him in one big burst, the idea, the rhythm, the flow of events and the tone, all of it—wham—just like that. He couldn't move his pen fast enough. It was as though someone was telling a story through him and he was just scrambling to keep up. It was a wonderful story, though, about a huge tall ship, a tea clipper on the China run "...a fortnight two days the ship laboured on with wind in the rigging that screamed a queer sound." The storm was bad, but there was hope "...of a sudden the captain cried shouting with glee, 'out there through the storm, shines a light to the lee'." The ship tacked toward the light but there was a reef that no one could see and then "...the shuddering shock of a ship run aground..." then "...down came the yardarms, five one man said, and fell on the captain...there he lay dead." By the end of the poem, everyone was dead. No happy ending. Mr. Swinson took the two pages crammed with writing on every line and read. As his eyes scanned the curious mix of iambic and anapaestic meters, the perfect end rhymes and the logical stanza breaks, the density and compactness of the imagery despite the occasionally juvenile and archaic word, the smile left his face, replaced by a look of utter contempt. Looking up, Jackie could hardly believe the change.

"Stand up young man!" he ordered. "Where did you get this?"

"I...I just wrote it!"

"Don't you be smart with me. You know very well what I mean. You read this somewhere. You memorized it because you liked it, and you wrote it down just now. Didn't you?"

"No, I wrote it, just now. It came to me and I wrote it!"

"Stop lying. You expect me to believe that in thirty minutes you have done...this?"

"What's wrong with it?"

"Nothing's wrong with it. That's what's wrong! What Mr. Northam has done class, is called plagiarism. It is dishonest. In fact, it is literary theft. Now don't let me catch the rest of you doing this kind of thing."

Jackie didn't write another poem for ten years. He had learned to fear his own inspiration. After that, only rage and unbridled wonder could prompt him to pick up a pen, but he would forget the reason he had not done so in so long and would try again and again to understand how a person who felt he had all the senses of an artist, could create nothing. Everything he wrote sounded like someone else's voice and each word made him more alone.

"Every grain of sand …knows. Grains of sand are solitary things. Put them together and what do you get? Stones. Stones are solitary things. Think bigger. Rocks. Rocks are solitary things. Think bigger. Mountains…the planet…oh my God" Jackie thought to himself as a rush of euphoria swept his mind and body.

Every grain of sand knows
every rock's alone
The words poured out of him onto the crumpled cigarette package
and every mountain in its pride
is sister to the stone
but he was afraid and lost the moment, remembering the class so long ago when it had come like this, and then it returned…
for mountains cannot make a beach
and deserts understand…
He had no idea what he was writing. Instinct told him to yield and be swept along. Soon he would learn what deserts understand and…who knows what else…

"Stand up you son of a bitch!" For a very brief moment, Jackie thought he would vomit as he felt an old hand reach into him from nowhere and squeeze his heart. Then he recognized the laugh.

"Sergeant?"

Barbara McLaughlan, Babs to her friends, opened the shuttered doors of her room which faced northwest across the Plaka. Somewhere out there, beyond the cafes, alleyways and tourist traps selling fake silver dolphin rings was the Acropolis. Syntagma Square was also out of sight off to the east a bit. The noise and smell of it mingled with a damp coolness that wafted up with the dry heat of the shade checked streets below. Horns honked, cats screeched, bazoukia music clamoured from passing taxis and underneath it all, up close, the footsteps of strangers coming and going. An endless procession of the simple, the exotic, the confused, the proud past and sometimes stopping at her door.

She worked her fingers through her long blond hair, untangling tiny knots with a supple deftness. In the wake of her touch, the strands lay free in loose curls. She glanced back over her shoulder smiling. The bed was a wreck. Sheets and pillows everywhere, mostly on the floor.

"Mmmmm" she sighed and turned again to the window. The sun, working its way down to the horizon, came out from behind a taller building across the street and filled the room with golden light. As it did, all that was imperfect, all that was perfect about the place was revealed in shades of mercy, the smudges on the windows and mirror, the relentless dust everywhere, the loose threads hanging from the delicate lace curtains she had found and hung with care. But the light was of a kind that infused what it revealed with a beauty that suspended judgment. Soft, forgiving, patient. She liked this moment, anticipated it every day. Unconscious of the act, she tapped a Kappa out of its blue and white package, fired off a match with gusto, inhaled deeply and blew the smoke into the room past the shutters. The steady rays of sunlight fanning out in the swirling cloud always pleased her. Suddenly she convulsed in laughter, started coughing and could not catch her breath. Each time it appeared she might, she started howling again. "The poor boy," she thought, remembering how the "Captain" had suffered a demotion to "Sergeant" within the last breath or so of orgasm and how she had put the screws to him by panting "Oh Sergeant, oh Sergeant." She could afford to. They had only been out of bed a couple of times in the last twenty-four hours. Canadian was he? She thought so by the cute attempt at humour sandwiched in between the insufferable good manners. Definitely not Sergeant material though.

The light breeze felt so cool on her skin that she opened her nightgown as far as she dared and stepped up to her Juliet balcony raising a leg to a rung on the railing, white folds of her night gown parting to reveal her firm and shapely thigh, golden in the day's last light. Another perfect evening coming. There were so many in Greece. Softly, she began humming "The South Wind", an old Irish tune her penny whistle playing father had taught her as a child. Her voice was light and happy, but a wistfulness shaded the melody and after a few bars, she sighed deeply. Her nails, she discovered, holding first her left and then her right hand up in the light, could do with some trimming. One didn't think of "manicures" in a place like this. The fingers and backs of her hands were rough from two years of cleaning floors and scouring pots.

"Oh dear" she thought "what's to become of you girl?" In the beginning, fresh off the plane from Ireland, she would do anything, pay any price to stay here far from the parochial thinking, the mind-numbing moralizing of her small home town near Donegal despite the green lushness that so many others treasured. She hungered for the unknown and the dry heat of a constant sun. " So go" she said one day and go she did, stopping one night in mid pour to the great consternation of a thirsty salesman.

"What's this?" he called out to her.

"That's it."

"What's what?"

"That's it. Yes, that's it darlin'. I'm out of here."

"What did I do?"

The smile on her face seraphic, she slipped free of the surface tension of her life as surely as a Zen student with an easy koan. Everywhere she heard the sound of one hand clapping. Seventy—two hours later, she was in Athens, incomprehensible currents of Greek in the air all around her, flooding her with hope and renewal. " Can't understand a bloody word you're sayin' she laughed to the first man who spoke to her in Greek " and I love you for it."

Now from her third floor room, she watched as Hiro came shuffling around the corner in his thong sandals, tattered shorts and Yomiuri Giants baseball cap. He was carrying a small mat and fanned himself with it as he walked.

"Hiro san!" she called "

"Nani-o...dare...doko?" he questioned, startled and looking about in confusion. Babs loved to use the little Japanese she had been able to learn from him. She liked to learn from everyone.

"Koko-ni...here" she shouted. "Koko-ni." Finally, as he looked up and saw her, his big smile spread out to a wide, gap-toothed grin.

"Ahhh Baboozoo" he yelled. Japanese, Babs had learned, never put two consonants together, so s following b was quite impossible for him. Still, she flinched. "Baboozoo" he repeated, genuinely glad to see her "what you do?"

"Not much, what you got there?"

"Mat."

"What's wrong with the one I gave you" she asked, since she had indeed given him one when he had set up camp on the roof, the first day he arrived.

"Broken."

"Should've told me. I'd have given you another one."

"No problem. I need for travel"

"Oh, so you're leavin' us then are you?"

"Hmmmm" he said, looking suddenly grave and staring into the shadowed alley. "Not so soon maybe but maybe soon...depend how I feel...wakarimasuka?...you understand?"

"Only too well...wakarimasu."

"Maybe you go soon too, I think"

"Really?" Hiro had a hard time with that one, falling into the l and r trap before he realized it.

"Leeowry."

"Jeeesus, have mercy on the language will ya' Hiro" she laughed.

"No mercy at all Baboozoo."

"Ya, no kidding" she chortled, "get in here before you get hit by a car or something. You're makin' me nervous."

"Okay, I home now."

"Maybe I go soon too" Babs thought to herself and left the window.

Chapter Six
A Black Man in a White Man's Skin

One by one they climbed the stairway and came out onto the roof making of the place an ebb and flow of languages and colours. Pablo the Argentinian philosopher had changed out of the straw coloured linen suit and sun hat he had arrived at the hotel in. Now he sauntered out to a low wooden bench in white drawstring pants and white, loose-fitting Greek shirt carrying a book on graffiti. He sat down, pulled out a pipe and absent-mindedly began to load up with a sweet, rich aromatic tobacco as he thumbed through the pages. Soon he was puffing away contentedly, immersed in his reading. He glanced up as the door creaked and Kirsten Jensen and Eva Sundstrom came out laughing away in Danish trying to balance a bottle of wine, bread sticks, towels, sunscreen and a newspaper.

"Oh no, oh no" the shorter and rounder Eva cried out as her sunglasses caught the doorframe and dangled precariously from her tiny nose.

"Eva you are so clumsy. Really. Don't drop the food" Kirsten called out.

"Oh, oh, help, help" Eva cried, and Pablo uncrossed his legs.

"Um, excuse me" he said.

"Yes?" Eva replied looking coy and mournful.

"I think the food is not a problem, but really, you must be careful with the wine. Such a pity to waste good wine."

"Oh Juan" she answered.

"Pablo" he corrected her.

"Whatever. Can't you see I need you?"

"Really Eva, you are such a tart" Kirsten cut in.

"You mind your own business" Eva responded, making a controlled crash onto the straw mat at Pablo's feet. "Here will do just fine for our picnic. Kirsten? Come here Kirsten" she said looking up. "Pablo is reading a dirty book and he is going to tell us all about it in exchange for some wine."

"It's not a dirty book, Eva" he said.

"Really? A DIRTY book?" Kirsten answered.

"It's about graffiti, graffiti, you know, writing?" Pablo countered.

"Oh yes, we know" said Eva, "like what you put on your bathroom walls. "For a good blow job, call Pedro Gonzales 922 0300 oh oh OH!"

"Stop it Eva, you will excite the man and philosophers do not respond well to excitement. It makes their brains...what do you say...hairy."

"Fuzzy" Eva corrected her.

"Fuzzy...whatever" answered Kirsten laughing.

"I can tell this evening will be typical" said Pablo humourously. "What has you two going so early in the day?"

"Oh nothing" chirped Eva "except Kirsten is going to fuck the Canadian. She thinks he's cute."

"Eva!" stormed Kirsten.

"I cannot hear you. I am cleaning up the mess you wouldn't help me from making, Kirsten. Did you say something?" With that, Kirsten unleashed a torrent of swearing, plopping down on a mat on the other side of Pablo.

"Pablo, tell me about graffiti" Eva continued.

It was now early evening and the sun was growing in the pollution haze on the horizon—a violet orange ball, the western sky suffused with a smoldering palette of rich pastels.

"What do you want to know?"

"What's graffiti?" she asked. "No, really, I want to know." Pablo looked at the sunset for a moment.

"Graffiti" he said "is what God writes on the bottoms of clouds at moments like this."

"I think we need a drink" Eva said after a moment, clearing her throat.

"Yo, Babs, you up here?" It was Ron Steicher, a.k.a. The Spacedemon sticking his head out the doorway with his longish golden hair, thick golden mutton chop sideburns and heavy moustache. Seeing the three on the roof, he paused. "Well now, what do we have here? Anybody seen Babs? I'm Ron. People call me Spacedemon. Crazy as a loon. Mamas, hide yer daughters. I just got in and I'm looking for that...Babs, you up here?....no, I guess not. My my my" he said walking over to Kirsten, " and who would you be?" Kirsten, unimpressed replied, "I would be Kirsten."

"Well now, looks like you're planning to have a party or something. You need someone to help you with that big old bottle of wine?"

"No"

"Right. Need company?"

"No"

"She's going to fuck the Canadian" chirped Eva.

"Shiiiit" Space Trucker sang out as Kirsten screamed something in Danish and chased Eva howling with laughter off the roof and down the stairs.

"They always like that?" Space Trucker asked Pablo.

"No" he said without looking up and the two settled into a strained conversation of infinite possibility—Spacedemon, the ex air force nuclear silo weapons expert, stonehead and now commercial cartoonist. Pablo, the Argentinian philosopher.

"If you knew what I knew" said Spacedemon, "about the drugs that are being used in nuclear silos as we speak, Pablo, you wouldn't sit around readin'. You'd do what I do."

"I see. And what is that?"

"I go like hell. When I was in Paris, I did the Eiffel Tower, Notre Dame, and the Louvre art Museum all in one day. Believe me, it could all go up any second. For real. See it while you still have your ass, Pablo. Technicians down in those silos are so stoned they might do anything. I know. I was one of them."

"Was?"

"Hey, what you readin' there?"

"Graffiti."

"No shit, they got that in a book? Well why don't you just go to a crapper and read it for free? When I was in Amsterdam -"

"It's not graffiti. It's a book ABOUT graffiti" said Pablo, irritated.

"You're reading a book ABOUT graffiti?"

"An analysis, yes."

"Well...why?" Space Trucker asked.

"Look, do you mind, I really want to read."

"No problemo. Can anybody just hang out up here?

"Yes" Pablo answered.

One by one, the waifs, strays and orphans of the Outside Inn found their ways out onto the roof, and the nightly party began. The Sergeant's buddy was painful to watch. New to the Med from his airbase in Germany, he had gotten drunk on Ouzo and fallen asleep naked in the sun. Now he was alternating tokes and shots to kill the pain, luxuriating in the growing shades of evening. Kirsten and Eva were back singing jazz and blues songs. From the din of conversations, their voices would rise every few minutes with "Gimme a pigfoot and a bottle of beer!"

In the background, the night sounds of Athens mingled. Bazoukia and clinking glasses in the tavernas, car engines and brakes, a thousand soft fragments of conversation rising between buildings. By nine p.m., the roof was full of people regaling each other with tales of the road. MorocCO had shown up with tray after tray of tomato, cucumber and lettuce sandwiches with feta cheese. And though he devoutly abstained from drinking alcohol, his own brand of logic had prompted him to bring, as usual, ten large bottles of Retsina for the others at his own expense. He lived for the party. The sweet aroma of marijuana wafted in and out on the night air. Candles in windproof glass holders created pockets of low light, each encircled by groups of five or ten travelers. As Jackie looked around each circle, there were five of them on the roof that night, they looked to him like living talismans. Cameos of good fortune. Light reflected in eyes, hands gestured for emphasis, faces leaned in and out of the light and darkness at the zeniths of their journeys like blossoms of some exotic plant. Just at that moment, life was everything he wanted, everything he needed it to be.

"I hear you play guitar" said Rosanna taking a seat beside him.

"Ya, I kind of hack around."

"I, too, play" Rosanna said in a soft Ethiopian accent, extending a brown hand with long, slender fingers in friendship.

"Alright" said Jackie. "What do you play?"

"Mostly my own style of jazz. Weed?" he asked, offering Jackie a joint.

"Thanks man, ya" said Jackie. He raised the expertly rolled joint to his lips and inhaled deeply, holding the smoke in for a few seconds. "Ho—leee" he rasped, "Where did you get THAT...whew!"

"Africa. Go ahead, I have other."

"Wow, thanks man. What's your name?"

"Rosanna. What's your name?"

"Jackie. Jackie Northam."

"I am just Rosanna."

"Rosanna...nice name" said Jackie exhaling a cloud of smoke. "I haven't seen you around. Did you just get in?"

"No, I am here for a while but I am staying with some people for a while and now I am back again. Do you play for a living?"

"No, just for myself and friends. Once in a while, I'll do a coffeehouse, but I don't want to make business out of it. You?"

"In my homeland, I was a professional" he said striking a match with his thumbnail and lighting another joint," but I had to leave." His hair was black and beaded with multicolored glass pieces. As he leaned back on one elbow, his dreadlocks clicked to the side. A choker of nails hammered into tiny fleurs-de-lis shone from his neck.

"Not my business, man -" Jackie started.

"What?"

"I said it's not my business, but why did you have to leave? Jesus Christ, this is good shit. Where did you get it?"

"Africa"

"Oh ya...so...you were saying about why you had to leave."

"Yes. There is revolution in my country, you know and my lyrics were a problem. I was accused of writing anti-government songs. They took away my passport and sent me out of the country."

"No shit" Jackie said.

"What is that?"

"No shit?"

"Yes."

"Oh, it's like... wow!" said Jackie.

They both paused, taking a long moment to take deep tokes. Holding their breaths, Jackie took a quick look at Rosanna who took a quick look at him. Both struggled not to laugh.

"No shit!" they both roared and broke loose in a coughing eruption of laughter and smoke.

"I think we will be good friends, Jackie" Rosanna said collecting himself.

"Maybe so, man" Jackie responded. "So, you came here from Ethiopia?"

"No, when they send me out of my country, I go to one country and another and—"

"Tell him what happened in Germany." It was the Sergeant. He settled in beside Rosanna who held up what was left of his joint. The Sergeant took it in slow motion.

"You stoned already?" asked Rosanna.

"Define stoned" the Sergeant answered dully.

"You're stoned" Rosanna said.

"What happened in Germany, man?" Jackie asked, sitting up and pulling his legs into half lotus position. What a difference a couple more feet of height made.

"Yes, Germany..." Rosanna trailed off into a silence that seemed to radiate from him. Jackie was staring intently to the northwest. The Acropolis, floodlit now, about two kilometers away, seemed to float in mid air. Rosanna, seeing the intensity of his gaze, traced his line of sight.

"Ahhh" he sighed.

"What IS that?" Jackie asked, transfixed.

"The Acropolis. This is your first time to see it?"

"Ya...well...first time at night...unbelievable..." Jackie droned.

"You are sitting " said Rosanna, "where the people lived who made it more than a thousand years ago."

"No"

"Yes, is that not wonderful?" Rosanna asked.

"Man" Jackie said, "I feel strange."

"Strange good or strange bad?" asked Rosanna.

"I don't know. I never felt like this before."

"Acropolis means high city" said Rosanna taking back his joint and inhaling the last of it. "There were many temples there, many for a goddess, Athena. A strong woman. Athens comes from her name."

"Who named it?" Jackie asked.

"The gods, because she gave a great gift to humans."

"What did she give us?"

"The olive trees."

"Hmmm" said Jackie trying to understand how a tree could be so important. "So," he continued, "what happened in Germany?"

The Sergeant produced a bottle of wine and passed it to Rosanna. Con McLaughlin pulled into the circle, wooden flute in hand.

"Jackie, this is Con McLaughlin" said the Sergeant. "Con…Jackie Northam from Canada."

"Oh, you're from America are you?" Con asked. Jackie was taken by the musicality of his voice.

"No. I'm from Canada" Jackie corrected him.

"What's the difference? It's all America."

"No man, it's not. Americans live in America. Canadians live in Canada. We are not the same."

"You tell him" the Sergeant cut in.

"Bullshit" said Sean, "Scratch a Canadian and you find an American."

"Don't mind him" Rosanna laughed. "He does this to every Canadian."

"I'm sorry" Sean acknowledged, "You people are so thin skinned about it, I just can't resist. What are we talking about tonight, boys?"

"*Boys*" Jackie thought to himself grimly "*If you only knew.*"

"Rosanna's miracle" said the Sergeant taking a long pull on the bottle. "The immaculate misconception!"

"You can laugh" said Rosanna "but one day you will wake up in hell and I will be the one to laugh."

"Why, what happened?" asked Jackie, reveling in the small group of characters that had gathered in this little place in the night from so far away.

"Angels" said Rosanna reverently, bowing his head. "Do you believe in God?" he asked Jackie.

"Yes" Jackie answered sourly. Rosanna noticed the tone but said nothing.

"In Germany -" Rosanna started.

"Ja, mein herr!" shouted the Sergeant. Rosanna gave him a bemused smile and continued.

"In Germany, I was arrested and put into jail. They beat me very badly everywhere. I almost died, I think, and I called out to Allah. They had taken away my music and set it on fire and then they put it out on my skin many times." He opened his shirt and Jackie stared aghast at the irregular scars all over his chest and belly. "Yes, they burned me with my own songs, my own children, but that night, after I called out to Allah, he sent his angels to me in the cell. They played all night."

"No way" Jackie said in awe.

"Yes. It is true" Rosanna continued.

"What kind of music did they play?" Jackie asked.

"Fucking jazz, man" the Sergeant said emphatically, hanging his head.

"Jazz" Rosanna repeated. All kinds. All night. Note by note, they dictated and performed whole compositions for me to replace my songs. Enough for a whole disc." He took a deep breath and the Sergeant passed him the bottle. Rosanna gulped the rest down.

"Then what happened?" Jackie asked.

"Then they blessed me and pointed to the cell door and one of them said, 'The journey is your guide.' And then they rose up through the ceiling and disappeared."

"What do you think he meant by that?" Jackie asked.

"IT meant that each thing teaches, each moment is holy, that there is a point to everything. We are not here by accident. This was clear when IT spoke."

"Why do you say IT?" Jackie asked, intrigued.

"IT was more than a man, Jackie. It was a woman too and a child and an old person. And it was smiling and crying, and its voice was like a gentle storm. Its eyes were this planet with the land a rich lime green and the waters indigo."

"Unreal" said Jackie, dumfounded. "It told you about life—"

"That too" said Rosanna, "but more like now, like on the roof, us...together from so many places...now."

An exaggerated East Indian accent insinuated itself into the serious conversation, "Oh the immense feeling of oneness with the universe." It was the Sergeant doing his best impression.

"If you don't like the conversation, mister military police, what are you doing here then?" demanded Con.

"Waiting for an angel" said the Sergeant. "Waiting for some kind of angel."

"Why don't you bugger off?" Con asked matter of factly.

"I don't want to bugger off. I like it here. You're just pissed because you found me in the sack with your sister."

"Bullshit" Con said in disgust getting up to leave. The Sergeant pulled him down again.

"I'm an asshole okay?" said the Sergeant. "It's what I do. I do it better than anyone. I bust big, drunk, stupid soldiers for a living, and I protect expensive fucking airplanes from the lunatics in this world." Suddenly a strong hand gripped his shoulder from behind.

"Hey, you air force? We gotta talk." The Sergeant froze momentarily.

"Who wants to know?" he asked warily.

"Ron Spacedemon Steicher." Everyone in the circle looked up. Even in the candlelight, it was impossible to miss his widely dilated pupils.

"Oh, just what I need" moaned the Sergeant, "another stoned freak."

"Stoned?" said Space Trucker with a laugh, "Is THAT why there's rainbows on everything?"

"Acid head" said the Sergeant pulling him down beside him, "Sit down."

"Eeeeaaach!" A scream arced in over Jackie's head, and Spacedemon, curled into a fetal ball, reaching up to fend off whatever it was with his hands.

"Fuuuck!" shouted the Sergeant as Con knocked over the candle trying to escape whatever it was.

With a thump, Hiro landed amongst them directly in front of the Sergeant.

"Ha!" he shouted, snapping smartly into a knife-hand-blocking stance. Spacedemon was giggling maniacally, struggling to calm his shattered nerves.

"Good evening" Hiro said goofily.

"Okay" sighed Jackie, settling himself.

"You crazy son of a bitch, you wanna give everyone here a heart attack?" snapped the Sergeant.

"Ha, ha, ha, ha, ha" mumbled Spacedemon, rocking back and forth, arms folded tightly in front of him, his voice high pitched and demented.

"It's okay man" the Sergeant consoled him, "Are you okay?"

"Okay? Okay? I'm sitting on a rooftop in Athens under the full moon, stoned out of my brains in this mystical candle light transient commune, an Ethiopian jazz musician is talking angel visions, Japanese doing flying side kicks are dropping from the sky..."

"It's okay man" the Sergeant reassured him, "It's okay."

"Okay?" asked Spacedemon, starting to shake.

"Breathe." It was Jackie from across the circle. "Just breathe man."

"What?" asked Spacedemon, turning wide eyed to him.

"Just breathe," Jackie repeated, and as he did so, the startled travelers looked at each other. Hiro, still standing, turned to Jackie, and snorted.

"Sooo" he said, surprised, and sat down in full lotus position on someone's straw mat.

"Shake the stress out of your arms." Jackie instructed. "Try to sit up comfortably with your back straight. Let your tongue rest on the roof of your mouth, your front teeth lightly touching. Keep your chin in line with your belly button. Yes. Good. Keep your eyes open, but unfocussed and rest your hands on your lap."

As he spoke, first one, then the others, followed what he said. His voice was soft and calmly reassuring.

"Now just gently, without forcing, follow your breath as it comes in, turns, and goes out on its own time. Focus on your breath. If other thoughts come, they come. If they go, they go. Do not force or hold onto any thought. If you notice that you have forgotten about your breath, just return to following it again. Be still. Only follow your breath."

Soon the group was quiet and as it drifted into the depths of silence, the other groups on the roof followed. Eventually, the whole bunch of them became an oasis of stillness in the bejeweled Athenian night. As though in sympathy with their efforts, the moon first swelled, then drew down amongst them, immersing itself in the calm center of the Athenian nightlife polyphony. Indescribable scents of a foreign land in subtler and subtler shades of fragrance revealed themselves to the travelers. The call of night birds, unnoticed all along, was suddenly there, small and precious in the darkness.

"Oh man" a voice whispered.

"Shhhhhhhh" several others responded.

Then, very quietly, and delicately, the notes of an old Irish tune, The South Wind, formed, slowly, like a lullaby. It was Con playing a small wooden flute. The notes passed through the silent sitters like light through glass. Not a muscle moved. Breath only. Time passed.

"Man, it's like..." someone started, and then, with a huge "bwaaap!" someone among them farted.

Suddenly the moon was in standard orbit, the traffic noise was back, and the entire rooftop convulsed in laughter.

By morning, Kirsten and Jackie had made love in the shed, emerging shining with sweat into the first rays of dawn and a gentle breeze. They did not hold hands or smoke a cigarette together. No promises were made, and love was not mentioned. There was no conquest. She had asked what he liked and had given it to him. He had learned to ask, for himself and for his lover. That was new. He emerged into the morning light almost ashamed. He was a little North American nobody who had just made it with a beautiful Scandinavian woman. She was so intuitive, rolling him out of the missionary position almost as soon as they had started, mastering him with a finesse that took his breath away. Under her touch, he felt the world melting away in all directions, surrendering, surrendering, exultant in her appetite. From there things blurred as they pleasured each other orally, and then he was astride her moving slowly and deeply, working hard to prolong the narrowing focus of the onrushing high, and then she was over him working up and down with great rich sighs, and behind it all, somewhere far away, dust flying as light worked its way through the cracks of the old wooden door. And then in spasms of ecstasy, Jackie arched his back up off the floor three times lifting Kirsten in the air squealing with delight and surprise.

As she rolled off of him and they collected their breath, she whispered to him.

"You are not like most North Americans."

"No?" he said, suddenly defensive.

"Oh, I don't mean in a bad way" she continued, taking his hand. "I mean you know what you want, or you seem to and you aren't afraid of letting go...and..."

"And what?"

"And you aren't obsessed with trying to impress."

"No, but...was it good...I mean did you...You don't find me..." Jackie stumbled.

"Too feminine? Oh God, forget what I said about you not being North American. You like what you like. I like what I like. We like the same. It is a moment only, a beautiful moment. Just sex. Don't read too much into it."

"No?" Jackie asked doubtfully.

"Shhhh" she said, "I go away today to Denmark."

A short time later, they opened the door on a new day and a roof full of sleepers. Kirsten disappeared with a smile into the building then and Jackie never saw her again though the images of their lovemaking would hover in his memory like a talisman for many years.

During the night, the others had been busy too. Moved by Rosanna's plight, someone had pledged a donation of cash to send one of the group to Turkey, where, it was said, an American passport could be bought for the musician on the black market. Others had followed suit. Jackie had kicked in three hundred dollars.

"When you get to Amsterdam" Rosanna had told him, "go to Poste Restante" an address used in every city in Europe when no specific address of a person is known. "Your money will be waiting, Allah willing." Jackie didn't believe it for an instant, but he was so sorry for what the jazz musician had been through that he bought in. In the mean time, it was decided, something had to be done. Without identity papers of some kind, it was only a matter of time before Rosanna would be arrested. Passports had to be given to hotel management when rooms were rented, and police at any time could ask to see identification. So, it was decided to get him out of Athens to the relative security of an island where the police were few. Jackie bought him a ticket on the inter-island ferry Portokalis Ilios leaving from Piraeus, the port of Athens, and together with ten of the rooftop crowd, they said goodbye to Babs, MorocCO, and the Outside Inn. Early one morning, backpacks loaded, they boarded the white, green and orange ship and set off for the islands to the south. That was how Jackie came to the island of Hydra. While the others set up camp on a beach down the coast, Jackie had called the cot on the balcony over the taverna at the harbor home.

Chapter Seven
Celeste

A few days after the crewing job on the yacht fell through, an elderly man walked up and sat down across from Jackie in one of the quayside cafes. He told him that there was a boat of some kind for his daughter, and it was sitting in a shipping container at the harbor. He motioned to an out of the way, fenced off area across the water. He knew that Jackie had tried to sign on as crew on the yacht which had been impounded. The man was paying—strong Greek coffees and ouzo with soda water. Jackie decided to hear him out and quickly took stock of him. White loafers without socks, soft white chinos with no belt, a short-sleeved, white, knit Ralph Lauren shirt contoured to his surprisingly muscular frame. His darkly tanned skin stood out in stark contrast to his clothes. He wore no jewelry, but his eyes, an unforgiving blue grey, reminded Jackie of a Finnish girl he had once known. She was humorless but breathtakingly beautiful. Like so many others, she had drifted into the periphery of his life, astonished him and just as surely and finally drifted out again. He remembered trying to get her to laugh over a drink in a Toronto bar. She had remained implacable, her eyes, he discovered to his surprise, seductive in their detachment. After a short time, they had risen as separate lives from the table. The similarity stopped there.

"I understand you know about boats," he said in a curious, crisp English spiced with tones of New England and somewhere else.

"It's true, but how..."

"Unimportant. I have a business proposition for you. You are enjoying your time in Greece?"

"Yes, but..."

"Perhaps you would like to be able to stay longer. A young American like you..."

"Canadian."

"Canadian" he corrected himself, "a young Canadian comes to Europe to..." He hesitated a moment.

"To what? Go on. You seem to think you know something about me."

"I apologize. I am being presumptuous and I have quite enough trouble already in that area."

"What area is that?" Jackie asked, uncomfortable that the conversation had so quickly turned personal with a total stranger.

"Thinking I know more than I really do about other people."

"No problem. I have the same problem. You may as well tell me why you think I'm here."

"The usual" he said, waving his hand to indicate the many young travelers passing on the quayside. "You are looking for something. Right?"

Jackie laughed nervously, "I admit to the cliche."

"Will you be able to tolerate what you find?" the old man started again.

"I beg your pardon?" Jackie said, trying to figure out how he had gotten himself into such a strange and unnatural conversation with the man. Being a polite Canadian, he could see no way to leave without giving offense, and accepting that working one's way through the "crazies" was part of being on the road, he decided to hear the man out. He willed his tense muscles to relax and inhaled slowly, deeply. The old man, anger rising in his voice, continued.

"Well if you don't know if you will be able to tolerate what you are going to find, don't you think it's rather dangerous and stupid to look?" Surprised and flustered, the man seemed taken aback by his loss of control.

"I am not looking for anything" Jackie blurted out.

"Well" said the man, pulling a weather-beaten Greek fisherman's cap over his shiny, bald head, "in my experience, when a person is on the move, he is either looking for or driven from.

If you are not looking for something, from what are you driven?" The eyes, a harder grey blue now shone opaline in the harsh light. Jackie felt the hand of an unseen path begin to close toward his life. Something much more profound than the man before him.

"Tell me about this business deal," Jackie heard himself say.

"It is very simple really" the man said, gesturing up the quayside to a shipping container. "Celeste, my daughter, has a surprise in that container. It is a racing sailboat of some kind. Don't ask me what kind. She mentioned the name of it once, but I don't remember. She has this fantasy of some day competing in the Olympics or some nonsense like that. And so I bought this thing in the States and had it shipped over. She doesn't know about it. I am told it is very complicated and there are many parts. I need someone to put it together. She is not...mechanical...She is not..." He strained for words that would not come. "She is not able," he said finally. "Would you agree to take a look at it and see if there is anything you can do? I can pay you whatever you ask, even get you a crewing job on another yacht..."

"How do you know..." Jackie started.

"It is a small island" he offered, avoiding Jackie's eyes.

"A small island" Jackie repeated, provoked, but struggling not to show it. Why did this guy know so much about him? He decided to yield to the moment for no more reason than it pleased his quest for adventure. "Sure, I'll take a look. What the hell. Now?"

"No, not now, there are some things I must take care of" he said, rising from the table. "Tomorrow morning. I'll meet you at the container. Shall we say at nine o'clock sharp? Oh, and don't worry about the bill. It is taken care of. Stay and enjoy a few more drinks." He turned, took a few steps then turned again and fixed Jackie with a piercing stare, "And, uh, you are not an artist are you, a painter, writer, anything like that?" Jackie, who was beginning to really dislike the way the man used his eyes, fixed him with a stare of his own and imagined boring through the man's eyes into his frontal lobe as he answered.

"Nothing like that," he said with a seraphic smile. For a split second, the man seemed not to know what to do. Then he produced a handkerchief from his pocket, wiped his forehead, turned and left with an aborted smile on his lips. Jackie watched as he walked away. Such an impressive person, he thought, would be known by everyone in such a small place, but the waiter just looked down and moved out of the way as the man passed. Several hundred yards down the quayside, the man stopped beside the entrance to an alleyway that was dark with shade. He pulled out a cigarette and started smoking, backing up slowly to the side of a building and leaning against it. He checked his watch and glanced up to the hillside surrounding the harbor.

As he appeared to scan for something, a figure quickly emerged from the alley and started to turn in the opposite direction from him. No sooner had the figure appeared than the man shot out his right hand, grabbed what now in the light appeared to be a quite large woman, in the back by her belt and struggled to steer her in the opposite direction.

A faint "shit" was all Jackie could make out amid the woman's flailing arms and bucking refusal to be led. Then she broke free, took a step back and gave the man a vicious kick in the balls.

"Jeesus Christ" Jackie heard himself say, draining the last of his ouzo. The man bent over at the waist, but managed to seize the woman again, and after a moment, forced her to go with him past the last buildings and up a path that led to the top of the nearest hill. There, he handed her over to a much bigger figure, which seemed to rise from the rocks themselves. Over the crest they went, the man pointedly gesturing, the woman flailing, and the massive figure holding on for dear life.

"Celeste" Jackie gasped, realizing that the woman was really a girl. On the way back to his balcony over the taverna, Jackie decided to check out the alley. When he got there, he found it to be a fairly short dead end. The blank walls of two buildings formed two sides. The third had a door with a small brass nameplate—D. Kalogiros, M.D.. As Jackie turned to leave, a click echoed among the walls. Looking down, he found a syringe driven deeply into the foam rubber of his left sandal, just beneath the toes. "Fuuuuck!" he said aloud, bending over for a closer look, trying to decide if he had been stuck or not.

"I'll take that," said a woman in a white lab who quickly but precisely took the needle from Jackie's grasp. Before he could get a good look at her, the door was closed and she was gone.

"Fuck this" he said to himself walking quickly away from the place out into the moving air and sunlight of the quayside again.

The next morning at precisely nine o'clock, he walked over to the far side of the harbor toward the shipping container. It was sitting in a small compound, which was littered with an assortment of crates, machinery, old pallets and rusting wire. Litter was banked up against the leeward side of the fence, which closed the area off from the public. The gate was open. The old man was waiting by the container and greeted him.

"Good morning. Look, I don't want to rush this, but I have things to do, so we will have to make this quick."

"No problem" said Jackie as the man removed the heavy lock, pulling the door open to the screeching groan of metal on metal. For a moment, he could see nothing.

"I had one of my men put the boat on, what do you call it, the little trailer?"

"The dolly?" Jackie answered, noting the use of "my men."

"That's it, yes, the dolly. Help me pull it out" he ordered.

Jackie and the man grabbed the handle of the light launching dolly and pulled the boat into the light. It was covered in protective foam wrapping. From his pocket, the man produced a tiny knife with a matte black handle and in a motion worthy of a ninja, sliced through the one band of taping that held most of the foam in place. It fell open in front of Jackie who made another mental note about the man.

"No need" said Jackie, "I know what it is. It's a 470 class racing dinghy...as in four point seven meters long, just over fifteen feet. It takes two to sail it, a skipper and one crew. The crew hangs out over the side on a trapeze when conditions require it. It definitely is an Olympic boat. There is a men's division and a women's division." The man's face paled visibly.

"It is so small. Who hangs out over the side, as you say," he asked.

"Usually the heavier person" Jackie said. He realized his mistake when the man bit his lower lip and exhaled loudly.

"Is it dangerous?"

"It is a very demanding boat," Jackie said.

"Demanding?" the man said, as though the notion did not fit somehow. Why would Celeste want a demanding boat? She resisted all authority. Probably she did not know the facts.

"Ya, the slightest mistake by skipper or crew...letting a sheet, a rope go too slowly, shifting your weight incorrectly, failing to read the wind or water just right...a lot of little things can dump it very quickly."

"Really" the man said, looking increasingly worried. "How do you know so much about this kind of boat?" he asked.

"I blast around in one for fun back home."

"You own a 470?" he asked incredulously.

"Yup! When the small craft warnings go up, I go out and blast around in the high winds and big waves."

"Do you race?"

"Ya, from time to time, but just at my own club."

"Are you good?"

"Yes."

The man was going to ask him just how good he thought he was, but decided differently.

"What does it take to master this boat?" he asked moving to face Jackie directly.

"Communication. After the training, it all gets intuitive. When each member of the crew knows how the other will react to all the variables of wind and water, they go beyond words. It gets very Zen. When the conditions are wild, I sail with my crew for hours, and we don't speak a word. We just act and react spontaneously, instinctively. There is no time for talk and no time for thought. You get very high, completely absorbed...It is very sweet. The communication happens at a very subtle level."

"Yes, I can see that. How odd that you are here just at this time. So, can you put it together?" Jackie agreed, pending an inventory of the hundreds of parts that would be necessary.

The next day, Jackie returned to the compound with a tool kit supplied by the man. It was delivered by a young woman who introduced herself simply as an employee of Dr. Silverton, Celeste's father. It did not particularly surprise Jackie that he had not learned the man's name. He was terrible with names. Besides, in his own family, Jackie's parents had rarely referred to him by name, and when they did, it was usually by his brother's name. He didn't take it personally though, at least not consciously. As often as not, they called his brother, Jackie. Only when Jackie was meeting with his first psychiatrists did he realize how hurtful the misuse of his own name by those who brought him into the world, truly was. So, it was Dr. Silverton. That was strange. To Jackie, he didn't seem at all like a medical man. As eloquent as he was, there was something of the street about him. Something hard and dangerous. Jackie thought of how sweet that notion was.

Danger, mystery, the unusual—how he craved it. He had never felt this good back home where life was so predictable. Anything could happen here, nothing was certain. He felt opportunity everywhere, even the chance to reinvent himself or to find a new self. In early high school, when his friends were dreaming of being lawyers or sports stars, Jackie had asked God simply to help him to be the most that he could be within God's law. He didn't know what he meant by that but it seemed radical and fair—a combination that pleased him well. Now he finally felt himself alive and engaged in that quest.

The gold monogramming on the black nylon kit bag read Carpe Spiritem, seize the spirit. "Strange to name a tool bag" Jackie thought to himself as he unrolled it on an old wooden crate. Everything he would need was there—pliers, wrenches, screwdriver, a small rivet gun and an assortment of rivets.

With a key, which the doctor had given him, Jackie unlocked the door and hauled the 470 out into the blazing sun, intending to rip the last foam coverings from the hull. Oddly, they just fell off, their fastenings undone. Backing into the container, he stared at the beautiful candy apple red deck and gleaming white hull. A bit further back, and his heel came down on something soft yet firm. There was a small cracking sound followed by an ear piercing scream that, magnified in the echo chamber of the container, scared the shit out of him as he convulsed involuntarily into a defensive posture and lunged toward the opening.

"Oh shit, oh, oh, you've broken my toe, you asshole!" a female voice shrieked from the dark end. There was a metallic thud and gong-like resonance as the person stumbled heavily into one of the steel walls. "Ow … damn, damn, mother-fucking, shit-faced, son of a…" Holding her toe in her hand, Celeste thumped heavily out of the container in four loud beats. Jackie recognized her instantly as the female he had seen the doctor drag off the previous day. Standing as she was on one leg, her eyes popping out of her head, Jackie could not help himself and doubled up in hysterics.

"You laugh? You laugh?" she screamed. "You broke my toe, you fucking faggot and you laugh?"

"Whoow, wait a minute" Jackie answered.

Celeste was looking around in panic, trying to figure out how she was going to get home or anywhere else for that matter.

"Move, asshole" she yelled as she made for the crate holding the tools. With a swipe of her hand, she sent them flying into a pool of grease and oil as she came down hard on the crate.

Unfortunately, the crate was badly weathered and came apart in several directions under her weight, one sharp splinter penetrating her shorts and entering the left cheek of her all too ample bum. With renewed vigour, she howled and already Jackie could see people running toward the compound from the cafes. But the more she howled, the more he laughed. It was just too pathetic. He couldn't help himself.

"I'll kill you, you stupid son of a bitch. When my father finds out, you're dead, dead, dead."

As she spoke, she struggled to her feet and Jackie could see the blood trickling from her white shorts.

"Oh Jeez, you're hurt" he said, suddenly serious.

"Well duhhh fruitcake. What was your first clue?"

"No, I mean you're bleeding, from your bum. There's a piece of wood stuck in you. Let me..."

"Like hell" Celeste said, feeling behind her until she located the fragment, yanking it out and throwing it to the ground with a grunt. By now several men had approached the entrance to the compound and slowed to assess the situation before entering. "What the hell are you looking at? It's just an accident. Go on, get outta here!" Celeste shouted. unconvinced they turned, looking back over their shoulders as they walked away. "Go on!" she repeated.

"So, how are we going to get you home?" Jackie asked.

"You aren't going to do anything. My father will already know about this. In about five minutes an offshore racing boat will be here to take me home."

"Where's home?" Jackie asked.

"For now, on the other side of the island" she said through her pain. Help me to the side of the quay." Jackie bent down so she could lean on his shoulder and they went out of the fenced area to a place where they could sit on clean concrete beside the water. In a few more minutes, the throaty roar of large engines being throttled down came from the harbor entrance out of sight to the right. Half a minute later the sharp, polished lines of an ebony Scarab glided beneath their dangling feet.

"That's confidence" Jackie thought, noticing that no fenders had been put down to protect the expensive yacht from the rough quayside. There was no need. Before it had come to a stop, the huge man who had taken control of Celeste the day before, reached up and scooped her into the boat with great strength and gentleness, lowering her slowly onto the edge of one of the boat's sumptuously padded seats.

"How do I get in touch with you?" Jackie called as the Scarab began to accelerate in a smooth arc back toward the harbor entrance.

"Just get the damn boat ready" was all he could make out over the rumble of the engines, that and the large man looking at him murderously until the boat passed from view.

That turned out to be a long but not very difficult task. Every part was present and by the end of the day the many lines that allowed the boat to be tuned for different wind and wave conditions had been threaded through the appropriate blocks and secured in place. Jackie set the trapeze wires on which the crew, secured to them by a fast release hook on his or her trapeze harness would hang. He then tested the gear, which would control the spinnaker, the balloon like sail that was deployed when the wind was abeam or following the boat. This one matched the red of the hull and as a light breezed filled it, there was a sudden blossoming of colour in the otherwise monochromatic compound. Satisfied, Jackie repacked the sails, put the canvas cover on the boat and sat down for a smoke. His shorts were grease stained and torn, his nails chipped and dirty and his hair a ragged mess.

As he inhaled deeply, his mind returned grimly to the last bubble bath he had taken. He did not want to think of that. Suddenly the image was just there, unbidden. The humiliation of wanting nothing more than to die and being unable to perform the act. It was strange how the whole gender issue had receded so far into the background until now. Now it came back with a vengeance. Maybe it was the hot, tough work on the boat that conjured the other side of his nature back into the foreground. It was always like that. He could spend only so much time in the world of rough and tumble until the softer side of his being asserted itself again. Most time spent in the presence of men was, for him, time spent holding his emotional breath. Men judged. Men consigned themselves and everyone else on the planet to tightly circumscribed roles. Why did they have to do that, he wondered. Moving from traditionally male feelings and impulses to their traditionally female counterparts within himself was as natural for him as breathing. In fact, doing so, living all dimensions of his being, was absolutely critical. He was beginning to understand that. Back home, the psychological brakes had to come on every single time he felt himself making that identity shift. He did not see it as a shift, but he knew that everyone who was not transgender did, and so for survival purposes, he learned to view it as a separate component of his being. When the two, which never were separate in the first place, could not be reconciled by reason, he realized he had ended up in the bathtub with a knife to his wrist. The relentless judgement of men had simply exhausted him to the point that the resulting intellectual, spiritual, psychological and emotional pain had become overwhelming.

He took another long drag on the cigarette, stood up slowly and scanned his surroundings for a full three hundred and sixty degrees. An island in Greece. Few people knew him. He would leave soon. Nothing, he thought would follow him from this place. The boat was finished. But "fruitcake," and "faggot," why had Celeste called him that, he wondered. Did it show that much? Who was she to judge, a fucked up, overweight brat with an attitude problem. After the incident in the alley, Jackie had wanted to check her arms for tracks, but he had forgotten. Maybe that's what she was doing in the container. It was pitch black inside and he needed a source of light. Looking around the yard, he found an old cracked mirror from a vehicle of some kind. Propping it up on a crate, he aimed it at the floor at the back of the Container. He found no needles, but there were the ends of several marijuana joints and an empty bottle of Metaxa, a Greek brandy. There were also the remains of a candle which had burned itself out, a blanket and a towel made up into a sort of pillow at one end. The candle was close to where the boat would have been, shining in the darkness.

"Ah shit" Jackie whispered as a lump rose in his throat. "Carpe Spiritem."

Chapter Eight
Fledge and Burn

Walking back along the quayside, Jackie stopped at a clothing store. Hanging on racks outside were floor length, hooded things. They looked like dresses, some more than others, except for the hoods.

"Can I help you?" the jolly, rotund proprietor asked twirling his black moustache.

"What are these?" Jackie asked.

"These are djalaba. Very nice. You like?"

"I like."

"Which one you like?" the proprietor asked holding up a serious dark one with heavier material and a very light white cotton one with intricate, salmon coloured scrolling and beads made of small shells.

"This one" Jackie said pointing to the more feminine of the two. The price was reasonable, but he wondered what he was getting himself into. "Are these for men or for women?" he asked.

"Women can wear. You can wear. Anybody can wear" the proprietor said, just wanting to make a sale. "You want to try on? We have place inside."

"No, I'm too dirty" Jackie said. "I'm staying just over there. If it doesn't fit, can I bring it back?"

"Sure, no problem" the man answered, handing Jackie his change. At the inn over the taverna, Jackie showered and washed his hair. He stuffed his dirty clothes into his backpack and resolved to have them cleaned the next day. The djalaba fit perfectly, the soft fabric smooth and cool against his skin caressing his instep and ankles as he paced back and forth across the washroom. The sleeves were long and widened at the cuffs. He flapped them to feel the cotton against his wrists, then flipped the hood up, inserted each hand in the opposing cuff and turned to the mirror.

"Saint Jackie the monk" he said with a laugh and tossed his head so that the hood fell back.

"Ya, right, Saint Jackie the tart is more like it sweetheart" he continued, fluffing his damp hair up with his hand and working out a few split ends. "Well whatever you are, you're me...I'm you...oh whatever" he said in teasingly sultry tones to the figure in the mirror. "Can you really do this? Are you crazy? The first gay basher you run into is going to beat the shit out of you. You know that." He paused a moment over that one. "Well maybe then, my dear, we have to learn how to survive a little bit better" he answered himself. "Maybe we need to learn to give as good as we might get." With that he went over to his backpack and withdrew a small black dagger with a four-inch blade and dropped it into a small leather purse with a thin leather strap. "You can let them drive you to suicide, baby, or you can be you and stand up for yourself." With that he reached into the backpack again and took out a choker made of rose quartz and silver beads. "Not bad" he thought as he looked in the mirror, turning so the light played brightly off the stones. "Let's keep this simple" he said to himself, "just downstairs to the bar, have dinner and come right back."

As he walked down the front steps from the front of the taverna, he was greeted by a cool and gentle evening breeze, the harbor ringed by a twinkling amber incandescence of candlelight and lanterns. On the one hand, he was hypervigilant, watching for the slightest signs of disapproval from passersby; on the other hand, the night was so sweet, foreign and magical that his heart was racing. It was like having one foot on the gas and one foot on the brake. Something had to give. The breeze picked up the folds of the djalaba and blew them across his calves, the coolness coming right up through the bottom and in through the sleeves. As the whole thing moved around his warm body, he felt his skin working with the night. No, he would just keep walking, maybe till morning. After two tours of the quayside, however, he was famished and started looking for a place to eat, having decided no male would be stupid enough to assault him in such a public place. For that matter, the whole quayside was public, even the balcony on which he slept.

Just below his cot, diners dined and musicians played nightly. Realizing this, Jackie relaxed, joyful at having found a small, perfect place in which he could be more himself. As the thought took form, even his body language began to change as he shortened his stride to a more feminine cadence and allowed a small turn of the wrist as he walked. Those who took notice of him, did not seem malicious. As he passed, the occasional couple would make a small, discreet gesture in his direction and words would pass, but there was no gawking and no dismissive giggling or twittering which would be standard fare in North America. Jackie was amazed at the cool maturity and acceptance of the people around him. Maybe it was the constant influx of tourists. Change was expected. Maybe it was just that Mediterranean and European males were profoundly different from their North American counterparts. Eventually, he headed for a restaurant that looked promising.

There was a pretty young crowd, and the place seemed lively enough. It was almost the last building on the quayside, at the far end directly across the harbor from the container compound. The patio itself extended out of the second and third floors of the building into the rough stone of the surrounding hills. Jackie climbed the steps. Speakers attached to the building were putting out some solid reggae. The waiters, of various ethnic backgrounds and young, were moving quickly because the place was packed. "What a great spot" he thought to himself, but try as he could, he couldn't find a free table anywhere and more and more people were arriving. A line was starting to form. "Shit" he thought, "this is going to take forever." By now he was starving and decided that this place would just have to wait for another day. He turned to leave.

"ToronTO!" a voice shouted from above. "Up here, up here." Jackie looked up and there leaning over a wrought iron railing with his arm around a girl was MorocCO. "Come up and join us."

The waitress who was controlling the line gave Jackie a nod and he made his way up to the second patio. He was surprised to find the chef from the Outside Inn with a bottle of Retsina in his hands and lipstick on his cheeks peering out from behind his amorous girlfriend.

"ToronTO, help, rescue me" he laughed, trying to disentangle himself from the girl. As he did, she turned around.

"I don't think so!" she said with a deafening finality as her eyes met Jackie's.

"Celeste" he responded cautiously, trying not to laugh, but it didn't last. The chef disappeared behind her except for his hands, one on either of her hips rubbing her into motion everywhere.

"Is she not beautiful ToronTO?"

Jackie had no idea what to say. It was the first time he had seen the girl smiling.

"Yes, beautiful MorocCO" he answered.

"Allow me to introduce…"

"We've met" Celeste said icily. "This is the idiot that broke my toe."

"You are the fruitcake, ToronTO?" the chef said trying to collect his half drunk wits. "Ha, ha, ha, ha, ha. You are the one? This is too good. Oh my God. Sit. We drink, we talk, maybe later we dance."

"Since when did you start to drink?" Jackie asked as they took their seats.

"This is all her doing" the chef responded.

The group that Jackie had come to the island with had gone off down the coast and camped out on a beach. Tonight was one of their rare forays into town to clean up, buy supplies and get a decent meal for a change. Spacedemon was there, the Sergeant, Hiro and the rest of the group. Some of them were at a nearby table and waved as Jackie looked over.

"Where's Rosanna?" Jackie asked, looking around.

"Shhhhh" said MorocCO leaning toward him. "Not so loud okay. We still wait for our friend to get back from Turkey. Until then, Rosanna has to stay out of sight, but so far, so good." As he spoke he looked around scanning the faces. The problem in Greece was you never knew who was a cop and a lot of people were more than willing to turn in a dirty long hair for the slightest thing.

"Who went, anyway?" Jackie asked, then noticing Celeste's interest, "Is she okay?"

"Celeste?" of course she is okay. She knows everything. She has spent a lot of time with us from the day we arrived. Sometimes she even stays at the beach. She is fine. The Danish guy went…Eric…did you know him?" That was a surprise to Jackie. They hadn't met, but everyone knew the Dane as a very quiet, soft-spoken intellectual more into existentialism and phenomenology than dangerous intrigues.

"Why him?" Jackie asked, bewildered.

"Who knows? He and Rosanna were always talking heavy stuff about identity and freedom and things like that. Maybe he is a romantic idealist.

"Does he know anything about the black market?" Jackie asked.

"Apparently he knows a lot."

"Who would have imagined?"

"I really like your dress, Jackie" Celeste cut in, "Where'd you get it? It really suits you."

"Yes" chimed in the Spacedemon from down the table, "It really is pretty. How come we never saw this before? Bet you didn't expect to run into us here. Don't mind her" he said nodding toward Celeste. "I knew a Sergeant in the service, tough as they come, had this thing for frills and velvet. Nobody gave him any shit. Straight as they come. Just had this thing for frills and velvet. Gay guy came onto him on the street when I was coming back from buying some smokes. Sergeant laid him out cold, right there in the street. Should have heard the crying when the guy came to...whaaa, whaaa, whaaa. Seriously...a grown man." By now everyone at the table was laughing over Demon's impression complete with pained expressions and limp wrists.

"Ninety-five percent of transvestites are straight" Celeste stated with a mix of authority and mischief.

"I'm not a transvestite" said Jackie acutely embarrassed.

"Nobody said you were, man" the Sergeant offered "but you do look kinda cute tonight, if you know what I mean."

"Fuck off Sarge" Jackie countered somewhere between hostility and humour, but the Sergeant Continued.

"He's just staking out turf. You know, making a statement, sending a message" he said seriously, following with a wry smile, "Just what statement are you making?"

"I'm not making a statement."

"Oh yes you are" the Sergeant replied.

"You may be hearing a statement, but nobody's making one."

"Uh huh" the Sergeant answered, not believing him.

"I don't know what problem is" Hiro but in, "You look very legal."

"Regal" MorocCO corrected him.

"Yes, legal" Hiro Continued, "Like king or movie star or something...very sophisticated."

"Thanks Hiro" Jackie said, pouring himself a glass. "To old friends and new" he offered, holding it high.

"To old friends and new" everyone chimed in.

I think you look like a Moroccan" said MorocCO, slapping Jackie's back too hard. You know what?" He drained his glass and poured another, pouting as the bottle ran dry. "Waitress, we need another Retsina. We must have another Retsina. We have many toasts to drink. Turning again to Jackie, he said "You know what?"

Dismayed at seeing the devout abstainer drunk, Jackie groaned "No, what?"

"You are just a black man in a white man's skin. Do you know that?"

"No" replied Jackie, "I had no idea."

"A black man in a white man's skin" MorocCO repeated with enthusiasm.

"He's cut off" the Sergeant laughed, grabbing for MorocCO's glass.

"And do you know why?" the chef continued, protecting his drink with his free hand.

As one, the group at the table, in an exaggerated, singsongy cadence asked "Why is he a black man in a white man's skin?" but the chef simply pointed, in slow motion to his own heart, held the other hand up to silence the group, and inclined his head meaningfully. For a second or two, at best, there was quiet, then one by one they broke into laughter.

"To the black man" said Demon, holding up his glass. As everyone followed with their own glasses, Celeste added her two bits.

"I think he's gay."

It was then that Jackie flashed back to the psychiatrists at the gender clinic. Each one finding something different. Something not true. Now, just for an instant, Jackie thought he saw why. Here was a group of people who instead of just accepting him, talking to him, taking him by gesture and word and action to know him, had instead to put him in a little box of understanding in their own minds. A genetic male appearing this way, had to be this, or this, or this, and so that is exactly what they saw, what they wanted to see, what they needed to see for reasons of their own.

"If they would just stop" Jackie thought, *"I would relax enough to speak softly, gesture the way I want, sit just so, be with the flow of conversation in feminine time, in feminine style, whatever that is."* But he could tell now, even with these, his good friends, that that was not possible. They needed him not to be transsexual, not to be such an...improbable woman. He sensed that they were afraid of something and as he sat there, speechless, his rage grew at being denied the possibility of being himself in the midst of others by the fears that others had and the scent of their fear caused his love for them to recoil. He feared it would always be so. To make matters worse, the more these thoughts pressed in on him, the more he was aware of the others staring at him. They finally sensed something was wrong. Jackie was staring down at his drink. When he looked up, he saw the faces of people, strangers now, who wanted him to be as they thought he had been all along...a North American guy with a story to tell, another blessing of the road. Like everyone, they did not like stories they could not understand. Such stories, they felt, diminished them in some way.

Serious most of his life, all Jackie wanted now was to be light, deliriously light and ...womanly...in this magical place across the seas. He felt the light, the water, the fragrances in the delicious night air, everything about the place, drawing that instinct from deep within him. And they stood between him and the moment in all its ripe possibility. How he hated them for it and loathed his own fear of disapproval. He could leave, he could tell them all to fuck off and unburden himself all over their smarmy heterosexual certitude, he could cry, he could turn the entire table upside down in rage. He decided to do all of these. Like a bomb going off, he erupted from his chair, mightily heaving on the table which, being secured to the Concrete patio with stout bolts, refused to yield. So abruptly was his great effort snubbed, that his hand ripped from the edge, sending an open bottle of wine spinning around on the table drenching everyone, and his own glass of wine up into his face. The almost animal-like howl that he loosed in the effort, combined with the unexpected shower, sent everyone lunging backwards, Hiro, actually head over heels.

"Try to get your small minds around this okay" he screamed. "I'm not what you think I am. I'm not what you want me to be. I can't be that. You can keep your oh so perfect little categories. I'm so tired of this shit. You self-righteous bigots. You smug bastards. I'm just so pissed off I…"

"Whew! Go for it!" Celeste shouted, rising to her feet as well and looking very excited. "Tell them! Tell them!"

"Oh shut up you little junkie brat." Jackie responded venomously, "Why don't you get a life? What are you so fucking afraid of anyway? No, we don't want to talk about that do we?" he shouted, watching her step back, blinking in momentary dismay. The damnable thing was that she was right. He did want to tell them. Something. What was it? Time. He would lose the moment, could feel it slipping away. Passion could take him there now. He felt it. The rage felt somehow…pure. Others could deny. He could not. Not any longer. "I'm a woman" he said simply, seriously, and then he sat down, took out a cigarette, held it with his wrist angled way back, took several deep swallows straight from a bottle that had miraculously escaped the chaos, crossed his legs and awaited the inevitable. There, it was out. Tears began to well up and somewhere he distantly heard the people. What were they now, friends, strangers?

"Staking out turf!"

"Legal"

"Straight…just bent!"

"Making statements!"

"As gay as they come!"

Only MorocCO did not immediately join the chorus. Jackie looked over to see him staring back pensively with his elbow on the table and his chin in the palm of his hand.

"Black woman in a white man's skin" he said with finality. There was silence as everyone helped to put the table setting back together, assiduously avoiding anything but the slightest eye contact with Jackie. The notion of Jackie being a black woman in a white man's skin was just abstract enough for the group to feel okay about returning to its former sense of self.

"To the black woman!" the Sergeant offered.

"To the black woman" everyone repeated, hurriedly refilling. Jackie raised his own glass numbly to his lips and thought of cages within cages within cages. For the others, the moment had been safely ushered by.

MorocCO may have been uncharacteristically drunk, but Celeste was well on her way to some bizarre, dark space that only she truly knew.

"Daddy would positively love you" she said to Jackie.

"Ya, why's that?" he responded defensively.

"My daddy, well, he's not really my daddy, anyway…" she said, trying very hard to collect her wits, "my daddy is very good, very, very good at knowing what makes people tick, he…"

"Uh, you told me" said MorocCO to Celeste, "that if you started talking about daddy, I was supposed to make you stop. So stop. You're talking about daddy."

"That was when I was sober. I'm better now. Now I don't give a shit, and I really doubt that you guys are a threat to anybody's national security. I mean, look at you all. Jeesuz Christ, get real. Be a mensch and pour me another glass, baby" she said to MorocCO. He was too far-gone to care. He had done his duty.

"Don't blame me tomorrow" he said.

"Sweetheart, if we do things right, there won't be a tomorrow" she replied with a sinister smile.

"Fuckin' 'A'" said Spacedemon without realizing what he was agreeing with.

"Anyway, at the rate we're going, nobody's going to remember anything anyway. Let's lay the whole thing out" Celeste continued.

"Again?" the Sergeant asked.

"Whuddya mean, again?" she demanded.

"Do you know how many times you've laid the whole thing out for us?" he countered.

"Well, I listen to you don't I" she asked. That shut him up.

"I know your father is a doctor" Jackie said "from what the lady told me when she brought the tools."

"Bitch" said Celeste.

"What kind of doctor is he?" MorocCO and the others shot him a glance that said not to ask, but it was too late.

"Daddy is a kind of freelance psychiatrist. Governments and organizations hire him to do psychological profiles of people. If daddy puts in the wrong word about you, you disappear or you just stop being a problem. There are lots of ways of making problem people into sweet, lovely, cooperative ...things. Think of daddy like a kind of psychological zit cream. When he's through with you, you just get less and less until you disappear." With that, she drained her glass and seeing MorocCO beginning to doze, poured herself another. Fascinated, Jackie wondered at the currents of life that one moment had him in the depths of depression and in the very next moment, up to his neck in adventure. This was good, even if it was only half-true. Even if it was tragic.

"*This is great*" he thought to himself. "*I'm sitting across the table from the daughter of a kind of spy or something.*"

Jackie asked "who does he work for?"

"I already told you...countries, companies" she said.

"Ya" he replied, "but I mean, like, what countries? Are you American?"

"What does it matter" she asked, "All passports lie. There are no countries. People fuck. They shit. They love. They hurt. That's all people are. Gimme a break, what the hell is an American? There are no Americans, and there's no Chinese, and there's no ..."

"Just faggots and fruitcakes and straight people?" Jackie cut in.

"Shit" said Celeste. "Got me there, partner. Daddy would be proud. Daddy would be so proud of that one. Daddy's girl does a good 'read' on a subject. To answer your question, daddy has not one single, itty-bitty moral in his body. No trouble there, no sir. Cut him a check and he'll sell a reading on anybody to anybody."

"But where do you live? Some place must be home?" Jackie continued, but for a moment, Celeste hesitated.

"We move around a lot" she evaded. "You'll see. There will probably be a message for you when you get back to your place tonight. Daddy wants to see you tomorrow about something."

"Is he angry about your toe?"

"No, he knows it was my fault" said Celeste.

"So, you're not angry?"

"No, I slept in the container. The great lock picker got what she deserved."

"You really have a thing for this boat, don't you?" Jackie said.

"How would you know? Maybe I just needed a place to get stoned in peace."

"You went to sleep looking at the boat."

"Now what the hell makes you think that?" she said, looking slightly panicky. "You're trying to read me."

"The way you placed the candle...too far to put out without getting up...close to the boat...which you had unwrapped. And when the candle..."

"Flickered" she said swallowing...her mouth dry.

"It seemed like it was..."

"Sailing...the shadow..."

"Was moving and moving..."

"Ya" she whispered, lowering her head. "You're just gonna love daddy."

When Jackie had returned to the taverna, the manager had given him the message. It was an invitation for him to call on Doctor Silverton the following morning to discuss something related to the sailboat. He was to take the main path that went up over the hills behind a particular church and across to the leeward side of the island. At the end of the path, someone would be waiting to take him the rest of the way.

So the following morning, Jackie shaved, put on the one pair of clean shorts he had and headed across the island. The higher he climbed, the freer the air moved. Tethered goats foraged in the dry scrub vegetation, and though the sun was well up over the horizon, unseen roosters crowed loudly. Light cirrus clouds blew across from the northeast. Reaching the crest of the hill, Jackie turned and looked down on the port. Nothing save one lone fishing boat returning from a night on the water seemed to be moving. How beautiful the little village clinging to the coast seemed from up here, the whitewashed buildings, bright in the morning sun like a long curving breaker frozen in time. Offshore, small flecks of white, whipped up by a fresh sea breeze stood in brilliant contrast to the deep indigo water. Somewhere upwind past the many small islands, which were just smudges in the hazy morning, was the Aegean Sea. Turning to the south, he surveyed the sea miles that led toward the Sea of Crete and the Mediterranean. A strong desire to be on the water gripped him as it had before and he promised himself then to do whatever it would take to make that happen. Then reverie gave way to remembrance.

"How could I say that?" Jackie thought to himself as he remembered the fiasco at the taverna. *"Now they all think that I think I'm a woman. Brilliant. Well that's what I said, so that is what I get. But I felt like a woman then. I was a woman, and so I told them. What's wrong with that? And now? Now I don't know what I feel like. There is the beautiful sea and the sunshine and I'm so high up. Birds flying, scrub bush all around, wild roses. I feel this place. Yes, the highest place on the island. When people need to get as high as possible, they come here. When they need a distant horizon, when they need to look down, when they want less between them and the sky. When they need a new perspective and a fresh breeze. They have always come here for those things. I feel this place. I feel the people that have been here. Is that presumptuous? Am I psychic? There is a psychic residue here. I am not imagining it. Layer upon layer, hopes, dreams, fears, layer upon layer. Why don't I feel like a woman now? Why does it come and go like that? Something's definitely wrong. Continuity would be right. Wouldn't it? Can we come and go within ourselves like this and still be sane?"*

As these thoughts pressed upon him, he steadied himself into seiza position, eyes closed, facing into the breeze. Thought led to thought, emotion to emotion. Drawing on his training, he let them all pass, all the makyos, the devils of delusive thought, the master had called them. Breathing only, he travelled a landscape more and more without time and sensation until from that place that such things come, he certainly didn't know where, seven white birds of thought appeared behind his closed eyes, sitting still on a dirt path.

"There are seven things you must do." The thought came from the group of them and not from any individual. But Jackie was unequal to the vision, becoming preoccupied instead with the fact of having it.

"Oh fuck, oh fuck, something strange is happening" he thought, unable to restrain his joy and opening his eyes though still in deep trance. There on the solid dirt path before him were seven pure white seagulls, motionless, staring at him, not ten feet away. When he saw them, his heart raced, and it was only something very deep within that caused him to close his eyes again and rejoin the meditation. He struggled to still his breathing but could not, tried to slow his heart but failed and when he opened his eyes a moment later, the path was empty.

Things like this had been happening all of his life. Strange psychic, spiritual events that happened, refusing all attempts to cultivate or control them, and then they were gone. As a child, he had burned his hand severely on a furnace pipe, but the burn was healed without a trace after the soothing words of his mother who read to him in calm, confident tones from the Bible. He had simply fallen asleep as she spoke, awakening an hour later to wholeness. As he drove through the White Mountains of New Hampshire, his grandmother had appeared to him at the moment of her death in Toronto, Ontario. He had seen books hurled with great force by an unseen entity in a university residence room barely ten feet square. The graduate student who had summoned him had been troubled by the spirit since she awoke to find it at the feet of her bed. To Jackie it was clear that the spirit wished her to make a phone call at that very moment. She did and reached the person, as she explained to Jackie later, that she had been calling for eight hours. Driving between cities, the man had stopped at his apartment only for the thirty seconds it would take to pick up a set of keys. She passed on the spirit's warning about becoming president of some new company. He confirmed that his father had just died and left him one. He was actually relieved to hear from this distant friend as he, too, had a bad premonition about it. The spirit, appeased, left the girl in peace after that.

And once, Jackie had witnessed a single, very large wave in a tiny, calm lake not much bigger than a pond. But he knew it signaled the end of a serious fight between his parents – and so it had. The girl friend that was with Jackie had been scared off by the knowing which had come to him with the sound of the wave. They would never grow closer than friends after that moment. Between the gender issues and the psychic events, he wondered whether his elder sister might be right. Maybe he was, in her words, a freak of nature. Still, feelings were feelings and facts were facts. No wonder so many people accused him of thinking too much.

"Do you think life is easier for other people?" a psychiatrist had once asked him.

"Yes" Jackie had answered. "I do."

As he worked his way around the last bend in the path, a tiny village came into view and at anchor offshore, a glistening, white motor vessel at least fifty feet long. Jackie wondered who the millionaire was. Two old women dressed in black and sitting in front of a weathered shack, giggled and returned his greeting with a curious wave, their hands curved like new moons.

"Yasou" Jackie said as he passed an old man leading a donkey up the path.

"Yasou" the man answered with a smile. As best Jackie could understand, the word meant hello but there was a certain joy in it that seemed to lift the spirits of everyone who spoke it. If a word could contain light, yasou was it. The man pointed back down the path and said something else in Greek. Jackie pointed to himself.

"Me?"

"Neh" said the man, nodding.

"Efharisto, thanks" Jackie responded.

"Parakalo" came the cheerful reply, and the old man trudged on up the hill.

The path soon turned into a rough stone trail, then a rough alleyway, then a better alleyway lined with houses, finally opening onto a paved quayside. There was a small beach with double-ended wooden fishing boats up on shore for repair. Red, green, orange, blue , yellow, they lifted the tone of the rocky shoreline with a riot of color combinations.

"Mr. Northam, over here" a voice called from behind him. When he turned, Jackie saw Dr. Silverton and Celeste waving from a nearby taverna. He walked over and joined them at their table.

"Jacqueline" Celeste said with a wide grin, "this is Peter Andrews. Peter, this is Jacqueline Northam.

"What are you doing?" the doctor demanded, grabbing her by the wrist.

"She can explain, if she has the guts" Celeste said, reveling in the tension. All eyes went to Jackie.

"Perhaps I..." Andrews said, rising.

"No, please, sit down" the doctor growled. "My Celeste has a very twisted sense of humour. I don't know where she gets it. Apologize, Celeste."

"Oh, you people are no fun at all" droned Celeste after a long pause. "Jackie dear, I'm sorry for suggesting that you were a woman. I just don't know how that thought could have come into my mind." One by one, she looked at the others, a sharp and caustic intelligence smoldering in her bloodshot blue eyes. She turned after a moment to Jackie and said with a note of pity, "men" then smiled mercilessly.

Andrews sank back down into his chair. Jackie sat fuming. How dare she play this game with his, his what, true nature, conundrum, neurosis, special calling? Part of him was grateful to her for using words that at least suggested she accepted him for what he was. Another part of him hated her for backing him into such a public corner. So, he sought refuge in cliché.

"It's okay, you had to be there" he said with a bewildered shake of the head.

"I guess" said the doctor as Andrews laughed with relief. " Mr. Andrews…"

"Call me Peter" Andrews cut in smiling too broadly.

"Peter is my good friend and business associate. He is staying with us for a few days. By the way, before I forget, we are having a party tonight. Why don't you join us?"

"Sure, where?" Jackie asked.

"Just a few doors up that way" he said gesturing vaguely to the left.

"Thanks."

"Not at all. Celeste, why don't you find Kurt and see if the repairs are finished?" With a roll of the eyes and a pout for all to see, she got up from the table leaning in until her cheek touched Jackie's.

"Say yes, dear" she whispered sweetly but sincerely in his ear. Then she looked away. "Kurt!" she screamed, freezing the blonde, powerfully built man in his track two hundred yards away and several startled people in between.

"Go to him, Celeste" the doctor half moaned, half ordered.

"Hummff" she growled and sauntered off with her hands in her jeans pockets.

"I don't suppose you are as good with electronics as you are with putting sailboats together, Jackie?" the doctor asked.

"What needs fixing?" Jackie responded, unsure whether he was serious or not.

"Something to do with the interface between a satellite navigation system and the steering mechanism of a yacht."

"Oh for Carpe Spiritem? No, sorry, that's way over my head." For an instant, the smile completely left the doctor's face and without it, his expression was brutal, like a pinched and tight version of a Samurai battle helmet. Then the smile was back so quickly Jackie doubted whether the change had taken place at all.

"Of course, the tool kit" said the doctor. "Yes, my life requires me to spend time on the yacht now and then, but we will not discuss that. As I was saying, I have a proposition. The 470 was only part of my birthday present to Celeste. I have also promised to provide her with training sufficient to try out for the Olympics four years from now. I had contracted with someone they say is the very best. Not the current world champion, the next champion. A bizarre young man from New Zealand."

"Tommy Elliott?" Jackie asked.

"No, he has too many problems just now.

"Eric Williams?" Williams was a comet in the 470 heavens, having come seemingly from nowhere. He was still little known. Only a few insiders were aware of his genius.

"Yes," said the doctor "that's the one."

"But how could you know about him?"

"It is my business to know about people" said the doctor coolly."

Taking the plunge, Jackie asked, "What exactly do you do, if you don't mind me asking?"

"Oh, I'm a sort of cross between a human resources manager and an executive recruiter, but I don't talk about my work much outside of the office."

"O.k." said Jackie "That's interesting. I used to sell people."

"I beg your pardon" coughed the doctor, drawing his glass of water safely away from his mouth.

"Ya, for a year, I sold corporate space planning and design services. I would tell you why you should hire our designers to create your new space. I sold talent. Design genius."

"Really, maybe tonight you would tell me exactly how you did that. Were you good at it?"

"Yes."

"Hmmmm, anyway, as I was saying, the problem is Mr. Williams has contracted a vicious little disease and will not be going anywhere for a while. I need a temporary solution. Someone to teach Celeste the basics until I can bring in another world class trainer. I can offer you a substantial hourly rate and safety boat to stand by at all times just in case." In case of what, he was not sure.

"Well, that's quite an offer" said Jackie, "U.S. dollars?"

"As you wish. It might be for days, weeks or longer" the doctor continued, "Of course, I don't know what your own plans are."

"Ya, that's the trouble" Jackie mumbled. "I'm not even sure myself…I've been travelling and my mind has kind of been on other things."

"Whatever" the doctor cut in. "Think about it. I don't make promises lightly. Let me know as soon as possible. Tonight would be good."

"Say yes" Celeste had said. It would not be easy. The doctor had no idea what he was asking. With this girl? The idea was nuts. It would be like teaching an orangutan to dance a pas de deux in a china shop. On the other hand, there was something seductively outrageous about the whole thing. And that was one of the points of the trip, he knew – to escape the tedium of his life in North America, the dragons of mediocrity as he had put it in one poem. Teaching the demented daughter of a mysterious millionaire how to sail in a little corner of heaven at someone else's expense. A girl who, he suspected, knew as much about him as he did about himself – maybe more. He would give it a few days and see how it went, but first he would go to the party. Every new scene, every new face and taste was a step away from life as he had known it. And that was good. At the moment, all the parts of his nature felt appealed to and the sweet sense of danger gathering itself on the fringes of what might be, filled him with relief and hope.

"Jackie, tell me, that symbol you are wearing around your neck" Andrews began, attracted by the silver pendant reflecting in the sun, "What is that?"

"This? Oh, it's an ankh. An Egyptian symbol of life."

"Do you have a personal relationship with Jesus Christ, Jackie?" Andrews asked as though it was the most natural question in the world. Jackie was aghast at the man's presumption.

"I beg your pardon?" he said in obvious shock.

"Oh don't mind him" the doctor cut in, "Peter's always on the lookout for souls to save."

"Do I have a personal relationship with Jesus Christ" Jackie repeated. "Well, you would have to define Jesus Christ and personal."

"*You sanctimonious son of a bitch*" Jackie thought to himself. "But tell me, Peter, do you?"

"Do I ?"

"Do you have a personal relationship with Jesus Christ?"

"Absolutely."

"How do you know you're not just talking to yourself and hearing your own thoughts?" Jackie asked, but the doctor cut in.

"Okay, okay if you two really intend to go into this stuff, you can do it later." A silence followed, and Celeste was back with an answer for the doctor.

"Kurt says the systems are up again and everything is nonimal."

"Nominal" the doctor corrected her.

"Whatever" came the bored reply.

"Fine, so thank you Jackie for listening to my idea. We'll see you tonight. Shall we say eight o'clock?"

"Sounds good to me" he said, taking the cue to leave. As he walked out of the restaurant, he caught an image of the group reflected in a window. Celeste was leaning forward asking the doctor a question. He answered with a hand gesture that said so-so. Dismayed, the girl pushed her chair back, shook an accusing finger at him looking toward Jackie as Andrews shook his head in evident disapproval.

"Shit!" The word exploded from the taverna behind him and just as quickly dispersed into the small sounds of the day as Jackie went off to think about the offer. On a huge rock down by the water, one that must have weighed tons, smooth worn and rounded by the sea's attentions, he pulled out his writing pad and watched the shadows lengthen.

"For mountains cannot make a beach and deserts understand"

How strange it was to glance down and read the line. It sat there like a milestone he had passed long ago. So much had changed since that line had come to him. Oddly, in reading it, he felt like a stranger to himself. There were so many things he could do right now. He could stand up and walk away, take a boat to the mainland and a plane to anywhere. Well, almost anywhere. In a month, surely, he would have to start thinking about how to make money to avoid going. Home? In some ways this island was home, these people, these changes, these unknowns. But he didn't feel pulled in any direction. If anyone had asked him where he wanted to go or what he wanted to do next, he would not have been able to answer. For what part of himself was any place home? Which part should he satisfy. Which was most him or her?

"You have given me a torment that anyone else in this world would find laughable and ridiculous" he said to the lengthening shadows "a pain that doesn't count...anywhere. I'm this for an hour or a day...I'm that for a minute or an hour...I'm all of it at once...I'm none of it. How the hell am I supposed to talk? How the fuck is anyone supposed to know me. The only clear thing you have given me is the black gift of being a bunch of contradictions and knowing it, and knowing they come from you. And so I am supposed to do what, go thumbs up or thumbs down on a part of me that's real and right? If you want me to live all of this, dear Creator, then please have the decency to make it possible. So much is out of my control. There is so much that is me that I cannot live." And as he spoke he completed the stanza.

for mountains cannot make a beach
and deserts understand
that sand and mountains will not serve
as stones in children's hands

"More nonsense that will end up in a waste basket" he thought to himself, and closed the book. He would rely on the moment and decide what to do when he walked into the party. "What was it MorocCO had said" he tried to remember... "The journey is my guide. Ya, something like that, well, easy to say. Guide to what?"

Chapter Nine
A Room Full of Certainties

"**A**ren't you going to ask why I'm wearing a dog collar?" asked Celeste sitting down across from Jackie and staring into his eyes.

"No."

"Does it excite you?"

"No, why should it?"

"Because" said Celeste, "there's even a loop where the leash goes."

"That should excite me?"

"The thought turns a lot of men on, but" she said, flipping her wrist, the fingers delicately splayed, "you're not like most men. What is it tonight, Jackie, Jacqueline, Jack, Judy, what?"

"Get real, Celeste."

"Me? I should get real. That's funny coming from a whore in training."

"Whore."

"Yes, whore. You know what you are and every time you cover it up to get something you want, you're giving it up."

"What the hell am I giving up? You don't know anything about my life."

"I know a lot more than you think. You and I are very similar. It's scary. You're giving up time. Minutes when you weren't you. You use yourself like money. You want something from someone who can't handle the real you, you play the cover up game. A minute here, a minute there, a day here, a year there. I've been all through it. So if you're going to teach me to sail, there are going to be some conditions."

"Ya?" said Jackie with a disbelieving laugh, "Like?"

"Like don't fuck with me."

"Why do you have to be so crude?"

"Oh I'm sorry, there's a lady present. Look, just don't mess with my head. I get enough of that. If you're gonna teach me to sail, you absolutely have to be you."

"Ya, right. Well what if I don't know who I am? What if I change a lot? Faster than you can keep up with? And who said I was going to teach you to sail anyway? I mean, look at you, you're hardly sailor material."

"You don't know who you are?" Celeste replied disdainfully, "So join the club. You change a lot? Well duh...I guess I know a little about that, don't I? Change faster than I can keep up with? I don't think so, and as far as not being your version of a sailor, what do you expect, whites and deck shoes?" With a leer, she waited for Jackie's denial.

"Ya, that's what I would expect. Would you expect whites and deck shoes at your vampire bar?"

"I don't go to vampire bars, but" she said hesitating, "whatever turns you on. So, you're saying that if I wear whites and deck shoes, you'll teach me?"

"No, I'm not saying that. You're too stubborn, too unpredictable, and too slow. The whole thing is wrong."

"I'm too unpredictable? Who's a man one day and a woman the next?"

"That doesn't matter" Jackie answered calmly. I sail equally well as a man or a woman, just differently."

The corners of her mouth drawn and tight, Celeste began to plead. "I'll lose weight" she said flatly, trying not to betray the anger rising within her.

"It's not your body that's slow. It's your mind." One of Celeste's hands moved abruptly to her dog collar and nervous fingers began to feel for the studs.

"You son of a bitch" she snarled.

"You do too much dope. Your reflexes are off." With that, Jackie took a page out of his small notebook. With his left hand, he held it between the open thumb and index finger of his right hand, letting it go and catching it the split second his left hand opened up. "Now you" he said to Celeste.

"What's next a Rorschach test?" she asked sarcastically.

"Just do it" Jackie instructed her, leaning forward with the page pinched between thumb and forefinger. Celeste grudgingly leaned forward and stuck her arm out. Her nicotine stained fingers were fat and the nails chewed to the quick. On each finger was a cheap metal ring with a different symbol...peace, yin yang, death skull, pentagram and around the thumb a big moonstone.

When Jackie let the paper go, it slipped cleanly between Celeste's fingers for a bit, but she had added a wicked sideways swiping motion with her arm which trapped the paper with centrifugal force until she could close her fist on it.

"Uh uh" Jackie said, "Can't change the rules to have your own way."

"Who's changing the rules? Anyway, rules are made to be broken" she countered.

"As I told you…too stubborn." Jackie said, scooping the paper up from the floor where she had dropped it in a crumpled ball.

"Okay, okay, one more time."

"The official way or your way?" Jackie asked.

"The official way. I promise." So Jackie took out a fresh sheet, held it between her fingers and dropped it. This time, she did not move her arm and the page had passed her hand by a good six inches before her thumb and index finger snapped shut.

"Shit…do it again" she ordered.

"This is going nowhere" Jackie answered.

"Well what's the point of this anyway?" she asked.

"The point is, you react this slowly on a 470 in twenty knots of wind, we are both going swimming, and I don't want you putting me in the water all over the Aegean."

"That's ridiculous."

"And that's the second thing. In a racing boat, you've got one skipper and one crew. You're so stubborn, you'd never be able to let someone else make big decisions affecting you."

"Like what?"

"Like whether or not it's too rough to fly the spinnaker, when to change direction to a racing mark, how to balance the boat."

"I don't want to be a crew. I want to be a skipper" Celeste said with force.

Jackie's face hardened, "Not without being a crew first."

"That's dumb."

"I told you" said Jackie, shrugging his shoulders.

"What?"

"You're too stubborn. It can't work."

A long silence set in. Static came from speakers somewhere. Music on the way. Beethoven's Moonlight Sonata. Jackie let out a deep sigh. "Ah shit" he thought. How incongruous it seemed with all the positive energy in the room. Laughter, smiling, the clinking of glasses, the shaking of hands. All Jackie could think of was being unable to cut deeply enough to end his own torment, and now here he was wasting his time with this, this punk brat. He felt he had betrayed the poignancy of his own dilemma by getting bogged down in all the trivial little irritations the kid seemed to exude.

"What's the matter?" Celeste asked. "Hello? You there?"

"Ya, I'm here. I'm right here with you in this place" Jackie answered in a monotone. A stream of cigar smoke enveloped them both. "Jeez, that's disgusting" he whined.

"What?"

"The cigar smoke."

"Touchy, touchy" she said, trying to lighten the mood.

"No, I'm really allergic to it. My throat closes and my sinuses shut down. I have to get out of here." At that moment, Andrews caught sight of the two of them, and carrying a huge brandy snifter, three quarters full, made his way over to them, stepping on the toes of a fashionably dressed artiste in the process.

"Celeste, Jackie" he said as he pulled a chair up in front of them.

"Mr. Andrews" Jackie acknowledged.

"You don't mind if an old fart talks philosophy with you do you? I'm in the mood for a really good conversation."

"Conversation or conversion?" asked Celeste with joyous sarcasm. "Doing the Lord's work again, are we?"

"Yes, to all of the above" blurted the man, singing in his high spirits. "So, Jackie, you asked me a question when we met about talking to the Lord."

"To? Surely you mean 'with' Mr. Andrews" said Celeste.

"To...with. What's the difference, Celeste. It hardly matters, child" said the man.

"Oh, it matters, Mr. Andrews. 'To' is lecturing, 'with' is communication."

"That's silly, Celeste."

"No, it's not" Jackie cut in, exchanging a conspiratorial look with the girl. "Anyway, as I asked before...how do you know it's God's voice you're hearing and not your own?" For a moment, the grin left Andrew's face.

"Do you know Jesus, Jackie?" he asked. "Have you been born again?" The man had power. Jackie had to give him that. There was a directness, an arrogant presumption about him. The man pulled his chair even closer to the two of them. "No, really, do you have a personal relationship with our Lord?" Jackie actually liked the man's simplicity. There was something of the salesman in him. Jackie felt he understood salesmen. They had a knack for overcoming objections and working around difficult situations instead of exhausting themselves meeting problems head on. Still it didn't stop him from seeing a dark side. *"You smarmy son of a bitch"* he thought.

"Yes I do. She speaks with me whenever She wants."

"She?" said Andrews with a twisted smile.

"Oh, this is getting good. Don't say another word 'til I get back with another drink" Celeste ordered.

"Your father lets you drink?" asked Andrews.

"Yes, and he isn't my father" said Celeste testily.

"Celeste, he does his best" the man offered, but the girl was already grabbing a martini from a tray as a waiter glided by.

"Celeste" Andrews reproved her.

"Oh, he doesn't care" she laughed. "Now what's this about God being a woman?"

"He's not serious Celeste, he's just pulling my leg" said Andrews.

"No. I'm serious" said Jackie leaning back and taking out a cigarette, offering one to Celeste, who lit both hers and Jackie's. "Doesn't it seem strange to you that God is portrayed as a male figure in most of the world's religions. Allah, Buddha, Yahweh, Krishna, Manitou, the Christian God. And the prophets are almost all male. Jesus, Mohammed, Moses, etcetera, etcetera. And the holy books are all written by males. Don't you find this just a little too convenient? I mean, come on, the mainstream religions are obviously just an attempt by straight males to explain the universe and the world in a way that keeps them in control of the world." Celeste squealed with delight and clinked glasses with Jackie.

"Absolute nonsense" Andrews said." Even if it was true, we are told in the Bible that men are to provide spiritual leadership and stewardship in the family and women as equal partners in faith are to provide…"

"Are men and women made in the image and likeness of God, Mr. Andrews?" Jackie asked. The smirk returning to his face, Andrews replied.

"The Bible says so."

"I see" said Jackie, "then tell me what kind of God it would take to make both males and females from itself" but before Andrews could reply, Jackie with a cruel look in his eye pressed on. "If we were truly made in the fullness of this god's nature, would we not have to be at least male and female, each of us? And don't you think it is just simple good business to come down to earth and appear as a male to crude civilizations when the decision-makers are all men? Who do you think would have listened back then in Biblical days if God had shown up as Christine instead of Christ?"

By this point, Celeste and Andrews had pressed back in their chairs as far as they could go as though hurled there by an explosion or repulsed by something hideous. Andrews' mouth hung open as he searched for words. Celeste's eyebrows reached upward for the middle of her forehead, one hand holding her martini, the other resting over her heart.

"Thought I'd heard it all" she said, shaking her head. Andews took a deep breath and decided not to fight.

"You certainly do have strong feelings about your relationship to our Lord" he said "Jackie, if you don't mind, I'm going to pray that HE gives you clear answers to all of your questions." With that, he hailed an imaginary someone across the room, feigning surprise. "Brad! Where did you come from?" Then he leapt from his chair, brandy slopping from his glass onto the floor.

"Do you really mean those things, or were you just playing him?" Celeste asked Jackie.

"Both" he replied.

"Do you mind if I ask you a question?" Celeste asked with an uncharacteristic sincerity. Jackie was on guard.

"No, what is it?"

"Do you really believe we are made in the image and likeness of God?"

"Yes."

"Then why do we do the shitty stuff?" Celeste asked.

"I'm no prophet, that's for sure, but a friend of mine once said that everything we do that's negative comes from fear."

"Are you afraid?" she asked.

"Yes. You?"

"Always. Teach me to sail, chicken shit?"

"Will you do what you're told?"

"I'll try."

"No dope while you're in training."

"No dope."

"Or alcohol before sailing?"

"Or alcohol before sailing. And you will be you?"

"I'll try" said Jackie

"Then this is gonna be real? It's really going to happen?"

"Is that what you really want?"

"Yes."

Jackie looked her in the eye, "I'll remind you you said that."

"Deal" said Celeste, grabbing Jackie's hand. "When do we start?"

"Grab your drink and join me outside" he said. They walked out of the building and across the quayside to its edge. It was an unspectacular evening with no moon. Low clouds smudged the sky, blotting out most of the stars. "Where's the wind?" he asked her. She turned to him impatiently .

"How the hell should I know. It's night time...duh."

"Close your eyes" he told her.

"This is stupid" she giggled.

"It's not stupid, close your damn eyes."

"Okay" she said, closing them and standing in a petulant slouch. "How's that?"

"Feel the wind?" Jackie asked.

"No. There is no wind."

"Yes there is" Jackie said firmly. "Feel your skin, the skin on your face, on your neck, on your wrists. Feel it....got it?"

"I...I...don't know." She stood motionless for a moment, then feeling nothing, squinted hard and raised her arms as though praying before a distant deity.

"Anything?" Jackie asked.

"Nothing" came the dejected reply. "Anyway, this is creeping me out."

"It's partly because of the drinking you've done tonight. It numbs the skin. Scratch your left wrist and follow the pain as it reduces on your skin. Focus 'til the pain is gone, then focus on the point where it disappears."

"You're sick" said Celeste looking at him sideways.

"Yes, that's right, now do it."

"You're really weird."

"You're the one who's skin dead. Humour me. Try it" said Jackie.

"Okay" She drew the nails of her right hand down her left wrist firmly, but not so hard as to draw blood. seconds ticked by as they stood, eyes closed, in the rich, damp air. Eventually, Jackie opened his eyes to make sure she had not snuck off, but there she stood, a tiny smile spreading out at the corners of her lips. Then she raised a hand to her face in slow motion, then held the palm up to the night sky. "Okay...I think I feel something...more a temperature thing, sometimes my face feels a little cool in spots."

"Yes" said Jackie "Good. Now slowly turn until you think you are facing straight into the wind." She did as she was told without question. She turned a little to the left, a little to the right, a little more to the left, still more to the left and then stopped.

"It's so light" she whispered.

"Yes, light" Jackie repeated.

"And it goes to the left and then to the right, back and forth" Celeste whispered.

"Yes...it's called an oscillating shift" said Jackie, "Some winds do that."

"Oh" said Celeste "Are there many kinds of wind?"

"Do you have a lot of different moods?" Jackie asked.

"Okay...okay...okay" she whispered with a curious tone of resignation. A moment of silence followed and then she said very simply, "Thank you" and then just walked away. When he called after her, she just kept walking, speeding up as he called her name, one hand swinging to the cadence of her flight, the other raised to her face.

Chapter Ten
Loose Ends

Doctor Silverton fought the tightness of the sheets at the end of his bed. With a sleepy heave, he attempted to roll over. Although his right leg broke free, a heavy weight pinned his left, stretching his instep and wrenching his hip socket as he turned, eyes still closed. Thinking it a dream, he settled down again, relaxing into the image flow, or was it a dream? In the somewhere between of sleep and waking, he began to think himself awake. At one of the portholes of his stateroom, the sheer lace curtain took on the form of a being, but just where curtain ended and being began he could not tell. A nice imagining. Squinting his eyes produced no more definition than rubbing them. He was seeing a wraith-like form several feet away, but feeling it as though it sat upon his feet.

"Talk to the one who mends the net" it said. "In holy darkness. Close…see…see" and filaments of its being seemed to float like silk in a breeze that was not there as it turned and pointed out the porthole. With a gasp, Silverton stifled a scream and ripped off the sheets. Nothing in his life had prepared him for this, and in his terror, he was entirely new, a stranger to himself. Heart pounding, the steps he took to the porthole were not his and a storm raged in his mind as he struggled against a kind of knowing that flew in the face of all his training and experience. Something in him began to understand that the spirit was no imagining and he felt at once enthralled and vulnerable. A part of him felt like he was losing his mind.

He had slept late. A glance at the bulkhead chronometer showed that it was eleven a.m.. The sun, rising on the opposite side of the island, would soon strike the quayside and Carpe Spiritem anchored close to shore. Both, for the moment, lay still in darkness. As he approached the porthole with its polished brass rim and locks, the ocean widened before him. Nothing but a heavy morning haze burning off and the calm untroubled waters of the Aegean. Half a kilometer up the coast, lay that odd little chunk of rock island with the tiny, whitewashed church. He had intended to take the launch over to it many times, to see if he could get into the building. But he never did. Why was it there? No one lived on the speck of stone barely thirty feet by thirty feet. But it had something. Even now the white cross atop the small, rounded dome seemed to burn with the day's first light. But he had seen that many times before. He was sure he had. No there was nothing. Beneath the cross, the rest of the church was still concealed in darkness. He watched and actually thought he could see the light descending the walls.

"Nonsense" he muttered and turned back to the room. "Nonsense." But the deed had been done and the knowing was firmly rooted in his mind, and he didn't like it one bit. What to do? One did things with knowledge. Knowledge was power. But this knowledge was dangerous, perhaps more a threat than the encrypted psychological files in his computer. The great Doctor Silverton starts seeing spirits. It would end his career, but if he really had been visited by a spirit, if such things really did exist, a whole new dimension had just opened in his life and already its attraction was irresistible. For men in their fifties, such opportunities were rare. Thoughts flooded his mind. How to make it happen again. Who to talk to. He was a consultant. One always hired a consultant for "special ops." This was a "special op." Time to be careful. If the powers that made deposits for him in his Swiss account found out he was talking to psychics or anyone else for that matter about this stuff he would soon find his life as insubstantial as the creature he had just witnessed. The studies for which he was paid so handsomely were derived from intuition, from recognition of subtle patterns in the thinking and behavior of his subjects. They were also based on careful observation and traditional psychiatric methodology. This was dangerous. He felt the first victim, objectivity, lying at his feet.

The next morning, Celeste made her way over to the compound and the dinghy, barely able to conceal her enthusiasm.

"Okay, let's go sailing!" she shouted when she saw Jackie. He had made arrangements for a small area of the compound to be set aside for the small boat. A narrow ramp for hauling out motor boats angled gently down to the water just beside the fenced off area.

"Did you bring something to eat?" he asked.

"No, why?"

"Because" he said, "You're going to need your energy from now on." A look of defiance came over the girl's face.

"I'm stronger than you are" she said, "anyway, we won't be that long."

"Eight to four every day with a half hour for lunch" said Jackie, "Bring something that gives you energy."

"You're joking" she said.

"Do I look like I'm joking?" Jackie asked.

"Lighten up, will you" Celeste said, "You don't have to be so serious. This is supposed to be fun."

"You're in training now. Don't expect fun for a while."

"Oh brother" she said, pausing to think over his changed tone and expression. "So when do we go sailing?"

"You won't set foot in this boat for at least a week, maybe two, maybe three. It depends on how fast you learn the fundamentals."

"Fundamentals" she repeated with a frown. "Wait a minute. It's my boat. You've been hired to get me sailing."

"My way."

"Your way" she said bitterly. "It's always everybody else's way. When is it going to be okay for everybody when things are completely my way?"

"When you're the skipper. If you've got what it takes" Jackie replied matter of factly.

"What does it take?" Celeste asked.

"You'll find out" Jackie said, fingering the lose strands of a frayed rope.

"I hate that" the girl blurted out, "that know it all and keep it secret attitude old people have."

"I'm not old" Jackie answered, surprised.

"You're ancient. You talk like a goddamned philosopher. Why don't you take the stick out of your ass and get real. You promised you would be you" she said accusingly.

"This is me. Did you bring the paper and pen I asked you to bring?" When it was clear to Celeste that Jackie would not rise to her challenge, she shrugged her shoulders in resignation.

"Yes, teacher."

"You have a whole new vocabulary to learn. Three days from now, I want you to know every part of the boat." To his surprise, she did not resist. "Can you draw?"

"No."

"Fine" Jackie said, "Draw the boat. Just the outline."

"I can't."

"Bullshit. Do it. When it's done, we continue" he said.

"Jesus Christ, I hate this" Jackie thought to himself as he went across the compound. How easily and quickly the tough talk came to him. He pulled his writing pad out of his bag and absently scanned the pages. He did not want to be harsh. He hated harsh people, but it came to him as naturally as breathing. To top it off, he knew what he was dealing with in the young girl and what was required.

"Here" she said, thrusting the drawing in front of him from behind. "It's ugly." It was true. The lines were thick. There were too many of them. Short. Unsteady. Semiconnected. Disconnected. Forced. Disproportionate. He looked her in the face. The expression was defiant but gaunt. The eyes a little sunken and surrounded by dark skin that almost seemed bruised. At the corners, crow's-feet radiated in deep furrows and small, premature wrinkles crisscrossed her forehead.

"So?" she prompted. He could not answer. "Okay, so give it back. I know how bad it is. Happy now?" She grabbed the pad and wrenched it from him. Jackie folded his arms over his stomach, staring at the ground. "What? What? It's ugly, okay? It's ugly. I'm ugly. So fucking what?"

"It's a boat" was all he could say, getting up slowly and walking over to the shining hull. "Port side" he said, patting the fiberglass and looking at her. "Port side. Write it down." After a long pause and a twisting of the corners of her mouth, Celeste began to write. "Starboard, bow, stern, traveler, magic box, cunningham, gooseneck, outhaul, downhaul, boom vang, hiking strap, centerboard, cleat, gudgeon, pintle..." The list seemed to go on forever.

"Stop...stop. I can't possibly learn all of this" she groaned.

"Every part and a lot besides, before you set foot in this boat. Here's a picture of the sails" he said producing a sketch from his bag. "Learn these part too please." She scanned the page which was filled with even more strange vocabulary – leech, luff, tack, clew, head, slot, and then she let go a long, heavy sigh. "And don't get frustrated" Jackie added. "With all the dope you do, your short term memory is probably fried."

"Well this is no fun" Celeste moaned.

"Does everything have to be fun?" Jackie asked.

"Something should be fun."

"Don't expect fun until we get on the water" Jackie said.

"When will that be?"

"Okay" said Jackie, "First, you learn the parts of the boat, then directions of sail, knots, the compass, basic weather, care and maintenance of the boat, swimming and treading water. After that." Celeste bit her lip, struggling to contain herself.

"How long?" she asked.

"That's up to you. Work hard and you could learn it all in a week. Can you swim and tread water?"

"Yes."

"Show me. Did you bring a bathing suit like I asked?"

"I'm wearing it" she said.

"Okay" said Jackie, "I want you to tread water for me...now."

"But" she began.

"Can't do it?" Jackie asked.

"I can...I'm just not ready"

"When a boat dumps, nobody is ever completely ready" Jackie replied. "In the water please." He pointed to the edge of the quayside where a metal ladder disappeared over the side down to the harbor water.

"It's filthy here" Celeste complained.

"Oh, I see, you're planning on dumping only in clear water," said Jackie. "Just keep your mouth closed and don't swallow any."

"You're just loving this, aren't you, getting paid to watch someone swimming in a sewer. Can't we do this somewhere else?"

"Yes" said Jackie with a sharp gleam in his eye, "but I thought you were in a hurry. How much of a hurry are you in, Celeste?" She did not answer, but stepped out of her shorts and pulled her t-shirt over her head. The suit was one piece, black and it concealed, as well as any bathing suit could, the rolls and folds in her flesh. She was very pale and Jackie suspected she would not have the energy to tread water for long, but a full thirty minutes passed before he instructed her to get out. She hadn't exactly treaded water, lapsing every five or ten strokes into a dead man's float, but it was clear that she would be okay if the boat dumped.

"Give me your hand" she said as she reached the ladder, but Jackie refused.

"You'll have to get back into the boat by yourself" he said flatly, but it was clear she had more staying power than he had suspected.

"Satisfied?" she asked as she stepped up onto the quayside.

It took her three weeks, but she gradually mastered all that Jackie asked of her. To do it, she had stayed sober. Despite her constant foul mood and jittery nerves, Jackie had prodded, coaxed, cajoled and nurtured her through the steep learning curve. Somewhere along the line, someone had told him that you learn what you use and so he intended to get her sailing now as soon as possible. There was one more lesson.

"The end of a rope is called the bitter end" he said.

"Ya, I know all about bitter ends" she said.

"I'm not talking in metaphors, Celeste."

"Of course you are. You can't help yourself, but go ahead."

"This rope is coming apart at the bitter end" he continued.

"Been there, done it" Celeste laughed darkly.

"Look" Jackie said, holding the rope up before her. She decided to humour him and studied the rope. The very end of it was smooth and uniform in the few, unfrayed places, clearly cut by something very sharp at some point in its making. But the strands had unraveled a good four inches and lay exposed, the imprint of their former winding now kinky and bizarre, individual fibers splayed out in all directions. For a moment, Celeste just stood there dumbly staring at it, then with great care, she twisted one strand, attempting to rebury the fibers and then she rotated the strands, trying to get them to lie down in their original positions. When she removed her hand, the end sprang again into disarray. She let loose a grunt of impatience.

"There are three things we can do with this" Jackie said, gently taking it from her. "We can whip the end…"

"What's that?" she asked.

"That's when you bind the end of the rope with thread."

"Why would you do that?" she asked.

"So it can be used as a rope again. So it can be tight and smooth enough to pass through blocks and pulleys, like here." Jackie tried to jam the end through a pulley but it would not go.

"Okay" she said.

"Or we can make an eye splice out of it… make a loop and bury the end back into the rest of the rope, making a loop like this" he said.

"Why would we want to do that?" she asked.

"Well, with a loop in the end, we could use it as a dock line to put around a cleat, or we could splice it around an anchor ring to hold an anchor" he said.

"Okay"

"Or we could make a long splice and attach this rope to another rope to make a permanent connection."

"Okay, but you forgot the fourth option" she said taking the rope from him and throwing it to the ground. "You can just fucking give up on it."

"No" said Jackie, taken aback, but slowly picking up the rope. "We only throw away the garbage. It isn't always necessary to throw a rope away just because it's come undone."

"Even when it's totally fucked at its bitter end?" she asked. Jackie had no idea what the expression on her face meant.

"That's right" he said, unsure of her direction.

"You know what?" she asked.

"What?"

"This is just like…"

"Like what?" Jackie prodded her.

"Oh, never mind" Celeste said, "How do you do it?"

"Well" said Jackie, "you need a needle and waxed thread to whip it, but splicing is more like weaving or plaiting."

"I want to whip it" she said. "Show me how?"

"Okay" said Jackie , pulling from a small bag, a long, thick needle with a big eye, a leather glove-like contraption with a thimble attached and some thick, waxed whipping thread which he had obtained from a crew member of Carpe Spiritem. "This is a seaming palm" he said, fitting the leather device over his right hand so the thimble was on the inside. "You use it to drive the needle through thick material." Taking a knife from his pocket, he held the rope up. "So, you've been there and done it" Jackie said looking at the rope."

"Well, figuratively speaking" Celeste said, shifting uncomfortably.

"Are you saying you are somehow like this rope?"

"Well look at the thing" she said with distaste. "It's falling apart. It's useless." The air was thick with self-pity.

"Ya, but we're going to change that" Jackie said. "I'm going to start it, and you're going to finish it."

"Uh huh" Celeste said uncertainly.

"But first, we have to sacrifice some of the rope."

"Okay" Celeste answered. Jackie let the rope unravel as far as it would and then held it firmly just behind the loose strands.

"We take it back to where the rope is still good" he said.

"Define good" she mumbled under her breath.

"Sorry?"

"Nothing" she said.

"There" said Jackie, laying the rope on a wooden block and slicing it cleanly through. "Now we tape the end temporarily so it doesn't unlay while we work on it" he whispered, expertly rolling a thin piece of tape around the end. "Now we bind it tightly" he said, squeezing the end of the waxed thread and passing it deftly through the eye of the needle. Unconsciously, Celeste had wrapped her arms around her stomach, gently hugging herself.

Chapter Eleven
Exoklisi - Silent Congregation

D r. Silverton felt good pulling against the oars, but it was
     odd, having no plan, no agenda, no profile to write for
     some nameless retainer. Just the sweet music of the
oarlock and the bite of blades angled perfectly to the water. But
there was something more, something not right. He felt...there
was no other word for it...anaesthetized. He should be feeling
things, a lot of things. His perceptions were acute, his intuition
flawless. He knew that. When he decided to know you, you were
going to get known. His encrypted files were electronic trophy
rooms where specimens of all kinds hung in the thin, charged air
of cyberspace. Hit men, money launderers, religious fanatics,
couriers, character doubles, would-be presidents, black project
functionaries. Neatly lined up, appearance and persona stripped
back with his crisp, terse prose to underlying impulses,
motivations and instincts that made them what they were
unbeknownst to themselves. He should be feeling things. Feeling,
not caring. He had not cared about anything since the moment he
had seen a newspaper photo of his first subject with a neat bullet
to the brain stem, lying face down on the ground in front of a
bombed out diplomatic limousine. Perhaps it was the bloody,
scorched and headless doll on the ground beside the man. No
matter. Now there was nothing but what nature presented to his
senses. No job, no Celeste, no concerns for tomorrow, no
memories. No thought for how many people he had sent into
harm's way.

"What's happening to me?" he asked himself, shifting around
impatiently on the seat to check his course. He had missed a
scheduled communication with one of his best and least forgiving
clients. The moment the apparition had manifested in his
stateroom, he had changed profoundly. The center had fallen
from his world, or now there were centers everywhere. His frame
of reference had been shattered, and reality would never be the
same for him again. He had seen the thing, had heard it, in the
stone cold sobriety of an ordinary morning. And strangely, he felt

blessed and released where he had not even known himself to be imprisoned. Now the bars of his former life stood in stark relief against the luminescent immanence of his new consciousness. "Fuuuck" he sighed quietly into the vastness about him. "Oh shit!" he screamed as a sudden black shape lunged toward him in the water past the oar blade and disappeared. "It's a cat's paw, wind, wind. Get it together" the doctor yelled at himself sinking back down to the seat from which he had jumped. "Relax...relax" he told himself, pulling a handful of pistachios from a pocket. His fingers trembled as he pried the shells apart with his nails. When he had opened ten, he scattered the shells in the water and stuffed the rest in his mouth. The thing, the person he had seen in his stateroom, was alive, aware and deeply intelligent, insubstantial as it was.

"We don't die" he whispered. "There is more, so much more. Life's not what it seems to be."

Someone sitting in the stern of the small boat would have seen the features of his hard face actually soften, the muscles relax and the intense, take-no-prisoners eyes widen as to embrace some show of beauty or goodness. "*Oh my God, I have been so angry,*" he thought to himself as he resumed rowing toward the island. The mist still swirled in patches that alternately revealed and obscured it as he pulled. Turning again in his seat, he went very still. The island was covered in a grey drifting upon which a small white cross, bright in the sunrise, shone like a brilliant marker buoy.

"What?" he asked aloud. "Talk to me. What do you want? I accept you, okay? Okay? Talk to me." Then he looked around, half expecting the spirit to rise up out of the water and talk to him. The thought that it might not, and that he would be left alone forever with only the one undeniable encounter fixed in his mind nearly sent him into a panic. How could he endure it? The visitation had wrenched him from his life. Things were not as they seemed, not in this world. He knew that now, but knowing that wasn't good enough. The knowledge had to be used. It trivialized everything that had come before in his life. "Fuuuck" he sighed with resignation and frustration, staring down into the dark mahogany bottom of the boat and shaking his head. He stayed that way for some time.

The sound of wood grinding on rock delivered him from his thoughts in a hurry.

"What the hell?" he shouted, assuming he had run aground, and the words came back to him a split second after he had uttered them…"the hell…the hell…the hell…" A current had swept the small boat along like a river in the sea. Now it was almost on the rocks and he pulled hard as a four-foot high wall of rock that was the circumference of the island, surged toward him from out of the mist, almost snapping off one of the oars. The sea was still calm though and he was eventually able to find a small place to draw the boat out of the water. He sat down for a moment and looked out to seaward. From the direction he had come, a small armada of pistachio shells swirled into view. He was astonished at the strength of that same current by which he had been carried without his knowledge, and more importantly for the doctor, without his permission.

Almost before he had made his way up the rocks onto the more level part of the island, the mist had dissipated. The sun had risen just enough in the east to have made its way down from the cross and now the whole east side of the tiny fisherman's church was in the light. It felt warm and comforting on the doctor's back. He paused for a moment to absorb the heat. He was no longer young and a little warming did wonders for his joints. In a moment, he turned to face the sun, stretching his arms to the sides and inhaling deeply. How beautiful the morning was. Carpe Spiritem sat quietly at anchor like a small, white cloud. Beyond, lay Hydra itself, green with olive trees and other low growth and the tiny village with its ramshackle assemblage of small, weathered shops huddled together at the shoreline. Blue, green, yellow and red shuttered buildings hung there and looked, from this distance, like beads on a Moroccan necklace. Still, some detail could be made out. The quayside was visible. That quayside. Even a person sitting on the edge of it. Yes, yes that was the place, the precise spot. It had to be. He had managed to keep himself busy enough for long enough, almost to have forgotten, at least for a while. A lump rose in his throat, and he swallowed hard to clear it. He could not take his eyes off the scene. Suddenly, as the figure moved, the doctor shifted toward it, then steadied himself. There was a small blink of light as the figure turned a newspaper page.

"Jimmyyyy." The doctor exhaled the name of his younger brother in the midst of a great whispering sigh. "Jimmy...Jimmy." It felt as though a red-hot poker had been thrust into his solar plexus, and he doubled over, resting his hands on his knees, shaking his head slowly, his eyes closed. When he opened them, black ants were pouring from a black crack in the rock on which he was standing. Before he could stop himself, he was stomping wildly on the outflow. "Bastards...bastards" he screamed, but the outpouring simply changed to a random swirling, apparently without direction, expanding from the center. No matter how hard and fast he brought his feet down, he would never be able to stem the flow. When he looked again at the quayside, the person was gone.

At that very spot, his brother had died. God, was it five years already? The doctor could not believe it. The news of his drowning was so vivid. The knock on the door. The expressionless eyes of the tavern keeper from downstairs. The wrenching preamble that only made things worse. The nightmare words. The silence. The surrealism. The healing back to something less than what he had had before – a world that included his brother. Drowned? He would never believe it. Jimmy went to that corner of the quayside every evening to watch the sun go down and to smoke his crooked little South American cigars. You did not approach him then. You could tell it was a special time for him. No one dared disturb his peace when he stared off into the setting sun, the shadow of his old straw hat huge on the stones behind him. He was always looking over his shoulder, always defensive. The doctor never pried. It would have given Jimmy the right to ask questions about his work, and the doctor could not, would not lie to his brother. Better they never discussed each other's work. Still, if it was foul play – a big gash and swelling had been discovered on the side of his head – but the police had said he struck his head on some concrete during his fall.

There was no blood on the quayside. It had been a windy and wavy night. The blood could have been washed away. It could have happened that way. A simple slip, unconsciousness. Cement grit from the quayside had been found in the wound. It could have happened. But the doctor hadn't been there. He had been within easy earshot, not forty yards away, listening as a very different Celeste told him in her then painfully shy way what she liked about visiting Greece with her father, with Jimmy. She called him Jimmy too. The doctor disapproved of that but everyone called him Jimmy. He was that kind of guy.

Exoclisi, tiny churches like the whitewashed stone building before him, were strewn across small islands throughout the Greek part of the Mediterranean. Their brilliant whiteness breathtaking against the indigo sea. Often they were built as a tribute by loving family members for one who had died. The doctor walked around to where he found a stout, weathered door hanging slightly crooked from its own weight. He expected to find old, rusted hinges, but no, these were freshly oiled, if somewhat pitted from the salty air. Where a handle had been, someone had attached an intricately woven rope loop. Look as he might, the doctor could not discover a beginning or an end to the work. A work of love, he thought. Such attention to detail was reserved for the prized or the lucrative. There was no profit to be made here. He took the chord in his hand and pulled. Nothing happened. He looked down. There were fresh scrape marks on the stonework under the door. Gentle, curved etchings. He pulled harder and the door yielded, groaning, wood on stone, the same deep notes that had made him think he had run aground in the boat. So, he expected to find someone inside. The darkness, however, was profound and he struggled to make out detail while his eyes adjusted.

"Hello, anybody here?" he called, but there was no answer. Gradually, the room revealed itself to him. There was a tiny window just a few inches across, the pane still intact. A piece of carefully crafted driftwood swept up and across the end of the room and served, it seemed, as a kind of free form altar. An oil lamp, an icon of the Virgin Mary and crucifix had been placed with care upon it. In fact, he thought he detected a trace of smoke. Maybe it was just his overactive imagination. In a small wooden box, he found matches. A hissing roar echoed loudly from the walls and domed ceiling as he struck one with his thumbnail. The small explosion of light settled into a warm, amber glow as he lit the lamp. There were no chairs. The doctor sat down on the floor facing the altar. With the door closed, man and room were still...silent. The flame did not waver and soon the doctor realized that he was holding himself very tightly. The silence, this kind of silence, the absoluteness of it, was unnerving. The place felt possessed. The silence, imposed itself like a solid thing, and the longer he sat there, the more insubstantial he felt. He wanted to get up and walk out, but could not. Already, a heavy inertia weighed him down. He breathed deeply, and when he did, one of his vertebrae popped. He raised his arms and twisted left and right. How odd it seemed to exercise in a place like this. But as he did, it was like whatever possessed the space receded into the background. But the silence. The doctor could never recall anything like it. It took a while for him to realize that the high singing sound he was hearing was the sound of his own pulsing blood ringing in his ears.

Looking at the stone walls and floor, the simple but graceful curve of the ceiling, he wondered what tragedy had caused the church, or memorial, or whatever it was, to be built. He looked for a flourish of detailing, some clever piece of construction or decoration, trying to tie in the maker of the rope handle. There was none. No, the handle was done by someone else. Someone skilled in the making of knots. A fisherman, he thought. Yes, a fisherman. What was it the spirit had said? The words presented themselves to him with the clarity of someone speaking from across the room.

"Speak with the one who mends his nets in holy darkness." A chill raced up his spine as he realized that whoever had moved the door across the stonework had to be on the tiny island still. How could he have missed him? He blew out the oil lamp and ran outside, almost knocking the door off its hinges. He tried to compose himself as he worked his way around the building. For curiosity's sake, he stopped and tried to see if he could feel the presence of someone else. Hell, if spirits were real, anything was now possible. He had always laughed at the American and Soviet research into remote sensing and chalked up their few successes such as the location of secret weapons installations to coincidence. Now, here he was, palms held up before him. What good it would do, he hadn't the slightest idea. It was clichéd as hell, but it did seem, somehow, right. Nothing happened. No sense of presence or no-presence. Nothing. He chuckled. "Idiot" he said to himself, then he strode forward, to make a quick tour of the building and have done with it. In mid stride, he checked himself so suddenly, he had to steady himself against the side of the church. There ahead of him, trailing out of sight around the curvature of the building, were the first brilliant yellow intersections of a net, a fishing net.

"No way" he thought, then as he considered what to do next, it jerked, ever so slightly away from him toward the shade. He had never been afraid of anyone. Why should he be so apprehensive now? But he was. The paranormal had never figured in his life in any way before. All the clandestine operations he had helped to set up, the operatives that he had identified for development and grooming – they were known quantities. Would the person around the corner know about the spirit too? He had never gotten himself involved in anything like this. He was out of his depth, out of control of events, and he knew it. Still, events had put him here. For the first time in his life, he yielded to circumstance, pushed himself cockily off the church and walked around to where the unknown surrendered a very old man sitting on the stones mending an enormous net, the canary yellow of it astonishing in the light.

"Yasou" said the old man without looking up. The doctor returned the greeting.

"Yasou."

"You didn't put out the lamp," the old man said.

"Yes I did" the doctor countered.

"The lamp is not out."

"Alright, I'll check it," said the doctor, who went back into the building. Even allowing for the contrast with the brightness outside, it was clear to him that the lamp was burning even brighter than it had been before. Shadows danced on the walls until, summoning a deep breath, he again blew out the flame, making certain this time. "You were right," he said, returning to his place beside the man. "How did you know?" The man did not answer. "Is the fishing good?" he asked.

"There is enough. You are from Carpe Spiritem. I..."

"How do you..." the doctor began, but the man waved him off and pointed to the shoreline. The dinghy was plainly in view and on its side was a plaque with "Carpe Spiritem" written in gold letters against a maroon background. Why had he not seen the old man when he dragged the boat up, he wondered.

"There is a better place," the old man said, pointing down the shore in the opposite direction. There lay his brightly painted, red, white and yellow fishing boat, double ended, higher at bow and stern, a kerosene lantern at one end for night fishing. It lay with the bow nudged up on the only sand on the island, the stern secured to an anchor. A blue, black and white eye, protection against the evil eye and malevolent spirits, was painted on the bow forever looking out over the boat's direction of travel. Another, the doctor could see, hung from the man's neck on a silver chain.

"So, you saw me come in. I heard you leave the church earlier, you know...the door on the rock...it..."

"Groans" said the old man quite plainly, not looking up from his net.

"I guess you could say that...yes, it groans" the doctor replied.

"We have things to say" the old man continued. The doctor wasn't sure how to take his words. The fisherman sounded like a complete imbecile.

"I am not an idiot" the old man grunted, threading and knotting without pause, "There are things we must discuss, things you do not know despite your satellite navigation array and your distant voices.

"Voices?" asked the doctor, his eyebrows narrowing.

"You know what I mean." Where the old man's hand had been, there was now a blur, a flash and line, cleanly sliced, falling to the rocks.

"No, I don't know..."

"You are doing a good job with the girl. She will learn to sail..."

"You know Celeste?" the doctor asked, surprised.

"Of course I know Celeste. She gives me no peace" the old man answered, a warm smile on his grave face for the first time. "The boy who teaches her. He is not very manly. Is he..."

"He is...safe" the doctor replied, choosing his words with care.

"How you mean...safe? Safe how?"

"What business is it of yours, old man?"

"Theodor"

"Theodor, why do you know so much about her? Why do you care?" the doctor asked.

"We will get to that" the old man grunted, his downcast eyes leaving the net for the first time, but his hands working faster.

"Safe how?" Something about the old man seemed kind and the doctor decided to go along with him for the moment.

"He will not have sex with her."

"No sex?" repeated the old man doubtfully.

"No."

"How can you be sure?" the old man pressed on. Losing patience, the doctor raised his voice.

"I have done a...he's a transgender."

"Trans..." the old man stumbled on the word then looked dumbly at the doctor.

"Ten years from now, he will probably be a woman."

"Oh, I see," said the old man, showing not the slightest surprise. "You know this?"

"It is the typical profile."

"So, because he will some day be a woman, Celeste is safe with him?"

"Well, yes."

"Tell me" the old man said dryly, "do you have shit for brains?"

"Listen" the doctor said, "I can hardly believe I'm sitting on this godforsaken rock talking to you about this."

"Not so godforsaken" the old man said defensively.

"I'm sorry, does this place have special meaning for you?" the doctor asked.

"Yes" came the reply. The finality of it warned against further questioning along that line. The old man returned to his knotting.

"So, what's the problem with my thinking?" the doctor asked.

"The sea is man's work. It is dangerous. Did you even think of that? Your Celeste with her tiny boat will be a speck out there." The old man motioned in an expansive arc to the water surrounding them. "A speck. You people with your big yachts, you make me crazy. And who will protect her? Hmmm? You? Me? The trans thing you said with his delicate features?"

"He is a good sailor and he's tough on Celeste" replied the doctor.

"Yes, she says so. She gave me this." As he spoke, the old man held up his knife to which had been attached a lanyard with an eye splice in it. The other end, he kept tied to one of his belt loops.

"She gave you a knife?" the doctor asked.

"Not the knife" said the old man impatiently, "the splice, the splice." The doctor took it in his hands and examined it. There was no seam, as the ends of the strands had been expertly trimmed and tucked under other strands. The effect was a tight, neatly turned eye splice that could have been sold in any marine store as decorative rope work.

"Celeste did this?"

"Of course, and she did not cheat!"

"How do you cheat at a thing like this?" the doctor asked, full of admiration for the work of art which he turned over and over in his hands.

"Once the splice is made, you roll it on the ground with your foot and all of the strands space themselves out evenly. This has not been rolled and it is perfect" said the old man with obvious pride. "She brought it to me when it was accepted by...what's his name, this sailing instructor?"

"Jackie."

"Yes, when he approved it. The doctor could barely conceal his envy and turned to look at the horizon.

"You are too hard on her."

"What do you know about it?"

"More than you think, more than I wish was true. She said the two of you were very different. He was so proud of you but very, very different." The doctor wondered if the old man was senile.

"What are you talking about?" he asked.

"Jimmy." The doctor stood amazed.

"You knew Jimmy? My Jimmy?" he asked.

"Sit down" the old man said. "Sure, Jimmy, your brother." He held out his hand and the doctor returned the knife. The old man looked distinctly uncomfortable and the fact did not escape the doctor.

"What do you know about Jimmy?" the doctor asked.

"He came here often. We talked."

"Talked? About what? Please, I want to know. You see...I miss..."

"Listen" the old man interrupted. The doctor began to pace.

"It is important to me. You see, I didn't..."

"I'm trying to tell..." the old man continued but the doctor was not listening.

Splicing the Light   111

"We never...he died."

"I know. God keep his soul. I...I have maybe done something very wrong." He threw down the net and struggled to his feet. "I don't know. Maybe I am wrong and it is not my business, but just yesterday, Celeste said you believe that Jimmy was murdered."

"Celeste" doesn't know what she is talking about" said the doctor, stepping back. "Listen, Theodor" he continued with a strong edge of distrust in his voice, "what I think...in fact, the whole business is none of your affair."

"Oh, but it is" the old man said. "I wish to God it wasn't." The man was clearly in anguish, twisting his frayed cap in his hands, his eyes on the ground.

"You know something?" the doctor asked, very much on guard. The old man could be anyone, in anyone's pay. In the doctor's world, you trusted no one. Observation and intuition were everything. The old man shuffled his feet and raised the cap with both hands, saying nothing. His body tensed, the neck muscles moved. His breathing changed. Dr. Silverton missed nothing. The old man was either a very good actor or ..."You do know something," he said, suddenly softer, moving closer.

"We talked" the old man said.

"You knew Jimmy well?" The doctor could not believe the coincidence.

"He was a...a friend."

"A friend" the doctor repeated. "Since when?"

"Every time he came to Hydra, he would find time to come here. He was a very fine man, a decent man, your brother. He loved you very much. Excuse me for saying, but you were very hard on him. He wanted to talk more to you. Heart to heart, brother to brother."

"It was for his own good," the doctor said. "What do you mean, you did something wrong?"

"I...I didn't realize you thought he was murdered."

"I don't know what to think" the doctor said, still unsure of the man. "He wasn't the kind to just fall in the water and drown."

"But he did. I assumed you would all know that."

"There were no witnesses. How would you know?" the doctor asked.

"I know because I saw it happen. I stayed longer than usual working on my net. I am old but I still see very well. Jimmy was in his usual place. He always…"

"Yes, I know," said the doctor. "He always went to that place on the quay at the end of the day to watch the sun go down."

"Just after it set, a little light still remaining, he just fell in."

"You saw it? It was getting dark" the doctor pressed, not wanting to believe the answer could be so simple.

"Gregorio's taverna had just opened behind him. All the lights were on. He was silhouetted against the lights and he turned and something made him stumble."

"Was there anyone nearby?" the doctor asked almost shouting. "There was a deep gash in his head…"

"There was no one," the old man said.

"Someone could have…"

"He was alone and he fell. That's all." By now the doctor was in a fury and turned to him.

"Why didn't you do something? Where were you?" he roared.

"I was here…here…watching. My grandson was supposed to have returned with my boat but he was late. It was useless, but I shouted. I screamed. I called without stopping, until I could call no more. I could see people in the light, in the tavernas just yards away from him. But he was in the darkness and they could not see him. I could see people in their rooms with their lights on. But when you are in the light, you do not see what happens in the darkness. I know, when I am fishing at night with my lantern, I cannot see even the water more than a couple of feet away. How do you think I felt?" The doctor began to turn and the old man moved with him to stay in his line of sight. "I could see YOU…you were so near…I'm sorry…it must pain you…but you were so near…and I was so far."

"My God" the doctor said, turning suddenly pale. "It was you…it was you…it was you trying to warn me about Jimmy."

"What?"

"I thought it was my imagination. We were having a party…it was so faint…I thought it was my imagination…a faint voice….and I felt fear. I thought I was imagining things, and it was you screaming your lungs out." Suddenly the doctor ran to the other side of the island. It took less than ten seconds. "Heeyyyyyy…heeyyyyyy…heeyyyyyy…" He screamed as loudly as he could toward the people walking on the distant mainland. There were people right where Jimmy had drowned. He screamed until his voice broke. No one broke stride or even looked in his direction.

He stood and stared in disbelief, a tight knot forming in his throat, until he felt a hand on his shoulder.

"I tried."

"I couldn't hear it. I didn't...pay attention...to it" the doctor rasped.

"I'm sorry," they said, almost as one.

"Do you forgive me for not telling you for these years?" the old man asked, shame heavy in his words.

"There is nothing to forgive. What could you do? When I think I'm hearing voices, I should listen," the doctor said, turning away.

"There may be more in that than you realize" the old man said as the doctor started toward his boat. "You said you heard me opening the door to the church. You said that was why you did not wreck on the shoreline." Doctor Silverton stopped and turned around.

"So?"

"I did not go into the church today. Usually I do. Today, I did not."

"But I heard it. The exact same sound – wood on rock."

"Then a spirit looks after you. It warned you of the rocks. Do you believe in guardian angels, doctor?"

"Jimmy deserved the help of angels more than I, and for me, if they exist at all, they are very distant voices."   The old man stiffened instantly. "I'm sorry Theodor, I didn't mean..."

"I know," he said. "Yasou" he called as he trudged back to his nets.

Chapter Twelve

Lessons

If Doctor Silverton and the fisherman had looked in a different part of the sea, they might have seen a pair of taut, white, dacron sails driving Celeste, Jackie and the dinghy at breakneck speed across the water. Celeste was not at the point yet where she could go out over the side on a trapeze wire to help to keep the boat flat. For now, it took all of her stamina and concentration just to hang onto the jib sheet, the rope Controlling the small sail at the front, and to keep her feet hooked under the hiking strap in the bottom of the boat so she could lean out over the water when a gust hit them. She had not stopped smiling since they pushed away from the quayside to the amusement of a group of shopkeepers who wished them luck and made gestures with their hands of something turning upside down. The boat was very sensitive, and Jackie showed her how a slight weight shift or a line pulled in too far or not let out quickly enough, could turn the boat over. Instantly, she became aware of some consequences for not staying alert and not following orders.

There were plenty of orders. With unskilled crew in a racing dinghy on a windy day, there is no time for pleasant conversation, explanations or polite requests. So, the change that came over Jackie was a shock to her. As the wind grew, the waves increased and the gusts became more frequent, accelerating the boat onto a wild plane, the boat rising up and flying on its own wave at maximum speed, his voice became harder and more urgent.

"Up! Get up! Hike out! Lean out! More...more...stretch out...In! Get in...get in...faster Celeste, unless you want to go swimming. Move back! Now forward...forward...more....out!

Stay out...inininin! Come on Celeste, look around, get your head out of the boat. Try and see what's coming. You're too slow. Look for the gusts on the water. They're the darker patches moving across the water. See them before they get here. And the wind direction changes just before the gust hits. Figure it out. Look up to windward. Call the next gust."

"But there are so many waves. How am I supposed to see wind? The surface is all broken."

"Forget shape. Think colour. Think dark. Watch. And for God's sake watch the waves we are catching up to at the same time. If you are too far forward and the bow digs in to the back of a wave, the whole boat can pitchpole, do a somersault, at this speed. Like now! Backbackback! Get back!" For a moment, the boat seemed to come to a halt, the bow buried into a wave. Skipper and crew lurched forward and Celeste's feet came out of the hiking strap. At the same time, a gust hit the boat and tilted it over on its side. Celeste screamed as she started an involuntary dive toward the low side of the boat. Jackie saw it coming and had the back of her lifejacket in a claw-like grip instantly, throwing her back onto the high side of the boat with one arm while the boat filled with water. The gust strengthened, breaking the boat free of the wave. Like a thoroughbred bursting from a starting gate, the dinghy sprang forward, spray flying everywhere.

"Oh my God!" said Celeste letting go of the jib sheet as she saw how deep the water was in the boat. "We're sinking!"

"I'll flatten the boat. Open the starboard bailer" Jackie said. In the bottom of the dinghy, there were two shiny metal flaps with thick, wire handles. One on each side of the boat. One just behind Celeste, the other on the opposite side closer to Jackie. Releasing the handle and pushing down opened a hole in the bottom of the boat, but the design of the fitting caused a vacuum to be established under water. Still it was against Celeste's instinct to open a hole in the bottom of what was to her, a sinking boat.

"Are you sure about this?" she asked. If they didn't take on any more water, maybe the boat wouldn't sink. There was some safety in that.

"Open the damn bailer, Celeste" Jackie yelled over the sound of the flapping jib.

"Ohhhhhhh" she moaned. Then she pulled the handle loose and leaned on the fitting the way Jackie had showed her on shore. Jackie did the same with the other bailer. Instantly, water started pouring into the boat.

"Oh my God, it's not working, should I close it?" she squealed.

"Watch" Jackie said with calm assurance. Trim the jib." As the two of them trimmed their sails, the boat accelerated again. Within minutes the water level in the boat had dropped so low that a loud sucking sound could be heard as the remainder sloshed around the bailers. "See?" Jackie called out.

"Unreal" Celeste said. Eventually, however, the wind became too strong and they headed back to shore.

"Right near the end there" Jackie said as they drifted back into the calm waters of the harbor, "you got pretty good at spotting the gusts." Celeste was worn down and was having none of it.

"You were like Attila the Hun out there. Yelling, shouting. I'm not deaf you know, and I'm not stupid. That really pisses me off. People are always telling me what to do. And don't tell me it's for my own good. I don't feel good. I feel bad when people yell at me. I mean, come on, can't you just get into it? That was fantastic...unbelievable...man, those waves. Did you see how fast we were going?"

"Ya, we went out" said Jackie, "and we managed to get back without dumping. Do you have any idea how hard I had to work to prevent us from going over?"

"Oh lighten up Jackie. You had a great time. You know you did."

"You're missing the point," he said. Celeste just rolled her eyes.

"Oh? And what's that?"

"The point is that when you start doing the right things at the right time, I'll stop yelling, but until then, you're just going to have to get used to it. Don't get me wrong. You're doing fine, but when conditions are this rough, it's not just a game, Celeste."

"So what's the worst that could happen?" she asked, still resisting him.

"You could get hurt, or you could die." Jackie said. "I can't believe I even had you out in this weather."

"It was calm when we went out" she answered.

"Ya, but it came up very fast" he said.

"Of course" she answered, "at this time of year, it often blows up like that in the afternoon."

"It does?"

"Yes, as long as I've been coming here" Celeste said.

"I wish you had told me," said Jackie.

"Well, you're the one who's supposed to know everything about everything. Anyway, you're not really afraid of the boat going over are you? You said it was easy to get it up. Now you're really making me nervous."

"Just let it go," he said.

"No, I won't let it go. I could die? What the hell was that all about? And do you think I give a rat's ass about my life anyway? I don't give a shit. So just teach me how to sail the goddamned boat will you and then you can fuck off!"

"You're not the only one in this world with problems, you know," he shouted back. They reached the quayside and tied up to the mooring wall. Dejected and angry, eyes down, they lowered the sails without speaking and stared into the bottom of the boat.

"What the hell is happening here?" Celeste asked after a few minutes. "How are we blasting around in the ocean one minute, I mean blasting! And the next minute, we're bummed out so we can hardly talk. I don't get it. We must be really fucked up man! Jackie...Jacqueline? Say something will you. That was too good to end up like this."

Jackie threw a line end into the boat and snapped a line out of a cam cleat, its serrated jaws snapping shut instantly.

"A friend of mine died. She was a 470 sailor. She hit her head when the boat went over, and she got trapped underwater in the rigging, and she drowned." He spoke in a monotone.

"Oh no, was she with you..."

"No she was in another boat. We were racing. They were behind us, and I didn't even see it happen. Didn't hear a thing, and I was concentrating on what was happening ahead of us and...I didn't know until later."

"Wow" Celeste said, "that's ...I'm sorry...Were you very close?"

"Ya" he said with a sigh, "very...so when I hear you say you don't care about dying...not worth a 'rat's ass' I believe you said, I.... Ah fuck it. Like I said in the beginning, this isn't going to work. Why don't you just go home and..."

"Don't do this" she said gravely.

"Why not? You're not the only one who doesn't give a rat's ass, kid."

"What are you talking about?" she asked.

"The same thing as you" said Jackie.

"Great! You want to die. You want to get out of this shit hole? What's the difference then?"

"The difference is I think it's impolite" he said "to take people with you."

"Even if they don't mind?" she asked soberly.

"Get out of here and leave me alone" he said.

"It's my boat. You get out of here. You're fired!" Jackie was too depressed to care.

"Fine. I'm gone" he said and climbed a ladder up onto the quayside. Celeste just jumped perilously from the dinghy to where her hands could get a grip on the concrete and pulled herself up.

"The Carpe Spiritem crew can put it away," she yelled.

"Fine" said Jackie.

"Fine" snorted Celeste. Two old men at a nearby table continued their chess game, shaking their heads in silence as the two walked off in separate directions.

Later that evening, Jackie wandered through the village to try out a little taverna he had passed a few times. It was a short way up the hillside and offered both a refreshing breeze and a decent view of the harbor. A lush green pine tree, like a trained bonsai, sprang seemingly from barren rock and trailed its length off at an angle over the patio stones. Through the whitewashed walls framed with lime green doorways, waiters in black pants and white shirts moved inconspicuously setting the tables with clean blue checked table cloths and candles. Jackie sat down where he could watch the sun set on the Aegean. The sunset was full of promise. A fine layer of broken cumulus hung just above the horizon. Its underbelly painted with the soft solar tones of a closing day, flickered in his imagination. His writing book lay open on the table and on that, the gold and black Parker fountain pen he always carried. He adjusted the long djalaba, gathered up a handful of long hair and tossed it free of the hood and off to the side.

"Yes ma'am, may I help you?" asked a deferential voice from behind. Before Jackie could turn, the waiter corrected himself. "Sorry sir, I..."

"That's okay," said Jackie. He ordered a bottle of retsina and chuckled quietly at the discomfort of the waiter.

"Hi" said a broadly smiling man about his age, dropping into the empty chair on the other side of the table. His jet-black hair was extremely short, like a marine cut, his features mildly Asian. "Do you mind?" he asked.

"Not yet" said Jackie. Instantly, the smile left the man's face as another expression began to take form.

"Oh, that's good" he said.

"Why is that good?" Jackie asked as the waiter returned with his bottle.

"I'm sorry," said the man, "are you expecting someone?"

"Shall I bring another glass, sir?" the waiter asked, nodding to each man in turn.

"No and no" said Jackie. The waiter hesitated for just a second as he studied the two.

"It's okay. I have some friends coming and we'll be taking our regular table. I'll order when they get here, Andreas."

"As you wish sir" the waiter answered and returned to the kitchen. The man then got up, excused himself, and went to the washroom. While he was gone, the waiter returned to Jackie's table.

"I know it is none of my business," he said, leaning close to him, but you want to watch yourself with that one. He's..." and he made a mincing limp-wristed gesture.

"Ohhh... I see," said Jackie, knowingly. "Thank you." Now he was really confused. "*I'm the one with the dress and the long hair,*" he thought to himself. "*Why doesn't he think I'm...I mean, he takes me for a woman and now he's warning me about a guy coming onto me. I don't get it. Strange.*" He poured himself a glass of wine and swallowing the cold, pine resin-scented liquid, went back in his memory to another time. A time in the drama department at the College of Education. There he had met Philip. Philip the painter and actor. Their imaginations had meshed like musical fifths. Evenings at the Lincoln House drinking jugs of cold, frothy draught beer. Their conversation weaving in and out of the New Orleans jazz played on the dowdy wooden stage by an unlikely assortment of players. The athletic Dutch trumpet player, the frizzle-haired clarinet player with the Kahlua bottle always under his stool --his eyes always so wide, his big grin demented as though he was somewhere connected to an electrical socket. The bass player endlessly swaying with his scarred and deeply stained dance partner, bowing exquisite tendernesses from it. Jackie still remembered, well, perhaps not so much remembered, as felt the first New Orleans jazz note he ever experienced. It was blown by the trumpet player and it was pure sex. A low, rolling, guttural, groan, four octaves down from a forest howl. Jackie and Philip had both stopped in mid motion as the note hit the air and hung there. They had exchanged a glance that said "Holy shit" and that's exactly what it was, some kind of really holy jazz shit. And that's all there was to it.

Some things are beyond comment. The first time they kissed was like that. An ethereal moment, a hole in space was how Jackie remembered it, a hole in space into which he fell backwards as the world rushed by and he, all desired and hungered for, and knowing, and knowing the hunger to be righteous. And he was astonished to discover that his body spoke a different language of intimacy with a man. A sinuous syntax of yielding...different. Well, there is an eloquence in the touch of any tender lover...he knew that. With his first and only man, with Philip, the voice was different – that's all. With time and God's grace, he hoped he would learn where his heart should be placed. To him, the love of a woman, the voice of feminine embrace, was...transporting...had always taken him, would always take him to a place which, if it was not exactly heaven, was at least, precisely, home. Here, he felt, on a rock turning in space, home was a very fine place to be.

"Okay, so, where were we?" the man enthused as he returned.

"Hey Jacqueline!" another voice cut in as a dark figure stepped between the man and the sun which was blazing just over his shoulder.

"Ya?" Jackie answered, raising his hand to block the sun, but the figure was wearing it like an icon's halo and the face remained dark.

"How ya doin' little buddy?" the voice demanded, full of enthusiasm.

"Spacedemon?" Jackie responded.

"I'm sorry" the other man cut in with an edge in his voice, "am I interrupting something?"

"Shall I bring another glass, sir?" It was the waiter drawing up to the table again with a shrug and a smile, impressed at the attention the longhaired foreigner was attracting.

"Hell yes" answered Spacedemon, working his way past the stranger to the table. "What are we drinking?"

"Retsina" Jackie answered.

"Pine sap!" laughed the American. "Okay, I can do that, but bring another bottle and menu will ya', I'm starving to death. Who's your friend?" he asked, turning to the stranger.

"I don't know," said Jackie, turning as well. "Who are you?"

"Richard." He said with a mild, hurt, dignity.

"I'm Ron Steicher. My friends call me the Spacedemon," said the American extending his hand.

"How nice for you" came the frosty reply. The tone escaped the American.

"Well, belly up to the bar, Rick and let's get this party going" he said, slapping the man on the shoulder. Richard leaned in to the table and, covering Jackie's hand in his, spoke smoothly. Something in Jackie melted a little, instantly.

"I live at the top of the hill, up there," he said, motioning with his arm. As he did so, Jackie noticed that the waiter looked up to the top of the hill and slowly shook his head before disappearing into the dark kitchen. "Come and visit me and my friends sometime...Jacqueline."

"Sure, okay" said Jackie as Richard drew away to a table partly out of sight around the corner of the taverna. As he rejoined his table, three strikingly beautiful women and a very dark, handsome man, looked in Jackie's direction. He wondered if they were actors or models. He sensed a strongly positive energy coming from their table. They were gesturing with enthusiasm and looked like they were having a great time. Well, it was the Aegean and there were always few frowns to be seen amongst the tourists and travelers. Jackie looked again to the hilltop. Through a tall, open window of the fieldstone house, a long, violet swath of curtain blew out, curling into the air like a Buddhist prayer flag, then drew back into the house, gold now in the last rays of the sun.

"That is a bad place," the waiter said, depositing another bottle of wine on the table. "A bad place." Then he returned to the kitchen.

"So, how ya' been?" Spacedemon asked, fiddling with the long hairs of his thick, blonde moustache.

"Oh, you know," said Jackie, evasively. "That kid Celeste is driving me nuts. I was making a few bucks teaching her how to sail, but she's so fucked up."

"That's funny," said the American, "She says the same thing about you."

"Ya?"

"Ya, so what gives?" Jackie sat back in his chair and looked him in the eye.

"What do you care?" he asked. There was no reply and the American buried his face in the menu. Without taking his eyes from it, he poured himself a glass of wine. "You're not!" Jackie said.

"Fuck off" came the reply.

"She's jailbait, you asshole" Jackie said, smacking the menu.

"That's not what she says" the American answered smugly.

"Well...duh...what do you expect? She wants what she wants," Jackie said.

"What is this, man?" the American asked, flustered, "I think I remember a rooftop in Athens where you and a certain Danish girl..."

"Swedish" Jackie corrected him.

"Where you and a certain Swedish girl got it on pretty good."

"Ya, but this is different, man" Jackie said ominously.

"Ah c'mon man, we're on the road. You know what I'm sayin'? It's Greece for Christ's sake man. How can you not do it here? Anyway, there's a lot more to her than you think."

"Her father's trouble" Jackie said.

"Every girl's father is trouble, man, if he's any good." The American said and smiled, pleased with the sound of his own philosophy. "Jeez, I should write that down. Anyway, he isn't her father."

"I'm serious, Ron" Jackie said, "He's dangerous."

"Dangerous how?" You don't believe that stuff she says about him do you? Ah come on man, she's just tryin' to impress. I'm not afraid of him."

"You should be."

"No man, you know what we should be afraid of?" he asked, getting agitated..."A nuclear event."

"Ah shut up," Jackie said as the sun settled into a blood red filament of cloud.

"No, man, you're gonna hear this" he said, downing his wine and pouring another quickly.

"Okay, tell me about nuclear events, but do you mind getting out of the sun? I really want to see this sunset." Jackie said.

"Sunset? Oh, ya, far out," said the Spacedemon.

"Why do you talk like that?" Jackie asked.

"Like what?"

"Like...far out. It's the new millennium," said Jackie.

"Ya, well this isn't going to be much of a millennium. You better get as much of it as you can" the American said.

"Why's that?" Jackie asked, closing his eyes and swallowing another cold mouthful of Retsina, the sun, hot on his cheeks and eyelids. "Mind if I look at your sketchbook?" The American pushed his large, black, hardcover sketchbook across the table. He always had it with him. He was a very talented cartoonist.

"Why's that?" Spacedemon asked. "I'll tell you why. Because in that missile silo I worked in, you wouldn't believe how many people on duty were stoned down there." Jackie opened the book. A huge yellow Tweety Bird was pulling frantically on a missile trying to dislodge it from the earth.

"Stoned?" asked Jackie, turning the page.

"L.S.D., speed, you name it, man. I mean, what do you expect? You have no idea what it's like down there. You go stir crazy after a while. It's not natural." On the next page, an arctic fox was urinating on a submarine periscope. "Man, it's all lights and data and plots projected on these big screens. Guys are shootin' the board with these data guns. Bang! You shoot a blip on the board and up comes the data readout. Bang, bang, bang! It's crazy man. People hallucinating, and the nukes right there ready to fly. Jeezus. If you knew what I know, you'd live every day like it was your last, man."

"Ya?" Jackie said, absently.

"I'm serious, man. Somebody is going to fuck up one of these days."

"So?" Jackie said, "What can you do about it?" It was hard not to notice the way the American fidgeted and shook.

"Me, I see everything I can before it all goes up in smoke, man. Countries, women, art, culture. I move fast. I live as much as I can. I did Paris in two days. What do you do?"

"Same thing, I guess, only slower. I just take it minute by minute."

"You play guitar, right?" the American said. "I heard you at the Outside Inn, didn't I?"

"Ya, man" Jackie said. "I played and you sang." It was obvious to Jackie that the guy's brain was fried.

"So, what kind of stuff do you play, again?

"Mostly my own stuff, some blues, but mostly folky type stuff." Jackie turned the page. The Tasmanian Devil was standing on the roof of the Outside Inn, howling at a full moon. Jackie looked up and saw the sun settling on the horizon. Spacedemon's sketches were brilliant, he thought. Strange products of speed and detail. Bare essentials communicating the forms and feelings. Like a Zen brush painting with more detail and attitude. As for the Spacedemon, he didn't quite know what to make of Jackie. There were no transsexual Disney characters, and America had no colors with which to reference the transgender palette.

"So, what's it like to be gay?" the American asked out of the blue. Jackie convulsed in laughter, slamming his knee on the underside of the wooden table, knocking it sideways and spewing a fine mist of wine everywhere.

"Oh Jeesus, Spacedemon, you really are something, man. Who says I'm gay?" Jackie asked.

"Well, well, I mean, look at you. You're very. You look like a woman."

"Jeesus Christ" Jackie muttered, shaking his head.

"No, no, don't get me wrong. I know girls who don't look as good as you...don't get me wrong" he said, pushing back a bit from the table and wiping wine from his moustache with the back of his hand. "I'm not attracted to you."

"You really have a screwy idea about gay people," Jackie said. "They hate people like me almost as much as straight people do. Well, maybe not lesbians, but gay men? They're as frightened of us as you are."

"What us?" Spacedemon asked, "I mean, if you're not gay, what are you, man? I mean, I don't get it. You make it with chicks, but you dress and act like one. I don't get it. You're doin' a real number on my mind, man. I'm really confused."

"Well," Jackie said, pouring himself another glass of wine, slowly and deliberately. "That's the first interesting thing you've said since you ruined my sunset." The American turned in his seat. The sun had disappeared below the horizon filling the western sky with a warm, orange-pink suffusion. "Never mind" Jackie continued, "it's gone."

"Ya, okay, sorry" said the American. "So help me with this."

"That's a riot" Jackie answered. "I should help you with your inability to deal with reality."

"Well, that's the point, man. Now, you're gonna hate me for saying this."

"Hey, in for a penny, in for a pound, go for it" Jackie said, his stomach hardening.

"It's just that you don't seem real, man."

The next seconds unfolded like a nightmare for the American. In an instant, Jackie launched himself across the table and had both ends of Spacedemon's moustache firmly in his grip as he pulled his hands apart...hard. One of the waiters turned and made for the table, but Jackie's waiter cut him off and drew him aside. They stood in the shadows, arms folded, grinning.

"Oh, oh, oh" Spacedemon howled. "Stop, stop" but the speaking only worked his upper lip against the strain and he was soon silent. Jackie smoothly drew his chin down for a one point landing on the table.

"I don't seem...what?" he asked. "What was that little word you said?"

"Nothing, nothing" the American moaned. Jackie tugged again, "Jeesus...stop" He grabbed Jackie's hands in his, but Jackie just rolled the hairs between his fingers like he was rolling a cigarette and pulled even harder. The American, finding no way to escape the pain, relaxed his grip.

"What was that little word?" Jackie asked.

"Real" Space Trucker groaned as the first of several course hairs rocketed from their follicles.

"And what did you say about 'real'?" Jackie asked like a mother correcting a wayward child.

"I said you didn't seem real. C'mon man, this is embarrassing" he pleaded. Jackie didn't need to look around. He could feel everyone looking at them.

"Really? And is this real...Ron?" Jackie asked, tugging again for good measure.

"Yes...yes" he grunted. There was the tiniest speck of blood where a particularly thick hair had dislodged.

"I see. Now I want you to think this next question over really carefully, Ron, if you ever want to smile again. Ready?" There was no response. Jackie pulled harder. "Ready?"

"Yes, yes" the American squealed, wincing, his eyes beginning to tear, but not with sadness.

"Good...what's my name?"

"What?" the American asked.

"What's my name...careful. You have five seconds."

"Fuck" the American growled, then a quickly stifled scream sliced the air as Jackie yanked hard.

"Wrong answer, Ronald. You're beginning to piss me off."

"Uh, uh, uh" came the response and then "Whatever you want it to be."

"I see" said Jackie "and am I real no matter what name I'm using?"

"Yes, yes" said the American.

"Oh, I'm so relieved" said Jackie suddenly letting loose and throwing his hands up in the air like a calf roper trying to beat the clock. "I guess I misunderstood you."

"Man, you're fucked up" was all the American could think to say as he rose from his chair, smoothing his moustache back into position. "You need to do some serious chilling."

"Bye Ron" Jackie said absently as he hurtled into depression. "And say goodbye to everybody on the beach."

"What? You leaving?"

"Ya. I'm outta here. Remember what I told you. Be careful." Jackie said.

"Fuck that. You can't leave. What about Celeste? She needs those sailing lessons."

"What the hell do I care about other people's needs? To most people, as you so beautifully put it, I'm not even real. So, why the hell should I care about anybody? I'm outta here" Jackie said with finality.

"Hey...whatever, but I'll tell you one thing. You're taking this way too seriously, and you're gonna crack up one of these days. I was only kidding around for Christ's sake." The American was backing away from the table and pointing at Jackie as he spoke.

"You smarmy bigot" shouted Jackie, rising to his feet. "You come in here and tell me that I'm not real, and then tell me not to take it seriously...you...you..." Exasperated, Jackie slumped back down to his chair and poured another glass of wine. Astonished customers at the tables pretended not to be noticing, taking furtive glances and working hard to suppress their laughter. People from other worlds. Dressed down creations of fashion designers from Europe and America. Designer sandals, designer jewelry, but not too much, perfect makeup, but not too much. Cool casual.

As the American left the patio, his words carved up Jackie's thoughts. He found it harder and harder to think. It was as though a plug had been pulled in creation and Jackie, soul and all, if he had one, was being sucked straight down into the blackness. "Not real?" Jackie wondered if it was true. The possibility that the American was right, terrified him. What if the whole thing was just one huge self-delusion? Jackie had wished that was true. If it was true, surely his years of psychotherapy would had unearthed it. But it hadn't. There had been no blinding, tear-filled moment of revealed truth. No big therapeutic breakthrough. No renewal. Jackie had not been born again in the crucible of honest self-examination. Questions had just led to ever more questions, while the rest of the nontransgender world marched confidently on in its certitude and judgment. How Jackie longed for answers. Why did he one minute identify so clearly as a man and in the next, as a woman? He was not bisexual. He had a clear preference for sex with women, strong women, women whose natures took them on easy flights above the gender landscape. The focussed, grasping of men, in his mind, paled by comparison to the diffuse, transcendent experiencing of life which so many more women could claim.

Maybe he was just a sensitive man in a time of brutish people. Maybe he was hiding something. Maybe the man had been driven out of him. Psychotherapists had listened patiently for months as he explored that possibility. Jackie wondered if he had been raped as a child. The trauma might have caused him to take refuge in some alternate reality. It could have happened. It could explain everything. As terrifying as the prospect was, Jackie had placed great hope in it being true and had invested huge resources of emotion in exploring the possibility.

He had remembered a fragment of imagery from when he was eight or nine years old. In his memory, he had been walking home from elementary school. A large, black car stopped. On the hood was a fancy silver ornament. Before Jackie knew it, he was in the car and the man driving it was asking if his parents had ever told him not to take rides from strangers. But Jackie had seen the man at his house and knew that his father knew the man. There was no more to the memory. As Jackie had recounted it to the therapist, his heart had begun to pound, his hands sweated and a huge sense of dread overcame him. He felt like vomiting and tears poured. Try as he might, Jackie could not advance the memory, if it was a real memory. Maybe it was not real at all. But it might have explained things. And it took so much energy to go there. On the day Jackie terminated the therapy sessions, much to the disapproval of the therapist, he tried to explain his reasons. Looking for psychological truth, for him, was like a miner working in a tunnel. The longer he works, the more tired and hungry he becomes. If the tunnel is deep, and he works too hard, he may not have what it takes to get back out again. The damned thing is that each time he is about to give up, his miner's light reveals another shining nugget, never enough to guarantee his future, but always raising the possibility that where that one came from, there may be others. The pathetic thing would be to discover a major deposit and die unable to make use of it. And so, one day, Jackie just gave up the pain of the search and tried to accept things as they were. For reasons he would never understand, he was as much a woman as he was a man. He had not tried to become that. It was what he was given to live. One day, he hoped to stand before his maker and ask why.

And so, he drank the night away, drank away his life and the feelings that went with it as thoroughly as he could. There was no longer any self-pity, just the impossibility of understanding, of knowing, of being. How he got home to his cot on the balcony above the taverna, he had no idea. He awoke to the heat of the sun on the blanket he had pulled up over his head. His mood was deadly and his throat, parched. After a good breakfast of eggs

and toast, however, he felt better and went for a swim in the sea.
The cold water took his breath away and restored his senses. As
he came up from one dive, a dull thudding sound from the
shoreline caught his attention. There, on the shore, a fisherman
was repeatedly hurling something against the large rock on
which he stood. Thwap, thwap, thwap the rhythm sounded.

"Kalimera, good morning. What are you doing?" Jackie asked,
swimming offshore from the man.

"Yasou" the man replied with a smile. "It is octopus. I make it
soft. You know how to make the octopus soft?" A wave turned
Jackie as he started to say something. "One hundred times. One
hundred times you have to hit him on the rock to make tender.
Then okay" he heard the man say behind his back. When Jackie
could get turned around again, the man was gone. For a moment,
Jackie wondered if that was what God was doing to him, to
everyone, slamming us against the rock of life until we
become...tender, until we become...okay. Jackie was, if anything,
well read. The thought of Soren Kierkegaard's Gospel of
Suffering flashed in his mind as he swam in the water. Maybe
everything in life was, indeed, a teaching. Every fibre of his being
hurt. Maybe, he thought, he was just the dumbest kid in the class,
the one who couldn't get the point while everyone else looked on
in thinly veiled derision. Left, right, up, down, girl's, boys, good
bad, black, white. Things were so simple, or were made so simple,
by other people. His mind would not stop trying to understand
itself. Not even in mid-stroke, on a beautiful morning in the
peaceful Aegean. He looked up at the coastline. Something
moved on the hilltop setting off a little flash of light. It was the
house that the guy at last night's tavern had invited him to visit.
He decided to check it out.

Chapter Thirteen
The House on the Hill

The flagstones of the quayside turned to cobblestones in the alleyways and the cobblestones to pebbles and the pebbles to dirt as Jackie walked along, angling up the hillside. As strange as Richard had seemed in the taverna, so sudden, so imposing, there was also a detachment, a benign loftiness. Jackie thought of his friends and his role models, the nonconformists – Norman Bethune, Salvador Dali, Miles Davis, Emilia Erhardt, Boudicca. He thought of shamans and witches, how it was said that they lived away from other people, on the fringes of human settlement. It was just a thought. The house on the hill was probably just put there for the view. Facing to the west, as it did, the sunsets must be spectacular. Anyway, Jackie needed diversion, time away from his thoughts. New people and experiences were better than drugs for that, he had learned years earlier.

The wind blew harder the more he climbed, tugging at the long, white, cotton tunic he wore loosely over a pair of short, white shorts. When the wind stopped and the tunic settled, it looked as though he was wearing a short dress. The deep brown water buffalo sandals he wore were well broken in, but any sharp stone could remind him instantly to watch his step. It was another perfect Mediterranean day. Again, below him, the tiny white houses, and people smaller still, moving like insects. For some time, he walked, looking down at the coastline and out to sea keeping the path in his peripheral vision. He had intended to visit the small island with the fisherman's church just in view off the next headland over. Well, it would have to wait. He wanted something, what, he didn't know. But it wasn't happening, and he knew he would leave soon, get in motion again, see how he felt in a new place with new people.

Suddenly, he was falling. For a fraction of a second, he knew he was dying or was about to die. The path had ended...suddenly. The compression set in...the trauma cliché...time slowing, thought accelerating...a moment for absolute authenticity before the breaking on the rocks below...the moment ripe for revelation. Instead, only a blur of grey rock, a temple with prayer flags. A face full of horror. He fell past these things. They did not belong to him. The thought did. Jackie thought it directly to God. Two words. "You lied."

"Hi there!" a voice said with studied indifference. "That was quite an entrance. We usually come in through the front door." The path, it seems, had split in two and Jackie had taken the one less travelled straight down a flight of stairs into the kitchen. "Try to keep the blood all in one place, will you. I'll be with you as soon as I finish this salad." A clean cloth was thrown to him. "Want a beer? There's some in the fridge if you didn't break it and it still opens."

Blood was pouring from a deep gash in Jackie's forehead. The room was spinning, and he felt like he was about to pass out. He sat up a bit and as he drew his head up, he painted the white refrigerator door with a great swath of blood. It was a huge commercial unit and the billows of cold air that engulfed him worked to clear his mind. As he steadied himself, hundreds of bottles of exquisite beer and wine from all over the world came into focus in rich hues of green and brown. Jackie took out a tall bottle of Dutch gin.

"Oh gin is it?" Richard said taking it from him. "No, I didn't take you for a beer man." From somewhere, he produced a fancy frosted glass and poured a clear viscous stream. "Come, sit. Cuts tend to get infected in this climate if you don't deal with them right away. From one corner of the kitchen, which Jackie could see was quite immense, Richard produced a black metal chair. Form over function, slick to the eye, hard to the touch. With one hand on Jackie's back and the other on his arm, he led him over and sat him down. Then he disappeared for a moment and reappeared with some wicked looking liquid in a bottle with a Red Cross insignia on it. Pulling another chair directly in front of Jackie, he cupped his chin in his hand and gently raised his head.

Jackie was feeling mildly euphoric, like he did when the guy washed his hair at the hair salon before he got it cut. He let his chin rest in Richard's hand and sighed. The room was cool and Jackie had worked up quite a sweat climbing the hillside.

"This will hurt, a lot" Richard said.

"Fine" said Jackie.

"Fine? Pain is fine?" asked Richard. "You are a strange one. Let's see how fine pain is, shall we?" With that he soaked a large hunk of cotton batten with the antiseptic. The caustic, stench of it fired up Jackie's nostrils like a mouthful of wasabi. As Richard touched it to the deep cut, the effect was, like the gash itself, "fine" to Jackie. It was a right or left turn in events. Something more intimately a part of his life precisely because he had no control over it. Something he did not have to think about. It was what it was and as such, he did not mind. But it did, indeed, have its own personality. To an alert mind, no two pains are the same. At this moment, Jackie was experiencing clearly.

"You're smiling. Why are you smiling?" Richard asked. "This hurts. I know how much this hurts. Why do you like this? Do you like pain, Jackie?" He asked the last question very seriously, stepping back and searching Jackie's eyes for the answer, which he knew, would precede the words. Richard was very good with eyes.

"I understand it."

"You understand pain."

"Yes" Jackie said.

"So, you like it" Richard pressed.

"I don't care about it."

"Okay, you don't care about pain" Richard said with an unmistakable air of sadness. Still, he laid the next swath down slowly and drew it along heavily, causing the blood ahead to ooze out and the trail of medicine to flow into the wound. Jackie's eyes, focussed elsewhere, were utterly empty. He had not one iota of pity for himself. This did not escape Richard, who felt his throat tightening and could not understand why. "There you go," he said cheerily. "All done...cheers...so you decided to visit us after all." Jackie looked around. There was no one else there.

"Us?" he asked

"Oh, quite a few of us share this house. Would you like to look around, that is if you're up to it?" Jackie nodded. After Richard bandaged the cut, they stood. "You have already met the refrigerator, so why don't we just go this way." They went down the hall and into the dining room. To Jackie's astonishment, what at first appeared to be paintings on the wall turned out to be, in fact, framed blue jeans, at least the portion from the bottom of the front pockets, up to the waist. Richard watched him for a reaction.

"What do you think?" he asked. Jackie scanned the room. There was one on each of the four walls. Just blue jeans in baroque, gold frames with red velvet backgrounds. "Oh, come now, you must have some kind of artistic opinion, even with that throbbing head of yours." With that, he held his hands up in mock shock. "Oh my God, did I say throbbing head?" Then he drew down the zipper on the nearest piece. "Go ahead, reach inside. I know you're curious."

"I'm not sticking my hand in there" Jackie said, suddenly panicked.

"No? It's just a little art piece. Okay, an anatomically correct art piece." With that, Richard reached inside the jeans through the zipper and pulled out a huge, red plastic penis, which he stroked a couple of times with his long sinuous fingers while watching Jackie for a reaction.

"Uh huh" Jackie said, simultaneously breaking into nervous laughter and looking for an exit.

"Good, I'm glad you appreciate the humor" Richard said. "We have such a talented bunch here. Wait 'till you see the ..." He searched for a word..."party room." Then he took Jackie by the hand and led him through a doorway into the room Jackie had seen from the harbor. The prayer flags, light diaphanous curtains of many hues, blew in and out past the solid, field stone walls. The floors were polished stone like mica or granite with flecks of gold that sparkled in the slanting light.

"And this" said Richard, motioning toward a huge structure in the middle of the room, "is our pride and joy...What do you think?" The object was an immense pyramid of what looked like mattresses or beds, each draped in a different color of rich satin...jade...burnt orange...ivory...violet. An incredible assemblage of earth and sky tones. As Jackie gazed at it in the afternoon light, the thing shimmered and flowed like a river cascading over a precipice. Suddenly, he realized just how out of his depth he was. Part of him wanted to throw itself into the rainbow of it; part of him wanted to flee.

"So, do you like it?" Richard asked.

"It's nice," Jackie said.

"Nice."

"Ya...nice" Jackie repeated.

"You do know what it's for, don't you?" Richard asked, looking Jackie up and down hungrily. "I mean, you seem like you would know. You know…" he said uncertainly after a long pause. "Maybe I've made a mistake here…wouldn't be the first time."

"What do you mean?" Jackie asked uneasily.

"Well" Richard said, stepping forward and looking Jackie in the eye. "I like you and, well, you're here." He moved closer until the two were inches apart and he caught the scent of Jackie's coconut sun tan oil. "And I just assumed, I mean…" His hand reached to the back of Jackie's neck, under his long hair "everyone knows what we're all about here. You do, don't you? I mean, that's why you're here?" Jackie was unaware of his own tightening, but Richard did not miss it. "Oh dear" he sighed, realizing his mistake, but thinking it less than fatal.

"Look, I'm not gay" Jackie said as Richard's eyebrows raised and a skeptical smile spread out across his face. "I'm not."

"No?"

"No."

"Then why are you here?" Richard asked, withdrawing his hand. "They told you about us. I know they did. They always do, and you're very perceptive. You don't watch where you're going, but you're very perceptive and, I think, very sensitive and…"

"Look," said Jackie, his heart pounding, "I'm here because you and your friends, you're so… different from everyone else. Hell, I didn't know, I mean I've worked with designers and dancers and…"

"You thought we were artists or something? Well, I do happen to be a designer, a fashion designer…quite good if you ask me. I told you you were perceptive. So you thought you would come up here and hang out with a bunch of artists?"

"Ya, something like that" Jackie said. He wanted to tell him that there was something about the place, something about the people that told him here he would be accepted and not judged – a little anonymous, exotic place on the far side of the planet where he could be himself, away from straight people, if only for a while. But there was danger everywhere.

"So, Jackie's not gay. What then? Straight transvestite, bisexual transsexual, male lesbian?" Richard asked sardonically.

"I don't think there's a name for it."

Splicing the Light   135

"Wrong, sweetheart. It's all been done. It's all been said. The lands have all been discovered and a flag planted on every one."

"I think we're mystery," said Jackie.

"Oh, please…darling…how long have you been feeding yourself that line?" Richard answered with clear disgust.

"What do you mean?"

"In my experience, people who say they're running into the sweet arms of mystery are really skidaddling from the truth."

"I see," said Jackie, "Like a man running into the arms of a man is skidaddling from the touch of a woman."

"Ouch, that's some stinger, baby" Richard responded, impressed.

"I'm not your baby," said Jackie.

"Are you anybody's baby?"

"I don't need this."

"Okay, okay, okay, I'll stop. You're just exploring. So, let me tell you a little about us. We are, in fact, I mean my friends and I, we're mostly gay. We're…friends and we are kind of like a family. We have a very nice arrangement. I own this house and one in San Francisco and another in London. All of my friends call all of my houses home, and the houses of my friends are my homes. Everywhere in the world. If I go to Cairo, I have a home there or in Tokyo or Paris or Rome, even Moscow and so on and so on. We have all been pretty lucky and we like the good life. You should see the houses. This place is nothing. I'm going to Cairo with some friends the day after tomorrow. Do you want to come?"

"No" said Jackie, "I'm going to Amsterdam soon, and anyway, I don't have any money."

It was a lie. He did have money and he hadn't decided where to go, but things were spinning out of control. Time to put on the brakes.

"Oh heavens, that doesn't matter, come anyway. I'll pay. It would be nice to have some new conversation for a change. What do you do, Jackie, for a living I mean?"

"I'm a writer, a musician, a sailor. Sometimes I teach."

"What do you teach? English I bet. You remind me of a teacher I had in high school. Boy, what an asshole. Oh, sorry, not that you're an asshole. So, you're a sailor. Well now. Can you manage, drive, oh what's the word…you know…a big yacht?"

"Skipper a sailboat?" Jackie asked warily.

"Yes, that's right…or a power yacht."

"Sail yes. Power no."

"Well, some of us have been thinking of adding a large yacht to our collection of toys and we will need someone to run it. Would you like to do that? Would that keep you in Greece for a while?"

Jackie wondered. Skipper of a big yacht, sailing rich artists around the world. Not bad. Adventure… a new life. So what was wrong? Partly it was the thought of being a toy keeper. He had never been told where or when to sail. But no, it was something else.

"You don't even know me. Why would you commit to something like this? I've told you I'm not gay" Jackie finally answered.

"Who's committing? Someone would have to check you out, but I get the feeling you can be trusted. You seem hungry for adventure and that's what we're all about here. You're just a little confused."

"Confused?" asked Jackie.

"Oh never mind. Do you think you'd be interested?"

"No, no, what do you mean, confused?" Jackie demanded.

"Look, I've got a big mouth, okay?" Richard said, showing genuine concern.

"Confused how?" Jackie insisted.

"Okay…okay," said Richard after a moment of silence. "You're not gay, but you dress, and if I may say so, move like a woman. No, no…" he said waving Jackie off, "That was a compliment. God, you're defensive. It's just that in my experience, such straight guys always turn out to be gay. You're in denial. There are gay people and there are straight people. Everyone else is…confused." He said the word staring at the floor, said it with a tone of certainty that conjured up in Jackie's mind the image of Dr. Silverton's fundamentalist brother. Jackie set his drink on a table, stood and made his way to a door. He paused, turned and surveyed the rich hues of the fabrics and the impeccable workmanship of the place. He tried to imagine it full of joyous people. Would they, too, find him "confused?" Here, least of all, had he expected to find the same old judgement.

"Yes, what are you thinking, Captain?" Richard asked.

"Yuck" Jackie answered with as much meaning as the word could carry. Then he stepped out onto the path again. It seemed somehow malevolent, and not just because of his head wound. Jackie stayed well to the inside edge and kept his eyes on the ground ahead.

Two days later, as the inter-island ferry Portokalis Ilios drew away from the island, Jackie was aboard. He watched the wake stretch out behind and the island shrink. It shrank on Spacedemon's broken body, where one of Dr. Silverton's men had hurled him over a cliff. It shrank on the bright red dinghy and Celeste's hysterics, shrank on the doctor's specter and his appallingly expanded universe, shrank on the fisherman's church and the old man mending nets, on the travelers on the shore, on promises made and events approached but never experienced, on the house on the hill and its banners flying. Then what Jackie thought had been real, existed only in his own mind.

The next few days found him flying from Athens to Vienna where he took trains through Switzerland, Germany, and Holland to Calais. Along the way, he traded his guitar for a black leather jacket, as the temperature grew colder. From Calais, he took a ferry to Dover in England and headed for the New Forest. Maybe Richard was right, Jackie thought. Maybe he was confused. Not about being gay. Jackie knew he was not, though sex with his own gender, whatever that was, was neither repulsive, nor unnatural to him. No, he was not confused about that, but he did wonder if the chaos in his emotional world was somehow tied up with the chaos in his spiritual world. He intended to find out. In typical dramatic fashion, he decided to go to the top for advice, or at least as close to the top as he could get. That meant Sybil Crowleigh. Sybil was a witch from a long line of witches. Jackie had read everything she had written. Books on astrology, palm reading, tarot, numerology, witchcraft.

Chapter Fourteen
The Old Forest

"So This Is Where It All Begins!"

In many ways, Wicca, the Old Religion, appealed to Jackie with its emphasis on healing and living in harmony with nature. The Wiccan Reede or credo spoke to his heart. "An thou harme none, do what thou wilt." It was, he knew, a philosophy not fully livable in human society. One person would always give offense, in some way to another, and offense was harm, if only emotional. Jackie's androgyny was an offense to many. Sometimes, he only caused others confusion, but was not confusion itself a form of harm? Maybe the confusion was something others brought on themselves in their refusal to accept the reality of others. Harm, he had learned, was a relative and political thing. If no blame attached to God for making us susceptible to decay and death and worst of all, the anticipation of it, then Jackie could care little for any discomfort he might bring to the world.

Psychics, prophets and apparitions often get it wrong. So does the weather forecaster, but the old crone on the bus was way off when she tapped Jackie on the shoulder from behind with her crooked, arthritic finger.

"This is where it all begins" she said, nodding conspiratorially and speaking in a voice that was at once both squeaky and gravelly. It mattered that she said that. It mattered that the sky had gone suddenly huge and dark, moments before and the thunderous explosion and flash of light that came from it. It mattered that just then the sign for the village of Stanbury was coming into view at the side of the rain deep road. From somewhere within him, an old protection spell surged and before he could think better of it, he wheeled in his seat, fixed her with his eyes and launched the words or the words hurled themselves from within him.

"Aski ka taski haix tetrax damnameneus aision."

It was a binding spell designed to cause all psychic energies in a small area to hold in their patterns. Negative energies would not be sent out and would, in fact, return to their senders. So too, with positive energies. The enchantment acted like a concave mirror reflecting energy back to a single point source, the sender. The woman's smug leer changed instantly to shock and she looked suddenly like she had swallowed something the wrong way. Instantly, she started gagging and choking. Jackie was as astonished as the old woman. Why had he done that, he wondered. The words, he knew, had come from an old treatise on white magic. Strange that he should remember them. Stranger still that he should blurt them out like that. Maybe his reaction was due to his reason for coming to The Old Forest in the first place. He had come for a reckoning. Maybe in the constantly shifting shadows and light of the occult, he would find a new perspective on his nature. Maybe he was a witch or a psychic born in the wrong place, in the wrong circumstance.

Maybe his transgender nature was what happened when a perfectly natural life force is bound by wires of fear, prejudice and judgment like some grotesque bonsai plant of the soul. Forced to grow and survive in a bizarre configuration of the imagination just to exist at all. It could be. From his earliest imaginings, he had wanted to be female, female in body, because he had always felt that he felt and thought like a female. But no, the wires were applied and twisted onto his life with the most exquisite care – family rules, church, schools, peer pressure, dreams. Yes, he knew that after a point, he had probably taken to binding his own life with the firm yet malleable wires of the norm. When dreams of soft dresses and feminine contour came to him, he would twist the wires of Christian salvation with a single-minded, desperate intensity, would sink to his knees in front of the televangelists he despised in the sickly television light and pray to a male god to forgive him and make him like the others – straight, normal and acceptable. And he pruned all kinds of new growth, stood waiting for it, alert always with the sheers of his intellect for the least signs of femininity when he would cut with great precision. The wrist cut back to only manly angles, the walk cut to a male gait, the eyes cut to an acceptable firmness, the voice trimmed to male range. His hopes he cut and his dreams as the bindings continued. He had learned a lot about bindings. He had not, however, understood the power that he was trying to bind. Not at all.

"Please" the old woman croaked, fear everywhere in her face and eyes.

"Oh my God, she's having a heart attack" a woman screamed from the next seat, "Somebody do something...driver!"

"Please, stop" she spluttered, grasping at her throat, an ugly blotched purpleness filling her complexion, the skin swelling.

"I'm not doing anything to you, you old shit. You're just getting a taste of what you sent out" said Jackie, his voice a strange, soft, yet utterly merciless instrument. Still, he was surprised, suddenly to find himself, white-knuckled, gripping the sides of his seatback as he glared at the woman.

Suddenly, out of nowhere, a beautiful, glistening knife blade that seemed to be made of clear crystal and emitting an intense blue and cranberry red flame at its tip materialized in the air directly between him and the old woman. As it took form, the resulting light revealed a black chord-like object that stretched directly from Jackie's solar plexus to the old woman's throat.

"I think everything is alright now, don't you?" a deep, resonant woman's voice spoke from behind Jackie. In the instant, Jackie saw the blade address the chord at its thinnest point and deftly burn or cut it in two. Both halves then turned rapidly clear and disappeared. Jackie collapsed into the seat in a stupor. "Better just let him sleep it off" the voice instructed the driver who backed slowly away.

"Yes, better that way" the driver repeated dreamily and sat down.

"Come along, Mother" the voice said, as a dark form leaned over the old woman and helped her to her feet. Jackie struggled to clear his head, but suddenly had the notion that he was asleep and gave up the effort. "Yes, sleep. We'll talk later," the voice said. It was the voice of a parent admonishing a naughty child. Jackie liked the voice. It then changed its direction as the old lady was helped to the aisle. "I told you to leave the tourists alone. Didn't I warn you?" The old lady croaked and gasped.

"It was nothing, nothing at all. Just a coughing fit you silly thing," she answered.

"It was not...nothing. You got three'd and you know it. The most basic rule – what goes out comes back times three..."

"I most certainly did not."

"You got three'd by a virgin," the voice said laughingly under its breath. "I can't wait to find out how you plan to explain this to the others. I mean, really, he didn't even know what he was doing."

"That's no virgin" the old woman snarled in a rough whisper as the two headed for the door.

"Careful dear" the voice said as they descended the steps.

"Oh stop fussing" came the testy reply.

"Three'd" the voice said with bass notes.

"Oh shut up"

"Three'd" the voice sang in soprano.

"Was not"

"Was…"

And the voices trailed off as Jackie sank deeper into a kind of sleep, his face smashed up against the window and the dark figure glancing up at him with a furrowed brow from under an umbrella as she passed. She was wearing a straw hat with a narrow, upturned brim circled with a chain of bright flowers.

Some time later, Jackie awoke alone on the bus. The front door was wide open, the sun was shining and a fresh breeze blew the scent of freshly washed trees and field grasses inside. There was bird song everywhere. He felt deeply rested but had no idea where he was. He sat up and checked his watch. Five p.m. It meant nothing. He had no idea how long he had been wherever here was. As he ran his hands through his hair, he withdrew a large daisy from next to his ear.

"Cute" he thought. The Old Forest. It slowly came back to him. The storm…Stanbury. Something about an old woman…then nothing. He wondered if he had had a breakdown of some kind. Nothing like this had ever happened to him before.

"Right, are you a waif or a stray?" the bus driver asked as Jackie emerged from the bus. "I was told it would be best just to let you be sir and because I was just at the end of my run, that's just what I did. Hope you don't mind, sir."

"Who told you to do that?" Jackie asked.

"Well that's just the thing, sir, I…I…don't exactly know. But I'm sure they were most insistent about it."

"Jeesus Christ" Jackie suddenly shouted and felt for his wallet. It was still there. "Thank God."

"Oh, no need to worry sir," said the driver laughing. "No one's going to rob you around here. Oh my goodness, no."

"And why is that?"

"Well" the ruddy-faced man replied, "no one here would dare. You never know if the person you're stealing from might be..." Then he thought better of what he was saying. "You're safe here sir. Safer than anywhere in the world." He was getting a head of steam up again. The man obviously loved to talk. "But never you mind, I'll just drop you off in town, if that's where you're heading."

Soon, Jackie was settling in to a room at the Godolphin Inn. It was a very old building, with a cottage look and gracefully sloping roof of straw thatch. Old, weathered timbers gave the place a substantial and warm feel.

"I'm sorry, sir" the neatly dressed girl had said at the front desk. "We have only one room left and it's a bit...tired. We usually reserve it for women anyway and I don't think..." With the events of the day, Jackie was about at the end of his patience. Something snapped.

"It's okay...Miss...?"

"Ross, Alexa Ross"

"It's okay Alexa because I'm transsexual," Jackie said in a sultry feminine voice.

"Oh my goodness, are you...oh my goodness."

"In the last few months, I have slept on a rooftop and balconies in Athens, a beach in Corfu, and very cold water pensions in Spain. I don't think this is going to be a problem. I promise to conduct myself like a lady. Anyway, all rooms look the same in the dark, don't they?"

Jackie's bizarre, flirtatious manner caught the girl completely off guard and she started to laugh, glancing around the room to see if anyone was listening to their strange conversation. There was no one else around.

"Well, jolly good then" she said straightening herself up, "Mr...Miss...oh what do I do now?" Jackie was oddly touched. No one had ever asked him for that kind of advice before.

"Why don't you just call me Jacqueline and register me as J. Northam. That way everyone will be happy" he answered.

"Right then... Jacqueline, if you would just sign here, please." She passed the register to him and Jackie signed, taking his time and working hard to make the letters round, open and nicely spaced. He often thought about how women's writing and women's speech shared a lot of similarities. Still, it took work to undo the years of pseudo male script he had learned to write in his self-consciousness. "You're Boudicca" the girl continued, then with a giggle, "That is, you're in Boudicca." Jackie looked at her uncomprehendingly. She was still quite flustered "The rooms, the rooms are named after famous people. Your room is Boudicca" she said and then sighed. Her mind was still struggling to place the man...he obviously was a man...in some manageable context. And yet, when he changed his voice like that and altered his mannerisms and facial expression, he was so...feminine.

"Relax, Alexa, I think everything's all right now" Jackie said without thinking, "I'm just a woman in a man's body. There are millions of us." As he said so, the image of his endocrinologist came to his mind. Sitting in his office one day, Jackie had asked him how many transsexuals there were in the city. The doctor gestured to the filing cabinets along one wall. There were hundreds of files. He was just one doctor.

"It must be difficult for you...Jacqueline" the girl said.

"You're a sweetheart, Alexa" Jackie said, resisting a huge urge to run around the counter and hug her. People were entering the lobby. It wouldn't look right, so Jackie headed off to the room of the warrior queen.

The door to the room was arched, solid oak, and beside it on the wall, a wooden plaque with the name Boudicca burned in pseudo Celtic script. In the low light of the hallway, the effect, if Jackie let his imagination go just a little, was mysterious. The room itself made him feel safe, secure and somehow excited. Good reproduction hangings adorned two walls. One immediately made him gasp. For years, he had practiced a psychic visualization exercise designed to bring a person into contact with his guardian angels or spirit guides. In such a trance, it was said, spirits would reveal themselves and instruct the seeker, answer questions, and comment on life decisions. Their ways of communications were enigmatic. Some left a calling card of fragrance suddenly pervading the air. Some drew pictures in the seeker's mind, some in color, some in simple black and white. Some used sounds. Some would touch. Some just gestured. Hallucination? Neurosis? Jackie had long known that if what is real is only what science and mathematics confirm, that which is measurable, then love and hope and faith were just wishful thinking. In the end, he knew, that is real which most speaks to the heart and having and holding onto and possessing were just impulses of minds terrified in a universe of unspeakable scale and complexity.

Surrender, he had always thought, was essential. The sine qua non without which all of man's endeavors were nothing more than fear inspired ego. Surrender to the beneficent unknowable. Faith in divine purpose. Faith that we are partakers in a greatness, in a poignant unfolding. And sometimes he could see so clearly that it was our adversary relationship with the universe, our insistence that nature yield to our questions, respond to our directives, our timetables, our agendas that actually cut us off from truth or created a feedback loop in which we got only those answers determined by our arrogant ways of asking. The universe, he knew, is very sensitive to tone. Of course, living among frightened creatures always shut these visions down. You cannot, he knew, commune with the elements or your own inner horizons, in a room full of clock-watchers, time being as it is, only a very earnest sleight of hand, which only the very best musical moments escape. Sometimes he wondered if his identity was like time. The hour hand of thought, the minute hand of feeling, the second had, in the case of the transsexual uncomfortable in his own skin – hypervigilance. Then his head would hurt and he would do anything as long as it was shallow and frivolous.

"Joy" he once wrote, "is lost in the place where sullen mind gnaws its metaphysical tail to the bone of contentions." One day, screwing his face into the most serious mask he could manage while looking in the mirror and deftly loading on the mascara to an otherwise exquisitely made up face, he delivered that line with deep, professional solemnity, then almost put his own eye out convulsing in laughter. Sometimes he wondered if that was what it was all about, the frivolous, unpredictable, mythical slut-imp part of his nature getting even with the controlled, logical, circumspect part. Good science coming to play in the fields of gender. Gender dancing on the workbench of science.

When Jackie called his spirits, in trance, he called them to a sanctuary of his imagining. One day, the elements of it just drifted together in his mind. The north Atlantic. A rock cliff of a hundred feet. An emerald green meadow a short distance inland thick with fragrant wild flowers. An altar of miniature standing stones. Two upright, one across on top at waist height. The upright stones carved with the crescent moon of the Goddess and the stag horns of the God – master of animals. The horizontal stone inlaid with a glistening quartz crystal pentagram. On it, tools of ceremonial magic lay carefully arranged. Surrounding this little oasis of the spirit, stood a magnificent grove of oak and willow in full summer foliage.

The tapestry on the wall before him was identical to this except the magical tools and signs were absent. Jackie was dumbfounded, but unable to explain it, he eventually decided that the proportions were off and his reaction had simply been based on surface similarities.

The subject of the second tapestry seemed very simple. Another medieval setting in which common folk, stood about laughing, smiling and clearly enjoying themselves at a country crossroads. Like the other, the rich colors had faded somewhat. Jackie found himself in a daydream imagining their conversation. They must live nearby to walk to their meeting. A celebration, perhaps, something to do with the countryside – planting or harvest. Maybe a celebration of the seasons. They seemed ready to dance. What could it be? His gear stowed neatly in one corner of the room, he lay down on the large bed and wondered, then wonder became that drifting place where images neither sharp nor fixed move in and out of the shifting tableaux that give place to dreams and deeper states. From this drifting place, passed through on going to and returning from sleep, Jackie had many times culled rich images for his poetry. Often, they were startling, presenting themselves with such force and vividness that he would awaken excited, gasping for air, scrambling for pen and paper to record the experience before it faded from memory. Only the very strongest ones lasted more than a couple of minutes.

From time to time, Jackie experienced what felt like prophetic dreams or visions. Six months before it happened, he had seen the eruption of a volcano on the island of Montserrat in the Caribbean. Sometimes, he just went places, flying like a bird, once, to a small town in the northwest part of Australia, past high hills to a dry, flat expanse and a small town over which he just hovered and circled. There seemed to be no reason for his being there, or if there had been one, it had not been revealed to him. Simply, there was the immense joy of flying, of going at great speed in complete safety in the direction of his thinking. The star filled night was like a part of him. When he flew, there was always a strong sense of rejoining, of reunion. For a moment, the image of the wall hanging came back to him and he knew for an instant that he was dreaming. Then that knowing slipped by and he found himself staring in pitch-black night. There was also the presence of a being, but he could not see who or where it was. Slowly, a rectangular picture frame of milky opalescence like liquid moonstone formed around part of the night so that it looked to Jackie like a kind of celestial blackboard. He knew it would be written upon and sure enough, an unseen hand or mind began to draw a shape, a line like a cross between Arabic script and occult symbols. Curiously, the writing did not move from left to right or right to left but began in the middle of what turned out to be the final graphic, and moved gracefully both left and right until the final strokes finished simultaneously at the beginning and end.

"Remember this!" a bold, male voice resonated. The script was like an etching on the night. As though someone had etched black paint from a light bulb with the intensity of the sun. Rays of light streamed out of the inscription. Jackie sensed something dramatic in the moment, different from the cacophony of sounds, the flowing pastiche of visual effects that made up the average dream. He sensed a psychic dimension to the event and hurled himself from sleep as he had taught himself to do. Immediately, he grabbed a pen and his sketchbook from the backpack and hurriedly drew the image. It took no more than a moment and when he was finished, he held it at arm's length and studied it, adding arrows and explanations for future reference.

"Script evolves simultaneously in both directions."
"Light streams through here."
"Remember this! [a male voice]."

Excited as he was, Jackie was exhausted. He had it written down. No need to try and understand it. That could wait for morning. Often he had to accept that important things were communicated to him in sleep and he was simply incapable of interpreting them, ever. This felt like one of those. He had done all he could for the moment and fell asleep quickly as soon as he got back into bed.

The next morning was glorious. Sun shining, birds singing. It was decision time. He headed downstairs to the dining room planning to take his time over scrambled eggs, toast and several coffees. After months on the road, it would feel good to indulge in a North American style breakfast again. As he passed the front desk, Alexa called to him.

"Jackie, someone left something for you." She looked suspicious, defensive.

"Oh really? For me? But nobody knows I'm here" he protested.

"Well, that's not exactly true is it" Alexa said, thrusting a business card toward him on the counter. The card was black with silver writing on it.

Major Arcana Antiques
And
   Occult Shoppe
   8 Sussex Lane

"But who's it from?" Jackie asked.

"As if you didn't know" the woman answered with a hint of disapproval.

"I don't have a clue," Jackie said.

"Well then, I guess you'll just have to go along to 8 Sussex Lane and find out, won't you?"

"Alexa, you know who this is, don't you?" Jackie continued, but she just held up her hands with the index fingers of each crossed as though to ward off a vampire.

"I'm not getting involved," she said. Jackie found it hard to tell if she was serious or just fooling around. She seemed both amused and frightened.

"Involved in what?" Jackie asked.

"Exactly" the woman responded patronizingly and seemingly much older. "Now you just have a good breakfast and go along to the …" She coughed, suppressing a giggle. "…antique shop."

Sussex Lane was located on the northeast edge of the village adjacent to an old stone warehouse, which was padlocked and no longer used. Along the lane, Jackie passed a quaint teahouse, The Penny Whistle with lace curtains and a huge tabby cat stretching in the front window. It looked briefly in his direction, yawned and went to sleep as he passed. Across the roadway and down a bit, he came across an old wooden building with two enormous barn doors, The Tack and Anvil, Blacksmith Services and Riding Gear since 1723. There was an incongruously modern building with canary yellow aluminum siding and two crimson doors. Between them, a silver lightning bolt reached down from the roofline. The sign on the left half read Toby's Cyberfix, the right half read Old Forest Ham Radio Operator's Club. It was eleven in the morning and no one was on the street. Life, Jackie smiled to himself, was a laid back affair on Sussex Lane. He took the business card from his pocket and checked the address. Number eight was a few doors away. Probably, the card was just a business promotion, some "type A" small business person promoting services to new arrivals in town via the inns and B & B's. A real nut case, if Alexa's reaction was any indication. Well, it was a place to start.

Jackie made his way past the warehouse. In North America, it would have been renovated, the stone sand blasted, the timber beams that must be inside, highlighted somehow, the exposed brick wall interior hung with fine art paintings – Van Gogh's café scene, and Starry Night or some such. The floors would be refinished hardwood. In North America any structure more than one hundred years old was very precious in a land of sterile modern architecture. Here, everything was old, except the lightning bolt building. Jackie glanced back at it. Antennae of various heights festooned the roof. He could see them now as he passed the large oak in front of the place. Jackie noticed that here, too, the doors were slightly ajar. He had seen that in many of the buildings he had passed. It had been hot for several days according to the local newspaper. No one seemed to have air conditioning. Still, it was odd to be in a place where doors could be left open without fear for one's safety. Jackie wondered how long it would last.

A few strides more brought him to Major Arcana Antiques. The name, he knew was drawn from the twenty-two key cards of the seventy-eight card tarot deck, used by gypsies, witches and psychics for centuries to tell the future. Jackie had learned how to do it in his teens. Over a period of years, he had committed all of the cards, their deeply rich visual imagery and assigned meanings to memory. It was not an easy thing. There were many ways in which one could lay the cards out. This was called a spread. Each position in the spread also had its meaning. If a card came out of the deck right side up, it had one meaning, reversed – another. The cards immediately before and after a given card affected its meaning, as did a preponderance of one suit in a spread. But these variables were all superficial. The real messages, the ones worth consulting the cards for, yielded themselves only to a seeker with the ability to reach a deeply intuitive state. Jackie had left the cards alone for years after thoroughly scaring himself off with them. It is important, when the cards are read, or when any other kind of psychic reading is done, for that matter, that the reader speak in an uninterrupted flow, the images and thoughts that come to his mind.

One must not hesitate, judge, edit, or in any way censor the input that he receives from the cards, with one exception – tragic news. This must always be presented as a possible outcome of the querent's current pattern of actions, something, which can be changed. However, to otherwise block the flow with judgement is to immediately shut down the stream of images. Jackie was very good at not interrupting the flow. So good, in fact, that he would often find himself completely spent and nauseous in a strange sort of way when the cards had too much to say through him. He was self-taught, except for the book on tarot cards written by the lady he had come to find in the Old Forest, Sybil Crowleigh.

"Oh my God" he thought, realizing that the store before which he was standing, could be and very likely was, owned by that same Mistress of the occult. In a large rainbow-like arc over the front door, the cards of the major arcana were fanned out in all their multi-colored splendor, large laminated prints on hardboard of some kind. There were many versions of the tarot deck. This was the Rider – Waite deck, the one Jackie used. He stood beneath the sign admiring it and glancing inside. It was dark and he could see little. Suddenly, there was a firm but gentle piercing on his left shoulder.

"Two of swords!" a screeching, rasping voice cackled and Jackie almost peed his pants.

"Jeesus Christ" he yelled, whirling around and ducking, but the piercing in his shoulder just increased.

"Two of swords!" the voice screamed again. Jackie instinctively struck out, dislodging the thing, which pulled away into the air from him in a black blur. It was a huge raven and it landed on a perch just inside the darkness of the building. "Piss off!" it screamed.

"Do I know you?" Sybil Crowleigh asked as she stepped from the gloom of her shop into the daylight. Her face was familiar to Jackie and her eyes seemed to suck the breath out of him. There was something so old about them. Old and momentous. Something like nobility or greatness of a kind glistened in their hazel depths. Jackie's shock must have shown. She eyed him with amusement.

"No, I d…don't think so."

"But you know me, I think. My face is plastered all over the books I've written and you have that disgusting starstruck puppy dog look. Sybil Crowleigh," she said, extending her hand.

"You've already met Pen. Penelope, get out here," she yelled, holding up her arm. As she did so, the great black bird hurtled from the darkness and landed in one great breaking motion with surprising softness. "Apologize, you horrible creature" she commanded.

"Sorrry" the bird rasped. Jackie broke out in laughter.

"No problem" he answered. "What did she mean by two of swords?"

"Oh pay her no attention. I made the mistake of giving her a few tarot lessons. Now she thinks she's the world's greatest card reader. Two of swords was it?"

"Yes, two of swords" he answered.

"Well, it is one of the cards in the deck. A blindfolded woman sits on a seat of stone, her arms folded across her chest, a sword in each hand. Behind her, the seas of the subconscious and in them, reefs. Above her, the new moon. Some say she is blind to her own situation. Some say she is the epitome of balance and sees in a different way." Jackie remained silent and simply blushed. It did not escape the woman's attention. "So what can I do for you? You're certainly not here for antiques, so it must be the other."

"The other?" Jackie asked.

"Oh don't be dull. I hate it when people are dull. It makes the time pass so slowly. What is it you want? To see a witch, maybe have your photograph taken with one? To have your fortune read? Maybe you want to join a coven? Sorry all the covens are full. So what is it" Come now, let's have it or I'll have to get it from Penelope and she's not what she used to be. Good, but not what she used to be. Psychic, I mean. You know that, I hope? Oh yes, animals are very, very psychic, except those that have been co-opted by humans."

Jackie was taken aback. Standing in the presence of one of the world's great witches, he found he suddenly had nothing to say. This was not how it was supposed to go.

"I've read all your books" he blurted out after a long silence. What he really wanted was for her to go past his words and bumbling awkwardness. Far past. He wanted her through some magical psychic gift to see him for what he was. To see him as he saw himself...as a woman. He wanted her to go where no drug or therapist had been able to take him... to the root cause...to why he was as he was. Seeing clearly, beyond all speculation, one could know, and knowing, be. Feeling like a woman in a man's body, there was always a possibility that it was wrong, something not meant to be, unnecessary, irrelevant. Science and medicine had not provided any answers. Maybe the occult would. For a moment, the woman's eyes glazed over, actually went from green to a colorless swirl.

"You ungrateful little bastard" she snapped. Then she returned to herself before Jackie could ask for an explanation. "Oh" she said, "I was just thinking of something someone said before you arrived. Don't mind me. I just go off sometimes." Jackie wondered if she was senile. She had to be over sixty, maybe seventy.

"Ya" he said, "I thought you were talking about me."

"You?" she asked. "Oh goodness, no. Why would I say such a thing to someone who has read all of my books?"

In the instant that she had just "gone off," the witch had seen, in compressed time, a slow motion scene in which Jackie walked down an embankment and under the bridge that was only some five hundred yards away from them. There he had taken out of a pocket, a bright silver medallion on a thick, brass chain. She recognized it instantly by the energy pulsing from it. It was hers! Her son had designed it, and she had had fifty of them struck for coven members in the immediate area and friends. A precious few she had given away in America to witches that had trained with her and had started their own covens. But there it was in the young man's hands as he slowly knelt beside the stream that flowed under the bridge. Then he took the amulet with its handsomely carved zodiac and Sanskrit words spiraling inward and tossed it in. Immediately, the energy radiating from it ceased. The sense of loss she experienced at the moment bordered on physical pain. *"Where did he get it?"* she wondered. *"Why would he dispose of it in this symbolic manner? Where had he learned how to neutralize a psychic tool in this manner? Why do it at all?"*

"You have questions" she said, suddenly kind, "and I have nothing to do at the moment. Why don't you take an old woman to tea?" *"It would not do,"* she thought to herself. *"First he nearly fries Mother's brain and now this. No No. This will not do at all."* She was very particular about her corner of the forest. Malicious influences were not allowed in, but if they did, somehow, manage to infiltrate, they were removed or rendered psychically harmless. There were ways for dealing with even the most tenacious threats, spirit – based or human. On the other hand, sensitives, as psychics used to be called, are often drawn, without being aware of the fact, to energy vortices, areas of dynamic psychic activity. Spiritually charged places. His being in this place at this time, could, she thought, be due to no more than the heightened psychic activity occurring in the area and the convergence of Mercury and Venus. Every one of her coven members had noticed that something very odd was happening.

Odd geometric shapes and sounds were being encountered in dreams and trance states with increasing regularity. A variety of theories existed to explain them, ranging from drunkenness to eating of the abundant hallucinogenic forest mushrooms to psychic attack from black magicians in London. Sybil Crowleigh was staying distinctly out of the discussion. Although she was a witch, she was curiously conservative and slow to come to conclusions on psychic matters until all of the facts were in. This alienated her from the more trendy wiccans who were just trying to fill an empty hole in their otherwise tedious lives. They came and went like the fashions they embraced. The craft would endure them. It always had. She felt sorry for them though, the naïve young men and women who had no idea of the kind of doors they were swinging open when they played with their ouija boards and half – baked incantations. Just like moths to a light, many would get psychically burned, some beyond help.

Tea was at the Bubble and Squeak, a smallish place with polished mahogany tables and white lace placemats.

"Ms. Crowleigh," the white haired proprietress said deferentially as the two entered.

"Ashton," the witch replied with some authority, "This young man is treating me to lunch."

"Oh well then" said the old lady, "I'll just…"

"I know the way, Ashton" the witch replied, "And bring me a vodka rocks."

"Well, I don't know" the old woman responded, flustered. "It's only eleven thirty and it's…"

"It's what, Ashton?" the witch asked showing her boredom.

"It's not…legal…or decent" she added with some strength.

"That's a laugh" the witch roared. "You're tippling away in here from the time you arrive. Not that I disapprove. I see you through the window, old girl. Don't think I don't. Now be nice to an old lady and bring me some vodka. Capisci?"

"Well, I just don't know" the woman replied and wondered off to the kitchen. Sybil Crowleigh, with Jackie in tow, took her usual table in the corner directly beneath a painting reproduction of Manet's Water Lilies.

"All right, young man" she said, "You're buying, so ask away. What is it you want to know?" Not knowing where to start or what to say, thinking he had nothing to lose, a stranger in this place that he would soon leave, he threw caution to the wind.

"You really are a witch, aren't you" he said. "I mean you're not playing at it, are you? I mean, you really don't have a choice, do you?"

"What a strange thing to say" the woman responded, unsure if she had just been insulted or complimented. "Of course I'm a witch, why do you think I wrote…"

"No," Jackie cut in. "I mean it's in your eyes."

"Oh you cheeky bugger" the woman laughed, "Want to talk about the lady's eyes, do you? Careful sonny, I could be your grandmother." Jackie turned red and squirmed in his seat. "Oh my God, and blushing like a young maid" she added.

"No, I mean you have a witch's eyes" he continued.

"I see," said the woman, her tone suddenly patient, indulgent. "And what, exactly do a witch's eyes look like...What is your name anyway? You didn't tell me your name."

"Jackie...Jackie Northam. Well, they look...like they see a lot."

"Oh boy, are you a romantic" the old woman said. "Sweetheart, there are witches in this town who can't see past the noses on their faces. No, no, eyes won't tell you if someone is a witch or not."

"Well, you can say so" Jackie said, "but there is something about your eyes. I can't describe it, but I look at your eyes and I just know."

"You just know."

"I just know."

"And does this kind of 'knowing' happen to you very often, Jackie?" She asked tenderly, and then suddenly it was as though someone had turned the world upside down. "AND JUST WHY THE HELL DO YOU WANT TO THROW MY PENDANT IN THE STREAM?" she screamed. The rage and viciousness in her voice caused Jackie to scramble out of his chair and across the room. The metamorphosis was so sudden and complete, the power of it so great, he could only stand and gasp. "EXPLAIN!" she commanded. "WHAT DID I EVER DO TO YOU?"

"Jeesus...shit...I'm outta here" Jackie stammered as he turned and headed to the door, his arms gathered about his solar plexus as though he had just been kicked.

"Oh don't mind her, she's nuts" the white haired lady said with a laugh as she reentered the room with a tray. But stepping between the two, it was as though she had run into a solid object. What happened then unfolded as though in slow motion. The single drink on the tray, in a high stem, crystal goblet, skittered across the polished surface toward the edge and tilted over, but before more than a tablespoon of the liquid could leave the glass, it righted itself. Jackie and the white haired woman exchanged glances, then stared at the glass, then both turned to the witch, whose brutal expression had not changed. Four people heading up the sidewalk toward the door suddenly thought better of it when the witch looked sharply in their direction, unseen through the curtains and reversed direction.

Suddenly, Jackie was excited. A psychic thing had happened. He had felt it. She had reached out and hammered him in the gut and there was no denying it. Now the force that had propelled him out of his chair ceased and Jackie visualized his crystal parabola turning the remainder of the witch's psychic emanations back on her. As he did so, he turned slowly toward her and the look in his eyes was old and cold and hard. He had never been able to visualize with such clarity. A light seemed to dance in the crystal, gathering itself into a single focussed point projected in the middle of the witch's forehead. For a split second, it seemed to him as though her skin began to lose resolution there, actually melting outwards. Sybil Crowleigh, however, merely laughed a crude, rolling laugh, closed one eye, and squinted back at Jackie with a smirk on her face. As she did so, Jackie realized he had lost control of the crystal. It was moving, floating, turning around and struggle as he did, it could not be stopped. Soon it was turning toward him and he knew that any thought he projected would soon be directed against himself. So he closed his eyes and focussed all of his attention on his own breathing and waited. The crystal flickered momentarily and then reformed and strengthened.

"This is cute," the witch said, examining the object that anyone entering the room would not have seen. "Crude, but interesting. Did you cook this up yourself?" She waited for an answer, but none came. "Quite so, whatever you think now comes back to you magnified greatly. An answer would be thought and thoughts have weight and shape don't they? Don't want to think ourselves to death do we?" Jackie remained silent. "Ah, focussed on our breathing are we? Well I want to talk to you, so stop it. I promise I won't hurt you." Jackie did not speak.

"It's okay," said the white haired woman. "If she says she won't, she won't." Jackie believed her. It was just one of those voices you could trust. As he opened his eyes, the witch turned away, leaving the crystal to fade away.

"Please sit down, Jackie," the witch said as though nothing had happened.

"Only if you'll tell me how you did that" he responded. For a moment, there was silence. He did not move.

"Nothing happened. An old woman got angry, and you ran away like a frightened mouse."

"And the thing you did with the crystal?"

"As you see, it was not really yours." Jackie balked at this.

"It was," he said, "to start with."

"No. You summoned its parts until they came together in your imagination and then you projected it with your will. But where did the parts come from? Are your thoughts something you call into being from nothingness? I think not...Anyway, enough of this. It's tedious."

"I don't understand," Jackie said.

"Well maybe there are things you want to understand that you just are not equipped to understand" the witch replied. Suddenly the frustration over Jackie's gender issues flooded into his mind and he grew angry.

"I have a right to understand!" he stormed. "I have a right to understand everything that touches me, everything that IS me!"

"Oh brother" the white haired woman said and meekly tip toed out of the room. "Here we go again" she muttered as she entered the front hallway. By now, Jackie's intensity had almost taken on the proportions of the witch's. There was a sparkle and a sort of grandmotherly kindness in her eyes as she watched him.

"That's such a male thing to say" she offered, but Jackie would have none of it. At the moment, he was feeling a special kind of violation, the kind that comes when someone enters your mind and grabs hold of your thoughts, moving them around and making sure you know exactly what went on. It was, in fact, a violation far more intimate than sexual rape.

"Male?" he screamed, cracking his voice in the process. The witch tried to assert a calm over his growing hysteria.

"Yes, male" she said in a slow, measured cadence. "Insisting on understanding things is just another form of control. Control is a very male thing. It is a vote of non confidence in the universe."

"Understanding is control?"

""Determining the means by which understanding will be allowed to come to you is control. I said control is a male thing. I didn't say it was a bad thing, unless you need to be in control to be happy. Men are often like that. Sometimes relinquishing control is better. Sit down dear." She pointed to the table and Jackie decided to stay. "Now, what is it that you are so desperate to understand?" Jackie did not answer. "I think we are going to be very good friends. Don't mind my temper. Does it have something to do with the pendant I made, the one you plan to toss in the stream?"

"I haven't decided whether or not to do that. Are you going to tell me how you knew?" Jackie asked.

"That pendant is a magical thing" she said with a straight face. It leaves behind a psychic signature in the air when it moves. I recognize the trail. I should know. I made the thing. How did you come into possession of it?"

Jackie told her of the witch he had met in Toronto, the one who had given him the thing. He did not mention that it had happened in the cafeteria of The Carlyle Institute of Psychiatry. The young lady had just gotten up from a table where she was in animated conversation with persons not present. Striding across the room, she had approached him boldly, studied him a moment, pulled his long hair aside and whispered.

"A very special gift, for a very special girl." Then she placed it around his neck and snapped the clasp closed. "It is a very special charm" she said "from a very famous witch friend in England." A moment later, she was back at her table, again immersed in deep conversation with thin air. That was how Jackie had first come to know of the name Sybil Crowleigh. First out of curiosity, then out of growing interest and fascination, he began reading her books. Even now, he had the thing in his pant pocket and knew she could not see it.

"So?" she pressed, downing the vodka that remained in her glass in one swallow. "Oh for God's sake, drink something will you. You're making me nervous." Jackie ordered a white wine spritzer. "A what?" the witch demanded.

"A white wine spritzer" said Jackie.

"That's a woman's drink."

"I don't care. I like it."

"Suit yourself. So where did you get the pendant?" she asked.

"It was given to me. A beautiful, young woman just walked up and gave it to me. She did say she got it from you. That's how I heard about you in the first place."

"And what was this woman's name?"

"Sorry, I don't know."

"Describe her."

"She was pretty, long red hair...crazy."

"Crazy how?" asked the witch.

"She spoke when there was nobody there. Long conversations."

"And where was this?" the witch Continued.

"I met her once in a café" Jackie lied.

"She meets you once and gives you the pendant" the witch said, incredulous.

"Just like that."

"Bloody hell! Ashton, bring me another drink…please" the witch called, but as she spoke, the old woman reached from behind her and placed the vodka and ice on the table. "Good God" yelped the witch.

"Gotcha" squealed the old woman, winking at her then pirouetting toward the kitchen.

"Don't you ever sneak up behind me like that again, you old hag" the witch snarled. "You're worse than my mother. So, where were we, yes, the pendant. I want it back."

"Too late" said Jackie. "No insult intended, but your vision was off. I lost it. I was thinking that I might put it in the stream because I read that that would neutralize the power, and I was coming over here anyway and I didn't know what kind of person you were. Who knows, maybe the thing made the girl crazy."

"No darling" the witch said with a sigh. "It was the one thing that kept her from going crazy for the longest time. She was my niece. I should know." She did not look convinced. To Jackie's astonishment, she took a large ice cube out of the drink, put it in her mouth and crushed it with one chomp. The sound echoed in the room. "Okay, you lost it" she said, "No sense in crying over spilt milk. Is that your book of shadows?" she asked disdainfully, pointing to Jackie's writing book. Jackie explained that it was just a writing book and not the collection of occult ceremonies and notes that made up the witch's personal workbook.

"I see," said the witch. "May I see it?" Jackie explained that it was personal and declined. "You're still angry," she said.

"Ya, well, it's not every day someone psychically knocks me out of a chair and across the room." The witch's eyes were on Jackie's black, hardbound book. It troubled her, and she didn't know why.

Chapter Fifteen
The Gift

If anyone had ever made a movie of Sybil Crowleigh's life, the opening scene would have started like this. The screen is black. There is a soft, rustling sound that is hard to identify. Leaves in the trees? Waves on a shore? A gentle round of applause, bacon frying in a pan, stones seaswept down a beach? A tiny golden light appears on screen and as it widens, we get more gold and more texture, but we still don't know what we're looking at. The camera pulls back and back until we see a very young girl with long red hair, gazing into a crystal ball and chatting merrily away. She is sitting with her long plaid skirt and jacket, white lace blouse, on a swath of flattened straw. The camera zooms back to reveal that she is sitting in the midst of a great crop circle, the finishing touches of which are just being applied by an unseen maker. She continues speaking to the crystal.

In the small village of Stanbury, some twenty miles southeast of The Old Forest, Sybil Crowleigh was born. Daughter of Shirley Donohu who was known far and wide for her expertise with herbs and potions. No one ever went to a doctor until they had gone 'round to see what the herb lady could do. More often than not, her concoctions did the trick and she never asked more than people could afford. Often she helped out for free. Charging high prices, she knew, would bring down the bad luck, and her abilities, trained into her from birth, would be taken away. She had seen it happen to many who had corrupted the craft. Anyway, that's where Sybil grew up and it was a strange thing because over the years, more and more people who felt like her about life and nature had moved into the area. Not all were practitioners of The Old Religion as witchcraft is sometimes called.

"Really Jackie, you must tell me what is in your little black book. I just know it's something interesting" the woman said.

"I told you" Jackie replied, "It's just poems and personal stuff."

"You came here to join a coven and find answers to things" the witch said leaning back in her chair, her eyes closed. "Do you agree with the things I say in my books?"

"Yes, mostly" he answered.

"And the part about there being no personal 'stuff'?" She said the last word with exaggerated distaste. "The part about all of us drawing from and giving back to universal consciousness? All of us contributing to the psychosphere that surrounds the planet? Child..."

and she said this with great compassion, "In one sense, there is no separation. We are all one. We breathe the same air and we swim in the same psychic sea."

"And what about people who are really different?" Jackie asked.

"Such as?" the witch asked, leaning forward.

Jackie thought for an instant about jumping in with both feet, declaring his transgender nature, getting the wiccan "take" on it, and having done with it one way or the other.

"Come on" she prompted in a gentle voice.

"I can't do this" Jackie finally said, his voice full of pain. He had backed himself into a corner half way around the world, had gone from person to person, group to group, looking for someone, anyone who would show understanding and acceptance of his nature. If this witch, whose creed was predicated on the joyous embrace of all things natural, should write him off, what could he hope for in this life? Where could he look for community, for companionship, for context. Self-acceptance, if it means isolation, was just another kind of hell, he knew. The witch sensed his growing panic.

"Look at me" she said with a laugh." A perfectly nice young man takes me out to tea and how do I repay him? Forgive me, I have a naturally enquiring nature, which is to say, I don't know how to keep my nose out of other people's business. Her eyes were fixed on the black book, her heart rate accelerating. "Do you like to draw, Jackie?" she asked quite matter of factly. Glad for the change of topic, the young man relaxed visibly in his seat.

"Yes, a little, why do you ask?"

As he spoke, the witch allowed herself to move into a deep trance. Jackie did not notice. Over the years, she had learned to do it almost instantaneously. She intended to know what was in the book, with or without his cooperation. If she could cause him to think the image clearly enough even just for a second, she, too, would see it.

"So, what have you been working on lately?" she asked. Whatever it was that was in the book that was attracting her so, was recent. She could feel it. In her mind's eye, she moved in a synaesthetic flux of sound, sight, taste, touch and smell, but they were not distinguishable sensations. It was hard to tell whether she was seeing or hearing a thought, tasting or touching a smell. One thing was certain now as she sat across from the curious traveler; he was suddenly relaxing inwardly and outwardly. She felt him breathe and let go of the present, felt a heat and a light flood over him. A cry...sadness?...no...seagulls...blue...indigo blue...a shoreline...a big yacht...a little sailboat...a dirt path on a mountainside...cascades of images...how clearly...how quickly he recalled the images.

"Just little things" he said. "Little sketches of places I've been, things I've seen." But nowhere was there the image that called to the witch from the pages of the book.

"Really?" she said. She decided on a more direct approach. "Such as what?"

"Oh, things in Greece. I was there before I came here." He ran through the list and it coincided with what the witch had seen. Either he was very, very good at concealing memories, or, and she could hardly believe it, he was genuinely unaware of the image that now shouted out to her from a page in his closed book, an image she could not decipher. Well, there was no rush. If it was to be, it would be.

"How long are you going to be with us, Jackie, in The Old Forest, I mean?" she asked.

"I haven't decided" he answered, "It depends."

"On what?"

"On whether I get what I came to find."

"And what is that?" the witch asked. Jackie hesitated.

"I know" the witch said at last. "You can't do this. Ashton!" she called, "Be a dear and bring me those silly psychic cards of yours, the ones you use for testing people."

"These ones" the old lady beamed, sticking them in the witch's face.

"Oh you just love doing that kind of thing, don't you?" To Jackie, she added, "She's such a show off." Turning again to the lady, she said "Ashton, are you still here? For heaven's sake, don't you have something to do?"

"Not since you scared all the customers away" the old woman answered. "I'll just stay and watch, if you don't mind."

"Watch what?" Jackie asked.

"I just thought it might amuse you to do a little psychic test, Jackie," the witch said. "Are you game?"

"Sure, what do I do?"

"Easy" the witch answered, shuffling the cards. "Cut the deck." Jackie did so, making three neat piles to his left which the woman reassembled. "Now move them counterclockwise on the table with your left hand please...good...that will do. Now, I must tell you that these are not ordinary cards, though perhaps you already know that. They are cards with various images in different shapes and patterns. There are two of each. Two with smooth circles, two with rough circles, two with triangles, two with squares and so on. Some of the shapes you may not recognize. I want you to draw twenty cards from the pile with your left hand so you end up with ten matching pairs. Two circles, two squares, et cetera. Do you understand?" Jackie nodded and pulled in tighter to the table.

"With my eyes open or closed?"

"It doesn't make any difference," the witch said.

"Okay" Jackie said and pulled a card out of the pile. He was hesitant, his movement slow and labored. A pained expression covered his face.

"Something wrong?" the witch asked.

"No...shhhhhh" he responded. He had worked his face down close to the cards and now slowly pulled back then stopped. "Ahhhhhh" he said with a sigh of relief and then pulled several cards out of the pile, turning several of them around lengthwise before continuing. His pace was quickening now. "Ah...mmmmm, oh" he muttered like a young Glen Gould at the piano. The pace increased until he spun the last two cards into alignment, completing two perfectly spaced columns. The witch shot the old lady a glance. The old lady raised one eyebrow and covered a grin with her hand. The whole thing had taken only a few seconds.

Splicing the Light   163

"Don't you want to think about this a little, maybe try it again and take your time. You're not matching socks, you know" the witch said with some irritation.

"I'm sorry, did I do it wrong?" Jackie answered.

"Wrong? Not necessarily" the witch said, "Just somewhat...abrupt and what was all that mumbling?"

"Mumbling?" he asked. "Was I mumbling?"

"Oh, get on with it!" the old woman called out.

"Patience old girl" said the witch, flipping the first card to reveal a star. The second card also was a star. Jackie smiled.

"Almost everyone gets at least one pair" the witch said. "Don't get excited. It means nothing."

"Spoil sport" grumbled the old woman. The witch simply gave her a look of disgust. The next two cards matched as well – two lightning bolts.

"Good" said the witch, "but it still means nothing. On the other hand, without these first two matches, nothing of significance can be shown. Are you psychic, Jackie?" she asked to no one in particular. Let's see..." The next card was flipped over and showed three undulating blue lines like waves, so did the next.

"Ah...good" said the witch. "We have something to work with here, at least a latent psychic ability. Nothing can happen if you don't have the raw material. So...how far does this go Mr. Traveler?" The next card revealed a cross...the next...a cross. The witch looked up at Jackie.

"Well, sir, you are beating the odds. Do you believe in luck Mr. Northam?"

"No" said Jackie.

"Well, we must talk about that some day." She took a long sip of her vodka and belched loudly, thoroughly enjoying herself. "Smile, Jackie, I'm telling you that you have something to build on, psychically speaking. That's quite a lot to come away with." As she spoke, she turned the next card. It was a crescent moon. The next card, she paused with and sat up a little straighter in her chair. "Well...well" she said dropping it face up on the table. "Five matches. Your psychic ability, Mr. Northam is more than latent. Now is it percolating away on its own or have you been working on it?" Jackie was looking over at the old lady. "That was a question, Mr. Northam" the witch snapped.

"I meditate a bit and I play around with psychometry. I started after I read one of your books." Psychometry is the art of taking a physical object such as jewelry, going into trance, and interpreting the images that flood into the fortuneteller's mind. Often, the client finds useful information in what is said.

"Hmmmf" the witch sniffed, unimpressed. When the next cards were turned, two squares lay beside each other. The witch did not hesitate, however, and moved swiftly to the seventh pair. The first card was an infinity sign, like the number eight lying on its side.

"Care to turn the next card over, Jackie?" the witch asked.

"Okay" he said and turned it over. Another infinity sign.

"I told you," the white haired lady said with great pleasure.

"Oh do be quiet, Ashton" the witch fired back. "You have not been quite honest with us about your abilities, Jackie" the witch said coyly. "This is well beyond chance." The next cards were a pair of golden cups. The witch drained the last of her vodka. "After you pulled the cards from the deck," she said, "you turned some of them around lengthwise."

"I did?" responded Jackie.

"You did. No one ever does that. Why did you do it?"

"I didn't realize I did," he said uncertainly.

"No?" the witch responded warily.

The next card revealed a triangle with one of the points facing up.

"Marvelous" she said, turning up the second triangle. "Really, very good, Jackie. I think we have a live one here Ashton."

"Told you so," said the old lady.

"Yes, yes" replied the witch crushing an ice cube between her teeth. Then she pulled up on the second last card, let it flap down again, and did the same with the last card. Looking Jackie in the eye, she took up both cards and placed them along with the rest of the deck in her purse.

"So, what was it?" Jackie asked.

"Nine out of ten is very good, Jackie. Be satisfied with that," the witch said condescendingly.

"Sybil" the white haired lady said, astonished. "What are you up to?"

"Did they match or not?" Jackie asked. The witch did not answer. In a flash, Jackie was around to the other side of the table and had the purse in his hand. Withdrawing the deck, he placed it on the table, drawing off the top two cards, placing them beside the pile. One by one, he tipped them over. Two blank cards.

"That's the hardest match" the witch said, "and you, you little runt, thought you could come in here and put one over on Sybil Crowleigh. Are you happy? Did you have a good time?"

"What are you talking about?" Jackie asked.

"Did you have fun?" the witch demanded.

"Sybil!" the old lady protested.

"Who are you?" the witch continued, "one of Blithestone's little hellions from London come in here to put one over on old Crowleigh? Well, you can bugger off back to wherever you came from. And if I so much as hear a whisper about you interfering with coven members or craft in The Old Forest, you'll wish you were dead. Do we understand each other?"

"Sybil" the old woman cut in, "I don't think-"

"Shut up Ashton" the witch commanded.

It took some time, but between Jackie and the old woman, they managed eventually to convince the witch that Jackie was exactly who he said he was – a North American just travelling around Europe trying to find out who he was. After she realized her mistake and her paranoia, the witch actually became intrigued with the young man. Why, she wanted to know, would a North American think he could find himself in Europe? Could a Martian, she asked, find himself on Venus? Suddenly the absurdity of what Jackie was doing started to impress itself on him. But what is a person to do when answers to life and death issues are not to be found where one is? Jackie had thought the obvious answer was to go somewhere else and look again.

"Well, I don't know what I can say" the witch replied, "if you won't even tell me what you're looking for. Why does Jackie Northam run around all over the planet looking for answers to some big, secretive question? Did you ever stop to think that if you're not getting an answer that makes sense, and I assume you have asked this question ad nauseum, that maybe you are asking the wrong question? You know, sometimes when people have a problem, they sink their teeth into the first question that seems to relate to it and they never let go. But that problem just refuses to die, and it's strong and it just starts to run around and carry you away. Next thing you know, your feet are off the ground and you can't even stand up straight long enough to let go. The problem just takes you along for the ride, and what you get to see is everywhere that problem calls home. You get enough of that kind of scenery under your belt and soon you start to think of that place as home, too. I take it the question, my young friend, is 'Who am I?' or something like that. Correct me if I'm wrong."

"No, it's something like that." Jackie said with a growing sense of excitement and peace all rolled into one. "How did you know?"

"Easy" said the witch, "Everybody wants to know that. Most people are afraid to ask the question. The answer is sometimes messy and there's a big, hairy irony that goes with it."

"What's that?" Jackie asked, full of anticipation.

"Obsessed with the question of who one is, my young psychic, one stops being. And true being demands the most outrageous bitch's brew of unlikely qualities."

In a strange state of euphoria, Jackie listened to himself as his voice drifted across the table.

"Will you teach me about that?" he asked.

"Ahhhhh" said the white haired lady as though she had just heard something for which she had been waiting a long time.

"We might be able to work something out" said the witch smiling. "You certainly know how to get a rise out of me." For a moment, it looked as if everything was heading off in a positive direction to Jackie. So he thought he would just seize the moment and run with it explaining that he would like to attend a coven meeting to get a feel for it. To be in the company of others who shared his interest in nature and the psychic arts was a very strong attraction to him. They would, he thought, have to be open-minded people, the kind who enjoy thinking and talking about life and living.

"Well, I know of one opening" said the witch, "but it's no good for you. They need a woman." Jackie's heart suddenly felt like it weighed a ton.

"Why a woman?" he asked.

"Because of the way a coven is made up. Six men, six women and a high priestess."

"Oh c'mon" said Jackie, "what difference does it make?"

"It makes a lot of difference" the witch replied. "Male and female energies are not the same and balance of forces is very important within the circle."

"That is so sexist" said Jackie.

"Yes, it is a decision made on the basis of sex, so I guess it's sexist."

"Are all covens like that?" asked Jackie folding his arms in front of him.

"They used to be" the witch replied with a sigh, "but things are changing. Occultism is growing and falling apart at the same time. No one observes the traditions anymore. Everything has to be new to be popular."

"Such as?"

"Such as in any city you can find gay covens, lesbian covens, bisexual, transgender covens, feminist covens. Everyone's messing with the balance of energies and it just doesn't work. Nature doesn't work like that."

"But I understand" Jackie said "that there are solitary witches too."

"Yes, for some, that is a valid and sometimes necessary path, but there are dangers in that. Coven membership has its advantages, you know, safety in numbers, being part of a community. Anyway, Jackie, what's the point in joining a coven here? Do it when you get home."

"I just wanted to get a feel for how I fit into the whole occult scheme of things. By the way, I know some transgender people. How do they fit in to the whole balance of energy thing?" Jackie thought he had nothing to lose. This great witch was as sexist and bigoted, he thought, as anyone he had ever met. His disappointment was profound as he decided to learn as much as he could about how a traditional wiccan saw the gender issue.

"The best and the worst. Queens and sissies, you mean?" she asked with a twisted laugh.

"No, I mean people who live very unspectacular lives, people who feel like a woman one minute and a man the next. Sometimes equally, sometimes more one way than the other."

"Well, that's it exactly! People like that are very unstable. You never know what you're dealing with. On a psychic basis, their energies are all over the place."

"But for some people, that's natural."

"Nature makes mistakes" said the witch. Like a tumbler falling into place in a combination lock, Jackie's heart froze. Still, he thought he could use her and come away with something for his trouble. So, when she offered to introduce him to some psychics in town, he accepted, deciding to stay on for a while longer. The first thing he needed to do was to find somewhere cheaper to live. He spotted an ad in the village newspaper and was soon moving into a small shed about seven feet by twelve.

"My husband built this cottage. I hope you like it" said Mrs. Turner as she pushed open the door. We rent it out mostly in the tourist season." The place was clean, if bare and Jackie had taken it on the spot. There was even a tiny washroom. On one wall, there was a map of Scotland, on another, a framed poem of some kind by Robbie Burns, something about whisky. He would read it later. When the landlady left and the door snapped closed, Jackie turned off the lights and lay down on the bed. He expected to fall asleep immediately but it didn't happed. For a long time, he replayed the day's events in his mind, or rather the events replayed themselves and he had no choice but to watch. Back and forth it had gone – up one minute and down the next. He had been thrown across a room by psychic power. He had aced a psychic test administered by one of the world's most famous witches, but what was it she had said, that he was asking the wrong question. What did that mean? What could be more important, especially for a person like him, than to achieve some semblance of peace about who he was? He considered the possibilities. Questions filled his mind, but none seemed as important as the one he had been asking his whole life. Maybe the witch was wrong. What could she know about it anyway? Male energy…female energy…she was as sexist as the rest.

As he drifted off to sleep, he tried to remember why he had come to Europe. Desperation, depression, a need to get clear about himself. Strange, he did not feel those things as acutely now. They were still there, but muted. He didn't hurt as much, no not nearly so much, something was better, somehow…sleep…when it came was a kind of gentle swirl…a gentle flight into a pattern that seemed almost familiar…up?…down?…around?…it didn't matter as sleep faithfully claimed its own. On the nightstand, his writing book fell open to one of his drawings, one of his doodles, rather – for he had given it no thought whatever. One day, mulling something over, he had just drawn it without realizing. A geometric shape. It was this shape into which he fell asleep, the same shape which had sent the red hair of a young witch flying in a long forgotten wheat field of the Old Forest.

Chapter Sixteen
Felicity and the Crew

"**W**as everything alright?" Mrs. Turner asked as Jackie answered a knock at the door the next morning. He told her that everything was fine. "Well if you do need anything, just let me know" the woman added, "My husband leaves early and gets home late. He sells spirits and his work takes him far and wide, I'm afraid. So, you'll have to deal with me." She was out of breath and her body was already turning to leave although she had not finished speaking. In her hands, she carried two pairs of cleated football boots and two footballs. She noticed Jackie suppressing a smile. "I'm a football mom" she said hopelessly. I have to get the boys off to practice. Enjoy your stay."

Not long after she pulled out of the driveway, a bizarre looking van pulled in. It reminded Jackie of pictures he had seen of the sixties. Large, petalled flowers, air – brushed with evident enthusiasm, swelled in great profusion all over the chassis. There were stars and comets racing across a polyurethane sky. Slogans and graffiti of various kinds flowed in fixed abundance – "circles are right – squares are human," "save the hedgehogs," nine to five sucks," "hug a witch – or else!"

"Well, get a move on, love, we don't have all day" called a large woman with a bald head as she exited the vehicle. When she was clear of it, the van lurched back to its normal position and voices inside jokingly let go together.

"Whoa" they laughed as though a huge wave had just passed under them.

"Knock it off, you two."

"Yes, Felicity" came the mocking reply of two female voices.

"Well, are you coming or not?" the woman called to Jackie. "You are Jackie, aren't you?"

"Yes, but who are you?"

"Oh, how bloody typical" the woman laughed. "She didn't speak with you first, did she?"

"Who?" Jackie asked.

"Sybil, of course" the woman said.

"No."

"She didn't tell him anything!" the woman yelled back to the others. Turning to him, she ran one of her large hands over her shiny head and looked down at the ground. She reminded him of a Buddhist nun he had known back home, except this woman was powerfully built, with massive tattoos on each bicep, one an ornately detailed anchor, the other read Love Boat. Jackie liked her immediately. "You're rather a cute little thing, aren't you?" she said, glancing at him. "Well, Sybil asked if we would mind showing you around a bit. She also said we should answer any questions you might have. Within reason. Seems she's quite taken with you."

"Is that so?"

"Jeesus, she's right, you do blush something furious."

Jackie was standing in his normal posture, one foot perpendicular to the other. The woman walked up in front of him, planted her feet widely apart and put her hands on her hips.

"You a dancer?" she asked.

"No, why?"

"Why do you stand like that? You a bloody poof or something?"

"I don't know. What's a poof?"

"A poof, a pansy, a faggot, you know."

"Shorten sail, Felicity. I like you and your tattoos, so don't make me angry."

"Shorten sail? Jeesus H. Christ. Shorten sail? He says I should shorten sail, girls and he likes my tattoos" the woman yelled back at the van. "You've got a way about you, Jackie. Get in the van and we'll show you around. Is there anywhere you want to go?"

"Sybil arranged this for me?"

"Don't get a swelled head, she's just trying to keep us out of trouble."

"Okay, look, I don't know anything about this place. I'm in your hands. Let's go." Jackie grabbed his wallet and writing book and off they went.

They started with a leisurely roll through the main street of the village. It was Saturday and being mid morning, the sidewalks were already thick with tourists. Jackie almost jumped out of the vehicle the first time Felicity hit the horn. He saw the fat Bermuda shorted man crossing the road with his nose buried in Europe on Ten Dollars a Day and expected something but not the ship's air horn that erupted in an ear piercing blast from under the hood. The entire vehicle shuddered and the man collapsed in a flailing of arms and legs, his glasses sailing through the air and a single page dangling between his fingers from which the book had fallen. It was a little piece of street theatre Felicity relished. That moment of panic in which a landlocked tourist actually believed he was about to be hit by a ship. There was no logic to it. The mind does funny things when taken unawares. Felicity counted on it.

"Ten" she said.

"Seven" said Kazuo from the back seat.

"Five" sighed Rosemary feigning boredom.

"Five?" groaned Felicity, "Bloody five? That was no five. He nearly crapped his drawers."

"Five" the woman insisted. "You jumped the gun. He wasn't in the zone. Never mind. The fish are spooked now."

"Smoke?" Felicity asked, banging a pack of cigarettes into Jackie's arm.

"Got my own" he said, "but thanks."

"Oh my God, bloody Froggie fags" said Felicity, spotting his Gauloises. "Ah well, each to his own."

"Let's take him to the tree" Rosemary said.

"Can we?" Kazuo asked, brushing her long, black hair out of her eyes and looking a bit alarmed.

"She said to show him everything within reason, but let's hold that for later. Hungry Jackie?"

"Ya, I haven't eaten yet."

"The Queen" all three said with enthusiasm.

The Queen, was Angelina Valente. Finding her took a bit of work. The soup stand she ran out of her converted delivery van was not exactly legal and mobility was the only way she stayed in business. Felicity knew her ways, though, and found her parked on the outskirts of town near a field where roadies were setting up for a rock concert. A hand painted sign hanging from her aerial read SOOP AND SANDWITCHES. With a great pounding, Felicity brought the "Star Cruiser," as Jackie had learned the van was called, to a stop everything in its own inertia, heaving to a grace note stop a microsecond later. Angelina's face went sour when she looked up and saw her customers.

"Oh, that's so corny!" Rosemary laughed, seeing the sign. Who made it?" The olive skinned lady in a long, red muslin skirt covered with tiny mirrors and bound at the waist with a bold purple sash, pointed at Kazuo.

"This one." Kazuo stood, mouth agape in a laughing denial.

"Sandwitches?" said Rosemary.

"Cute" grunted Felicity. "What foreigners do to the English language!"

Everyone who came to the Old Forest knew that it was famous for its association with Wicca. Every souvenir shop had at least one coffee mug with a witch of some sort on it. Brooms in hardware stores bore wiccan images and bookstores were bursting with volumes of the most secret rituals. There was the newest best seller The Ten Minute Wiccan Self-Initiation Guide for those with little time to spare. Occult shops sold everything from pungent moon goddess incense to voodoo dolls and athamés – the witch's ceremonial knife.

"So, what is it today, Your Highness?" Felicity asked.

"Why does she call her that?" Jackie asked Rosemary.

"People say she was a leader of a large band of Romanies...gypsies."

"Was she?"

"God knows."

"Lamb stew or chicken curry. The regular sandwiches" answered the woman, adjusting the velvet band that held her long black hair out of her eyes. The group ordered curry and someone produced beer from the Star Cruiser. There was hammering and sound checks from the P.A. systems on stage, feedback now and then ripping through the landscape.

"Check, check, check, test one...two...three, test, test, test. Down one, up on two" the musician called to the sound engineer.

"How do you like the music business, Your Majesty?" Felicity asked.

"I told you not to call me that, and this is not music." From somewhere a lead guitar let out a high bending note and sustained it from a screech to a whisper. A thunderous bass chord followed, then abruptly stopped as the player swore. "That is not music" the woman said, pointing to a speaker. "That is a nightmare, torture. There is no music in it. Where is the heart?"

"Ah Angelina, you are such a romantic" Kazuo cut in.

"And you," the woman said, slapping Jackie on the shoulder, "I suppose you would call that music." In fact, he liked it very much. The guy obviously had talent.

"I think it sucks!" he said. "This is music" he continued, holding up the bowl of curry.

"So you like Angelina's food?"

"It's brilliant" he said, following a mouthful of the fiery dish with a swallow of the rich dark beer.

"You know cooking?"

"I know you make your own curry powder, you fry your spices in oil and I know that you know how to keep mace and cardamom from overpowering the cumin."

"For that, I read your palm for nothing." Sitting down beside him, she took up his hand and pressed the palm flat..."Such trouble...and such fear. Not everything has to be lived, you know. But you will insist. You must experience everything. Do you know what I'm talking about?"

"Yes."

"You don't need to tell everybody everything. Don't give away too much."

"I've been told that before."

"You are very psychic, but you have done nothing about it. You wish to kill yourself but cannot. Good thing. In suicide, there is no answer. And as long as there is no answer, there is repetition." Jackie began to pull away but the gypsy tightened her grip.

"I don't know what you're talking about."

"Yes you do dear soul, but you are confused."

"How?"

"Spirit comes upon you...frequently...and you are transformed but you...you misunderstand what is happening to you."

"I...I."

"Listen, the question is not whether you are a woman or not..."

"Jeesus Christ!"

"You are a man. You are a woman. You are both...you are neither. It doesn't matter."

"What do you mean it doesn't matter!"

"Something happened to you. A very dirty trick, a very evil person. Long ago. Do you remember?"

"No"

"Since then, you have misunderstood everything."

"Can't you be more specific?"

"It is not clear. Several times, you have come close to the answer. But you do not really need it. Develop your psychic ability. Your answer comes to you before you go home, an answer, not necessarily the one for which you are looking."

"Am I going home?"

"Of course. There is much for you to do. Enough. So you really like my curry? Tell me how you make yours."

An hour later, the Star Cruiser with Jackie and the girls gabbing away, came over the crest of a hill and pulled to the side where three, loose gravel roads came together.

"Why are we stopping?" Jackie asked.

"This is a very special place" Rosemary said. Jackie got out and looked around. Field grasses swayed in the breeze, accentuated by patches of wildflowers. Birds catching insects wheeled and spun in the air, diving and soaring. Twenty yards into the field, an old bleached and broken tree stood like a splintered whalebone. Jackie walked in. The girls stood at the roadside and watched. The silence was deep and borderless. Jackie closed his eyes and breathed deeply. He turned to look at the girls. They were motionless, staring at him, intently. He thought about calling to them but the thought drifted away. His hand found the surface of the tree and he was astonished at its smoothness, as though it had been polished. In the instant that he touched it, a wave of comfort and excitement washed over him, feelings he could not explain. He felt a part of something. He had had the feeling once before. Two years earlier, driving home from a bar, he had snapped out a turn in his brother's Mustang GT, the engine howling to a low bass note. To his amazement, a huge full moon loomed above an old stone church across the intersection in which he found himself alone. Instantly, he was flooded with a sense of purpose which he could not understand, only that everything was right and the moment felt packed with meaning.

That, too, was an intersection of three roads, now that he thought of it.

Slowly, the thumb and index finger of his left hand formed into a crescent and those of his right into the sign of the horned god.

"So you do know" Felicity said with relief as the girls approached.

"Know what?"

"The routine."

"No, what routine?"

As one, the girls stopped.

"In the appointed meeting place, the first of us to arrive, signs to the others that it is safe to approach."

"Is that what I did?"

"Wait a minute, what is this?"

"Honest, I don't know what you're talking about."

"You gave the recognition and safety sign."

"I know...I...it felt right. I didn't even know I was doing it."

"You do know where you are, don't you?"

"What do you mean?"

"Oh brother" said Felicity, "will you stop screwing around?"

"Look" said Jackie, "I know about the sign from a book I read, that's all."

"Okay, fine, whatever you say, but you did the right thing in the right place at the right time, even if it was for the wrong reason."

"This" said Rosemary who had been listening with a frown on her face, "is the meeting tree. For centuries, we have used it as a meeting place."

"You mean you're wiccans, all three of you?"

"Well, duh" said Felicity.

"I didn't know!"

"You really do need to work on your craft, Jackie" Rosemary said. "We can help you."

"I'm not a wiccan."

"Suppressing gifts and callings is nothing to be proud of."

"Who's suppressing?"

"Why don't we sit down and talk a bit?" said Kazuo and they settled into the lush, fragrant field flowers and the gentle sweeping sibilance of waving grasses.

Splicing the Light   177

"You know" said Felicity, "I wasn't always the wonderful specimen of womanhood you see before you now."

"No?"

"Absolutely not, Jackie, if that's your real name" she said biting a rough edge off a fingernail and spitting it into the wind. It landed on his cheek and she quickly removed it. "Sorry, love. No, my parents found me a proper terror. Sent me off to a private girl's school. Aunts and grandmothers were instructed to do what they could to help me become a nice little lady. Sweet, feminine, Church of England, privileged. Me, I wanted jeans and a good punch up if anybody crossed me. I guess I was quite a handful. Drank like a fish from the time I was fourteen."

Suddenly, Jackie was aware that he had been looking at a picture of Celeste in his mind. "Are you there, dear? Yes, well, where was I…ah yes, drunk and stoned and raunchy…oh my god. It's amazing I didn't pick up a disease somewhere along the line. And they knew, they all knew what I was like. It wasn't like I hid anything…" her voice trailed off as she scanned the small clouds moving quickly across the sky "…until I started hiding everything. I was always a very lonely person, you see, and they, everyone pulled away…slowly…you could hardly see it happen…one by one. No one would argue anymore. I used to love the arguments. I guess they just got tired or gave up. Felicity wasn't going to be what they wanted. And it took me a long time to learn this, so listen up. People want what they want, and that's very rarely reality. Fears and fantasies get in the way. They were afraid of what I was and what I might become and I sure as hell didn't fulfill the fantasies they had for my life. No sweet, obedient, apolitical housewife there. No sir. Daddy was the best, 'You just be whatever you need to be, sweetheart' he would say, and that would be the end of it. He thought that handing out his carte blanche was the easiest way to avoid discussing anything real. Like my fucking life."

"What did you do?" Jackie asked.

"Why sweetie I did just exactly what you're doing" she said, delicately severing a wildflower bloom from its stalk and handing it to him. "I went into years of oh – so – clever denial. I thought anything would be better than living unloved by those who are supposed to love you more than anyone – your own blood relations. So, I tried to be what they wanted. Went to church, sang in the choir. Went about in cutsie little dresses, wore a smile, dated future captains of industry and commerce, kept my mouth shut about anything that would show I had a brain. And the biggest lie of all – I stopped sleeping around. Oh, the lies the mind can make the body tell. Christ! And the lies the body can make the mind tell itself! Unbelievable. I stopped talking to spirits, threw out all of my books on the occult. Can you believe it, one day I actually got down on my knees one Sunday morning in front of the television and prayed with the minister that Jeesus would enter my life and show me how to have a decent life." Jackie grabbed his left wrist with his right hand. "What I'm trying to tell you" she said, taking his hand gently in hers "oh bloody hell." She sat bolt upright. "Don't ever do that again."

"Do what again?"

"Try to kill yourself. You tried to kill yourself. The Goddess wouldn't answer the way you wanted, so you tried to kill yourself. You gave up on Her...on yourself...oh my god."

"No...I...I" Kazuo and Rosemary quickly drew nearer and reached out to him.

"I'm so sorry."

"It's okay, Jackie."

"It was a long time ago, okay?" he said.

"Not so long ago" said Felicity. "Within the last year. Jeesus, I knew there was a reason for this somewhere. Look, Jackie, sometimes the answers we get aren't what we want to hear. You know? And Her silence doesn't always mean we're unworthy. And you don't have to be anything you don't want to be. Don't ask me why I said that. It just seems important somehow. Look, you've just met us and if you don't want to talk, that's okay. It's just that I get a feeling that you need to be here just now and maybe we can help you some way. Sometimes, you know, it's easier to get on with strangers than with friends. So, what's bugging you?"

"I'm working out a lot of stuff."

"Like what?" Kazuo asked.

"Like the nature of the universe. Little stuff. You know." There was a brief silence, then Rosemary piped up.

"Maybe he should come aboard for a while. All in favor?" The three shot up their hands. "How about it, would you like to stay with us for a while? There's a lot more to show you and..."

"Oh do shut up Rose" said Felicity.

"You mean, in the van?"

"Goodness, Jackie, what do you take us for? No, no we live in much grander circumstances, don't we?"

"Oh yes" the others answered unconvincingly.

"I don't know" Jackie answered. They seemed nice enough and were definitely his kind of off-the-wall people. Their interest in him seemed genuine. The end of his trip was in sight. His money wouldn't last forever and he still hadn't found what he was looking for. Strange, it seemed to matter less now, but he knew the need would surface again.

"We could live under a bridge for all he knows" said Felicity.

"Well, come along with us and if you don't want to stay, we'll drive you back to your place tomorrow."

"Okay" Jackie said, "sounds good."

"Well, that's settled then, you do like –"

"We live on a ship!" Kazuo proclaimed proudly.

"Now Kaz, I've told you before, it's not a ship" Felicity corrected her as they got to their feet.

"Felicity is a famous captain, Jackie. Isn't she, Rose?"

"Yes, a real legend in her own mind."

"You see what I have to put up with Jackie" Felicity said as they got into the van. "You do like boats, I hope."

"Boats are my life"

"That so? Ride up front. Kaz, get in the back."

As the afternoon turned into evening, Star Cruiser was heading into the cool, dark fringes of the less populated part of the Old Forest. Scrub and course bushes gave way to larger, darker trees and the bigger the trees, the more dappled the light...the greater the silence. Several miles later – there seemed to be no need for it – Felicity slowed down. Jackie saw that Rosemary and Kazuo were sitting with their eyes closed.

"Okay?" Felicity asked.

"Yes" said Kazuo.

"Clear" said Rosemary, "but...oh never mind."

"What?" asked Jackie. "What are you talking about?"

"They see our home and that all is well" Felicity answered.

"Really?"

"Really."

"Will you teach me how to do that?"

"Sure, if you want. It's not perfect, but we usually get it right."

Soon, they turned off the asphalt road onto a gravel track. When Jackie was beginning to wonder if the track could go any farther, it turned again, this time onto a dirt path overgrown with bushes that brushed the side of the van. Through the foliage, he caught sight of a flash of sparkling blue. It had to be a river or a stream.

"Where are we?" he asked.

"At the approaches of the Ravenshead estuary."

Felicity noticed how he leaned forward. Through the scent of leaf and flower came an undercurrent of salt air. Like a drug, it infused him. He sighed deeply. He hungered for the stopping of the van, the turning off of the engine, the cascade of silence and subtle sound that would envelop them. Beauty was a thing he lived to surrender to and suddenly the thought became strikingly clear to him in a way it never had before. He opened his book and despite the lurching, started to write, *the need to surrender to beauty as much as possible!*

"We're almost there, Jackie" Felicity sang out. Just then a gust of wind poured into the van. Jackie's thumb caught the whirling pages of his book where he had doodled the spiral shape just as she turned to look at him. She saw it and a gasp escaped her. She couldn't take her eyes off it. It couldn't be.

"Felicity!" the girls screamed from the back seat, the truck slamming directly into a huge willow tree..

"You okay? You okay?" Jackie was asking. Felicity came around slowly.

"What happened?"

"We crashed into a tree!" She reached for her neck and groaned.

"Felicity, what were you thinking?" Rosemary yelled. The page that she had been looking at had blown out of Jackie's window onto the aerial where it was hung up, fluttering like a flag. It's sound drew everyone's attention.

"There!" shouted Felicity who raced to roll down her window only to have it jam after a couple of inches. Stretch as she might, she could not reach the paper through it. Jackie was surprised at the desperation of her effort. "Sybil's circle!" she shouted. "It was Sybil's circle. I saw it! On the paper! Grab it!"

In a flash, Kazuo and Rosemary had flung their doors open and made for the page which shifted on the bouncing metal rod. Felicity, too, had quickly gone for the handle, but found the door, too, jammed. With a mighty lunge, she smashed it open to a groaning of metal and cursed in her pain. Just as she reached for the sketch, however, it slipped up the aerial and lifted about ten feet into the air.

"Bring it down!" she commanded. The others froze and stared intently at the paper. For a moment, it seemed to dance in place, then tore off up past the treetops and away. "Shit, shit, shit!" she roared.

"It's nothing important" Jackie called out to them. "It's just a bunch of doodling. Don't worry about it!" The women seemed to confer for a second and then Felicity raised her arms in frustration.

"I know what I saw."

"You know how similar some of them are" said Rosemary. "Maybe it was just a coincidence.

"Coincidence, my ass. Come on Jackie, it's not far. As a matter of fact, we've just wrecked in our own bloody front yard." When he joined them, she wasted no time. "The drawing on that page, the one you were looking at when we crashed, what was that?"

"I told you, it was just a doodle."

"Where did it come from?"

"Where does any doodle come from? I don't know."

"Did you see that image somewhere?"

"No."

"What were you thinking when you drew it? Why that particular design?"

"Felicity, back off. It was just a doodle. I don't think when I doodle. I just doodle. You know? Doodle? And what the hell is Sybil's circle?"

"Never mind. Forget it. It's just an expression. They had continued along the dirt track another thirty yards or so when Jackie was sure he heard the sound of a boat moving through water.

"What's that?" he asked. Felicity looked at her watch.

"That will be Tim Wyn-Jones coming home from work. He's an architect. He has a tree house kind of place just around the next bend. Toot toot!"

"Toot toot?"

Two shrill blasts erupted from an old steam whistle.

"His kids like him to do that." Then, motioning for Jackie to catch up to her, she added, "This is home." As Jackie stepped forward, a boat came into view just on the other side of a hedgerow that had been obstructing his view. It was resting on a massive timber cradle, right at the bank, not ten feet from the water.

"You really do live in a boat?"

"High and dry for now. It's a coastal tug, built like a brick shit house. Like her?"

"She's amazing. Is she yours?"

"Every rivet."

"How big is she?"

"Fifty feet."

"What's her name?"

"Asylum."

"What's she draw?"

"Did you hear that girls, he wants to know what she draws. We got a proper sailor here. Four foot ten, luv. But she needs work, that's why she's out of the water. A friend of mine lifted her out with a barge crane – set her down neat as you please. We built the cradle. What do you think? Want to bunk with three crazy women for a while?"

"Absolutley."

"Good then, after I fix Star Cruiser , we'll go back and get your gear. Till then, you'll just have to make do, I'm afraid." After they had walked around the vessel, Felicity led the way to the boarding ladder. "Now you" she called down to him. As he reached the top rung, however, she blocked his way. "Not so fast. We have a little ceremony for anyone who intends to spend the night. You have to request asylum."

"What kind of asylum?"

"Hoi polloi asylum. Asylum from the common man."

"Okay."

"Well, go ahead, ask."

"I formally request asylum from the common man."

"On what grounds?"

"How should I know?"

"Think of something."

"On the grounds that they want to kill me" he said with a laugh, "How should I know?"

"I'm going to remind you that you said that. Asylum has been requested on the basis of personal safety" Felicity shouted down to the others. "What say you?"

"Granted" said Rosemary.

"Granted" said Kazuo.

"What's your name?" Felicity demanded.

"You know my name."

"Humor me."

"Jackie Northam."

"Asylum is officially granted to Jackie Northam on the basis of personal safety, unless by conduct injurious to the vessel or her crew you forfeit the right. So mote it be."

"So mote it be." the others repeated.

"Come aboard then."

This was no plastic toy boat that blisters and cracks with age. Quarter inch plate steel with massive rivets and solid welding saw to that. There was no cosmetic radiance as in the gelcoat of luxury yachts to chalk and fade in the sun.

"Now don't expect much. This is a working tug and we keep it ready for sea...just so you know." The scarred and worn bumper on the bow told Jackie as much, that and the old tires hanging over the sides. "What are you doing?" she asked as Jackie jumped up and down on the deck.

"It's so strong. I've never been on a steel boat before."

"Well you haven't seen anything yet" she said, lifted by his enthusiasm. "Wait 'till I show you the engine room. Are you any kind of mechanic?"

"Can't get a nut on a bolt. I'm hopeless with anything mechanical. Sorry."

"Don't say that, please."

"Say what?"

"Sorry. Don't say you're sorry. Not knowing engines – that's one thing. Apologizing – I can't stand it. It's a condition of asylum. Nobody ever says they're sorry. If you make a mistake big enough to talk about, just tell someone and get on with things. Mistakes happen. It's not like we plan them." Behind her words, Jackie sensed a deep hurt. So, the rough and tumble Felicity wasn't so tough after all. "Come below." She unlocked the heavy metal door, pulled the latches aside and swung it open. The rubber gaskets that kept it water tight looked a bit ragged. Jackie made a mental note. Maybe he could replace that. A couple of lines in the stern looked frayed at the ends, too, but salvageable. The smell of the main cabin instantly took him back to the sailing yacht in Greece. Diesel and teak oil, musty, secure. Felicity had her own captain's cabin aft. Rosemary and Kazuo had single berths forward in the foc'sle. Jackie was given a bunk mid way between the two. The whole place was spotless, not what he had been expecting at all. Someone had been very careful about polishing the brass. No paste residue anywhere. The head, as washrooms on boats are called, was as clean as the one at his old Zen temple. He should know. He had kept it that way for the edification of the Buddhist community. Cooking, tending gardens, cleaning the washrooms – all activities were of equal merit – all performed with absolute concentration, oneness of effort, as a living meditation. Oh, the sutras he had discovered in the removing of cobwebs, the scrubbing of toilet bowls, the replacement of dirty towels.

His community got his best effort, until the day he heard the head monk making homophobic jokes to a rapt circle of laughing devotees. *Like Christian, like Buddhist,* he thought as he left the temple, never to return despite his years of hard training. Yes, there was an almost religious devotion in the cleaning of the brass. A faint smell of incense was just barely noticeable, too. He checked the fire extinguisher in the hallway. It was well within the expiry date. Along the top of a white pipe which ran the length of the hallway ceiling, however, he could see a gray matting of old and new dust. Well, it was a tug, after all, a working tug, and not the Royal Navy.

"You don't have any drugs on you, do you?" asked Rosemary from down the passageway.

"No, sorry" said Jackie.

"Oh, it's not for me. Felicity won't have it on board and Sybil won't tolerate it." She approached and sat down on a crate across from him.

"Does she live here?"

"Oh my God, no" she laughed nervously. "Who could bear it? No, no. Don't get me wrong. She's very important to us all, really. Anyway, she hates boats."

"What, exactly is your relationship with her anyway?"

"She is the high priestess of the Hengest coven. We are part of that coven. It is one of the oldest in England."

"You must be very proud."

"Very" she said, and the word radiated peace and strength. "Are you religious, Jackie?"

"Yes and no. I've read most of the world's holy books, Quaran, Bible, Talmud, Vedas, Buddhist sutras, but nothing feels like home."

"What would home feel like?"

"I don't know. I just know it'll feel right when I get there."

"Have you looked anywhere else?"

"Looked? Looked for what? I don't know that I was ever looking for anything. Maybe I was. I've done all the drugs..."

"And?"

"And I stopped."

"Why?"

"It got scary."

"Do you mind talking about it? I'm curious."

"No, I don't mind. I started seeing and hearing things that I just wasn't ready for." He sat down on his bunk and faced her as she drew her crate toward him.

"Like what?"

"You'll think I'm crazy."

"Maybe you are."

"Rosemary...ya, maybe I am. Jesus, you're direct."

"Who decides who's crazy?"

"Ya"

"So?"

"I heard Tibetan temple instruments and I saw things – Egyptian hieroglyphs on the sides of buildings. I could read them. One day I saw eight sunrises superimposed on top of each other, and I thought I saw how everything is connected...like a web...psychically connected...like I actually thought I saw the connections...psychic connections."

"Jackie"

"It gets better. One day, on peyote, I was looking at this huge candle that we had and suddenly, I had this strange sense that I was somehow understanding the thing on another level. My friends all freaked out. They asked what was happening to me, but I was so far off somewhere that I put my hand in the freaking flame and kept it there. For a full minute. In the flame."

"And you didn't get burned."

"And everyone saw it. They never talked to me again. I saw the auras of everything. The rainbows between everything. They said it was just me, projecting, you know, from the drugs, but I can tell you there is an energy field between everything. How do you know I didn't get burned?"

"Just a guess."

"I'm not a prophet."

"No?"

"No, and I'm not some deep, spiritual, shaman or something."

"You got scared off."

"Big time. More than once."

"Sybil says psychics shouldn't use drugs."

"Why?"

"Because it's hard enough to work with what we see and hear when we're sober."

"Are you very psychic?"

"I'm pretty good at remote sensing, but I can't tell the future at all. Like today, I wish I could have seen the accident coming. Hungry?"

"Do you know where Felicity is?"

"Out working on the van. She'll have it up and running in no time. She's a great mechanic – fixes everything around here by herself."

"Why was that stupid drawing so important to her?"

"Sometimes we know things that we don't know we know. Know what I mean?" Rosemary asked with a chuckle.

"What's to know? It was just a brainless doodle. And what does she mean by Sybil's circle? This is really creeping me out." Rosemary started to speak, then stopped.

"Not to worry. It's a long story. I'm sure we'll all sit down and have a good talk about it. Are you any good in the kitchen?"

At the Major Arcana, Sybil Crowleigh was scanning the sky for Penelope. Never before had she just taken off like that. She recalled how first her dark eyes had rolled in their sockets, then widened enormously as the great bird lifted into the air and raced out the door. Where did she find the energy? Penelope was old. She had no right moving like that. Sybil wondered if the bird had eaten some of the poison mushrooms that grew around the edge of the village. Poor dear. Well, she had been a good and novel companion over the years. It would be hard to lose her. Still, the witch squinted up at the sky.

On the far side of town, hedgehogs winked and ground squirrels sniffed at strange doings above them. A dark object, too small to have anything to do with humans, too erratic to be an animal, veered and sheered in the air. There seemed to be no intent. Not a hawk hunting or a gull riding the thermals back to the sea. Just sharp curves and sudden alterations in speed. A kind of purposeless frenzy. There was only one constant. The thing was getting lower. Eventually, it came into view over the antique shop, where it caught the witch's eye.

"What's this?" she muttered.

She thought it must be something just drifting in the wind, its passage being so chaotic, and so she looked away. But something made her turn again to it. Unconsciously, her index finger mirrored the flight of the thing on the dusty tabletop by her side.

"What the – " she muttered and jammed her finger into a pot of black paint that she had opened to refinish the table. As she watched the thing in the sky, she continued to trace its movements on the table. Curve for curve, change for change. Whatever it was, it was getting nearer, the pattern it expressed descending over the village. A shudder caused her shoulders to tighten and her jaw to lift toward the sky. "Penelope" she whispered, and then again with some excitement. She glanced down at the table and recoiled as if a snake had crept up beside her. "Cerridwen! Great Goddess!" There on the surface were the intricate interlacings of what many had come to know as Sybil's Circle – a crop circle pattern that had been made in her presence as a child and twice again in her lifetime. Now it seemed to be dropping out of the heavens right on her head. As the great raven flared to a nimble landing on its perch at the shop's entrance, Sybil waited for its cackle. Landings were always accompanied by a cackle. This time there was none.

"Explain yourself!" she commanded. "Where the bloody hell have you been? What's gotten into you?" But the bird just stared at her with a coal black fire in its eyes, tilted its head to the side and opened its beak revealing a small, white roll of paper. The witch started to reach for it, but hesitated. "Spit that out, you stupid bird! What on earth..." The raven, however, just extended its neck. "Oh, very well then." She extricated the roll with great care. She pressed the paper out on the table, and there, to her utter confusion and consternation was a hastily sketched image of her circle. Immediately, the witch jumped back and went into her psychic self defense posture – left hand as the crescent moon, right, as the horned god – and visualized pouring psychic energy like flecks of pure gold from a fountain which issued from the top of her spine, up through the crown of her head and into the air, cascading down through a deep lapis aura which she projected around her physical body.

I am protected by thy power
Gracious Goddess, every hour
I am protected by thy power
Gracious Goddess, every hour
I am protected by thy power
Gracious Goddess, every hour

"You've got some explaining to do, you old fart" she said to the bird, offering her forearm. The raven hopped onto it. You're going to tell me where you got that thing and how you knew where it was, or I swear I'll pluck you feather by feather and make soup stock out of what's left."

Chapter Seventeen
Sea Changes

Some days had passed since Jackie arrived at the Asylum. As the sun came up, cobwebs, spun in the night, turned into dew jeweled geometries at several places along her railings. Across the estuary and down a short distance, Mike Tuff's alarm clock went off. In the kitchen of his plush, waterside condominium, an electric timer kicked in and water trickled down over the finest Colombian coffee.

Aboard Asylum, Jackie came out on deck and found the women sitting on small Persian carpets, meditating. He joined them as quietly as he could.

Across the water, Mike playfully slapped the bum of the naked woman beside him.

"Okay hot stuff, I'm going to the club to shoot a few holes."

"Ah, baby, not yet, what time is it?" came the muffled reply from under the covers.

"Hey, it's the weekend. Be a sweetheart and pour me a coffee will ya? I've gotta get movin."

"Oh, okay" the woman moaned. "Are you playing rugby today?"

"No, that's tomorrow. We're gonna give Predator a workout, maybe run up the coast to The Blue Fox and back."

"Today?"

"Yes, today, as soon as I get back. I'll tell you what, you pick up some groceries and beer, you know – the usual stuff. Oh and could you get me a carton of cigarettes, too? Terrific. Stow them in the boat, make it nice, and we'll leave as soon as I get back. Okay?"

In the washroom, he paused to look out the window that afforded a view of the estuary. There was a dull cast to the water – not surprising for the time of day. Absently, he pulled open the drawer where he kept his razor. *There it was, sitting on the cradle – that abomination – what was it called, Asylum? Lunatic Asylum – at least the freaks on board knew who they were,* he thought. *What an eyesore*. When he withdrew his hand, his fingertips were bleeding from two parallel lines where he had grabbed the blade.

Forty minutes later, he was in his Mercedes heading for the Fairhaven Golf and Country Club. Classic rock was his music of choice and he fed one of his favorites into the CD player. The high-end sound system found itself digitally as the volume numbers sped up to where they had last been set. The roar was ear splitting. Drunk. He always forgot to turn down the volume before getting out of the car when he was drunk. Still, at thirty-four, his reflexes had remained sharp and he deftly reduced the sound levels.

"Big Mike!" the greenskeeper called as he drove through the gate acknowledging the old man with a movement of his index finger.

It was early enough for him to be able to play on his own. Sometimes, he liked to do that, but given the choice, he would play with his friends or a client of the brokerage firm he represented. He was good at driving himself – better in direct competition with others. Golf. He loved everything about the game – the long game, the short game, the private world of it all, the manicured nature, the way it took him away from everything he didn't like. It was the subtlest thing in his life. In golf, he had learned, the smallest mistake had profound consequences. It was a finesse sport and its unrelenting honesty fed his need for control at all levels. Control meant success. He was a very successful man, he knew. He had the toys to prove it. "*God*", he thought, "*life is good*."

In a Zen temple, Jackie would have been meditating with his eyes open, facing a bare wall. Here, there were too many distractions. In a Zen setting, the slightest fidget would instantly be noticed by everyone in the room.

"No moving!" the Master would roar, and the 'encouragement stick' would come crashing down on the offender's shoulders. Over time, Jackie's sitting had become...simply...still, profoundly still, his breathing...soundless. Every errant thought, every devil of distraction, every 'Makyo' was met with instant return to a following of the breath. Over time, this resulted in great paradox. He was, as he sat among the women, aware of the tiniest disturbances of grass blade and leaf at surprising distances, and he was, at the same time, utterly untouched by the hearing.

After a while, he went below and made a batch of omelets, a bit runny, the way the women liked them, the insides stuffed with ripe tomatoes, old cheddar cheese, green onions and thyme. The others were indifferent cooks. Even Kazuo had no real control over Japanese cuisine. Rosemary and Felicity were fine with basic fare, but the fragrances that issued from the galley, burst upon the meditators in a deluge of delectable overtones – there were the omelets themselves – deep and homey, punctuated by the rich, roasted complexity of properly percolated coffee, and the familiar undertones of light toast. It was the least he could do in return for their kindness. He even broke out a bottle of Tobasco for Felicity. As filaments of the culinary bouquet wafted across the deck, one by one, the women opened their eyes.

"Incredible" said Kazuo. A moment later, Jackie came up the companionway and onto the deck carrying an enormous wooden hatch cover with the food laid out on it. He had taken time to fan out a rainbow of wildflowers that he had picked nearby.

"Good morning, ladies, breakfast is served." It had been quite some time since anyone from the outside had done such a selfless act for the three of them. Breakfast took a long time. There was much to discuss.

"Are you ready to go, babe?" Mike called to his girlfriend before the car had even come to a stop. Aboard Predator, she jumped a bit as the tire squealed on the driveway. She steadied a small vase of flowers that she was in the process of knocking over.

"Are you sure you want to do this? Look at the sky. The marine radio forecast is calling for southeast winds at twenty knots. That means rough, right?"

"Nothing we can't handle, babe. Long before any bad old weather gets here, we'll be long gone. Worst come to worst, we can duck into plenty of places along the way. You know what, come to think of it, we're faster than the weather, sweetheart. Predator will do over seventy knots. Even in big waves, we do forty to fifty knots. You know that. Weather systems don't move that fast. Hey, it's Predator!" Then he hummed the overture to Ride of the Valkyries by Wagner with great gusto. "So, let's do it!" Resigned, his girlfriend took her usual position on the dock, cast off the lines, then jumped aboard. Mike followed the canal that belonged to his exclusive condominium project out to where it joined the estuary and looked over his shoulder toward the Asylum.

"Mikey, don't." the woman said.

"Just once."

"Mikey, please."

"Ah, c'mon, it drives them nuts."

"Oh, baby, you are such a goof."

He punched the throttles up to one third speed and steered the boat into a hard turn, the low, deep rumble of twin Mercury four hundreds thundering ominously. Aboard Asylum, Felicity was the first to notice the vessel heading toward them and knew it for what it was. The onshore breeze carried the sound and Rosemary and Kazuo looked out over the water. Jackie noticed how Kazuo sneered before she raised her head.

"What is it?" he asked.

"You'll see soon enough" Rosemary said.

The distance closed rapidly and soon a brilliant, yellow hull was in view, followed by a huge, white rooster tail. The boat overtook the waves, pounding into their backs, sending sheets of spray flying out to the sides. To his astonishment, Jackie felt the vibration of the machine, but whether it was resonating in his heart directly or coming up through his feet and legs, he could not tell. His whole body seemed captured by the sound. It did not take long for his blood to begin to boil. It was everything he despised, violation on a huge scale.

Mike carried his speed close to the shore, closer than he had ever come before, close enough to carry on a conversation with people on the land if he wanted to and he did want to. He cut the throttles and spun Predator sideways, the white wake disappearing in the dark water.

"Get a life!" he yelled. "Get a job!" But no one aboard Asylum was about to allow their joyous meal to be ruined. Slowly, they packed up their knives and forks. "Bloody freaks. Aren't you girls tired of each other yet? Now there are four of you? What are you doing, starting a bloody commune?" No one responded. The women looked at Jackie. Expressionless, he piled the plates on the hatch cover and carried them below. The others went back to their work, except for Felicity who joined him below.

"So, what do you think?" she asked.

"He's a guy. A garden variety guy. Tough and terrified."

"Why terrified?"

"Terrified of life. You know what I'm talking about."

"Maybe. Maybe not. I'd like to hear it from you."

"Guys are about control. Life can't be controlled. Guys are afraid of anything they can't control. And a guy who gives up power is, to use a word from the Bible, an abomination to them."

"Is that what you are, Jackie, an abomination?"

"My sister had another expression – freak of nature. So, I guess it's not just guys. One day, I told my mother that I identified more with women than with men. You see, I couldn't stand the idea of her passing on and never really knowing who I was. I guess it was selfish. Anyway, it was a mistake."

"What did she say?"

"Just two things: 'I wish I was dead' and 'Please don't tell your father – it'll kill him.'"

"I'm sorry."

"Ya, so, anyway, guys are worse, Captain. They think we're throwing away something that makes you a guy and if it can happen to one of them, it can happen to any of them. It scares them shitless."

"It's strange, Jackie"

"What is?"

"You seem pretty masculine to me."

"Years of training, skipper. Now, even when I want to, it's hard to drop the act."

"Hmmm. What would you be like if you dropped the act as you call it?"

"Well,   let's   see.   How   about   a femdykeshamanChristianscaredasshitmysticairhead?"

"The guy really got to you, didn't he?"

"No kidding."

"They help you forget your loneliness, don't they?"

"Who?"

"All the people you have nothing in common with. The same people who cast you out. Hate is, at least, a connection, a relief from your relentlessly unique existence. Do you know what I'm talking about?"

"Yes."

"Well, hate can be turned to pity, pity to compassion, compassion to love. Come on, Christian, you should know that."

"That's a strange thing for a witch to say."

"Why? Been there. Done that. Understanding and compassion don't belong to anyone. It's just life, Jackie. If I told you, that that man and his girlfriend were going to be dead before the sun goes down, how would you feel?"

"Glad."

"Too much hate, Jackie. He can no more help being who he is than you can. Not overnight anyway. Change is usually a slow thing. Be patient. Have some compassion, for the others, and for yourself. And while you're at it, you might ask yourself why you made us breakfast."

"I underestimated you, Fella." It was Sybil Crowleigh descending the companionway.

"Hathor's blood!" Felicity yelped, "How long have you been here?"

"Long enough. Nice neighbors you have, but I think you're a little out in your timing."

"Oh really?"

"I give him less than four hours. Don't suppose any of you would know anything about this" she said unrolling the small sketch of Sybil's Circle on the chart table.

"How on earth did you get that?" Felicity asked.

"Penelope coughed it up yesterday. Don't suppose you know anything about it?"

"Jackie?"

"Yes."

"Do you recognize this?" asked Felicity.

"You know I do, that's the little doodle that you people got so excited about."

"You saw this?" the witch asked Felicity, "and you didn't call me?" The woman started to answer but the witch cut her short. "And you" she said, turning to Jackie, "What are you doing with my circle?"

"It's not your circle, it's mine."

"What do you mean, it's yours?"

"I doodled it. It's mine." The very idea of an argument over something so stupid appalled him, but he just didn't like the woman's attitude. There was something so mean spirited in it.

"Well it means a great deal more to me than just a doodle as you call it. It's a very complex figure, young man, and here you are with the very same thing right down to the last detail. In these parts, this is known as Sybil's Circle and for very good reason." She felt her anger rising, felt control slipping away at the edges. She never acted like this, like a petulant school child. But the discovery of someone else with her symbol felt like a violation of some kind. She had struggled so long to understand its meaning. And it felt so…personal, something special, for her alone…a puzzle for her own life. Maybe something from the gods. "You doodled it, you say? Nothing more to it than that?"

"It was in his notepad" Felicity said. "The wind blew it loose in the van. We had an accident over it. Last thing we saw was the page taking off over the trees. I was going to call you."

"A thing like this? You should have called immediately. When are you going to get a cell phone? I keep telling you –"

"No phones!"

"Alright, alright." Whatever the reason, it was clear that if Sybil Crowleigh was in charge of the Old Forest, Felicity was sure as hell in charge of Asylum. "Signal the family – we meet tonight – no, not tonight. You'll be too tired. Tomorrow night."

"And just why am I going to be so tired?"

"You'll see." Felicity made a show of mock intrigue. "And I got in here without you even knowing. You girls had better shape up or some London Satanist is going to have your brains for breakfast. Just a doodle, you say" she asked, turning to Jackie who nodded. "Well, there's more to it, far more. Bring him, tomorrow."

"You're joking" Felicity said, "to the meeting?"

"Bring him! This touches everyone. You know how this is unraveling."

"Yes, I know, but shouldn't we – "

"Bring him! There will be no harm to you, Jackie…just some…questions. I believe you know more about this than you realize."

"And if he doesn't want to come?"

"Oh, he'll come. Or do you just want to pass this by, too, young man?"

"I don't have a broom" Jackie replied with a smirk.

"Cute."

"Will somebody please tell me why this thing is so important to everyone?" The only response was a wind that blew suddenly down into the cabin and scooped up the drawing. Before even a muscle twitched in the others, the old woman had plucked it from the air with a motion that was too fast to be seen.

"Not again, my little darling" she said to it. "This time, you are going to talk to me." For a moment, Jackie wondered if she was losing her mind. He looked at Felicity, but her raised eyebrows and wide stare told him to leave it alone. "Have a lovely day, ladies" she said and disappeared back up the companionway.

"Why do I get the feeling that I'm the only one who doesn't know what's going on around here?" Jackie asked. "And why do I get the feeling she knows more about me than I do about myself?"

"Because, she does. You think you're lonely? Try knowing more about people than they know about themselves. They beg you to tell them and never trust you again when you do. A good witch knows more about you than your own mother."

"Is she a good witch?"

"If you don't cross her. She can do terrible things." Fear radiated from her downcast eyes. After a moment, she reached into the navigation station and turned on the marine radio, setting it to the weather channel. The announcer was warning of a low-pressure system building rapidly less than fifty miles offshore from the mouth of the estuary. Fortunately, he said, the winds would blow it off to the south.

"See, I told you babe," Mike shouted over the engines. "No problem. It's all blowing down to the south. We're in the clear. Just to be safe, we'll run around out here for a while, okay? If it's still good half an hour from now, we'll go. Deal? His girlfriend nodded, grateful for his concern for their safety, even if he was a bit reckless at times. She looked up at the sky. The gathering overcast did have a lot of breaks in it and shafts of sunlight poured through here and there. Reassured, she switched the marine radio off and brought up some rock 'n roll on the FM set. The waves were up to three feet, but if she was honest with herself, she had to admit that she actually enjoyed playing around in the bigger seas with Mike at the controls. His confidence and willingness to take clever risks had provided them with a lifestyle that was full of excitement and all the good things of life. So he was insensitive at times and rough around the edges emotionally, what guy wasn't? He was great in bed, he knew how to treat a lady and the future felt as secure in his presence as she did in his arms. That was enough for her. Under her feet, a rising Irish Sea swell passed unnoticed, lost among the lesser waves. Sunlight highlighted the small whitecaps that sprang up randomly as the wind piped up to twelve knots. "You know what" he said, "I think I'm gonna teach you how to drive this thing." An hour later, they were still at it. Aboard Asylum, a high pitched alarm went off.

"Now what?" Rosemary asked, as she pressed a button on the weather radio to get the report.

"...and the area of the Ravenshead Estuary to the north are experiencing sudden gusts to fifty knots with extreme oscillation in wind direction. Severe downbursts have been reported along the coast from Whimsy Point to the estuary. Small craft are advised to seek the nearest shelter at this time. Repeat...the fast developing low pressure system has changed its track to seaward and is rapidly increasing in intensity." Out of curiosity, Rosemary switched over to the VHF calling channel to listen to the pleasure boat traffic. Barely more than a few words were broadcast by one boat before they were talked over by another panicky skipper.

"Mayday...mayday...mayday...this is –"

"Whimsy Point Rescue, this is the motor vessel Alice B. My vessel –"

"All stations...all stations...all stations...this is Burnside Coastguard Radio, Burnside Coastguard Radio..." The more powerful transmitter cut through the chatter with ease. "A weather warning has been posted at sixteen hundred hours Greenwich Mean Time for the west coast from Wellington to Ravenshead Estuary. The low pressure system that was expected to track south and seaward is developing rapidly and has stalled. Future direction of this system is uncertain at this time. Current conditions include severe oscillating shifts in wind direction, downbursts and gusts exceeding fifty knots. Small craft are advised to seek nearest shelter at this time." The radio went silent for a moment, then continued. "This is Burnside Coastguard Radio, at sixteen zero three Greenwich Mean time, an emergency is declared until further notice. Vessel calling mayday, go ahead..."

"Felicity, you better hear this" Rosemary called out.

"What is it?"

"Something is developing right on top of us. People are getting their shorts in a knot all up and down the coast. Rescue sounds overextended and it looks like things are only just starting." Sensing the events unfolding around her, Felicity made one of the instant changes for which she was so well known. In a split second, her voice and movement hardened around a calm core.

"Call Tony. Tell him I'm calling in my markers. He owes me big time and he knows it. If he's forgotten, remind him. Tell him I want to be in the water in one hour."

"Felicity, he can't."

"In the water. One hour. Then get things squared away. Run all the usual checks and make ready for small craft rescue. Tell Kaz. You –" she said, turning to Jackie, "better walk up the path to the architect's place. This could get messy."

"I can help" he protested.

"I'm sure you mean well, but the deck of a tug in a sea way is not the cockpit of a yacht."

"Let me help. I know what I'm doing."

"It's your neck."

On board Predator, the throbbing drumming of a classic rock tune flowed into the roar of the engines and the crush of spray on the ocean.

"You're doin' great, Liz! Throttle back, throttle back. Come on, you gotta watch the rhythm of the waves. Keep control. Look ahead. See what's comin'." He was a good teacher. Tough, but he knew what he was talking about. She could tell. She renewed her grip on the throttles with her right hand and steered with her left. Looking downwind, the way they were going, the ocean looked so calm. With the wind at their backs, the ride was almost comfortable. The motion was so much smoother, the sound gentler. With the boat in this attitude, waves were things to be played with. Some black cloud wisps scudding under the overcast, caught Mike's attention. A moment later, the boat was thrown sideways so violently the woman's hands came off the wheel and she fell into him.

Splicing the Light   199

"I'm sorry…I'm sorry…What did I do?"

"It wasn't you" Mike grumbled, edging her out of the way and taking over. A gust then ripped down the boat from bow to stern, a hundred and eighty degrees from where it had been. It was so strong the beer can he had left in the holder started to whistle eerily. "Jeesus Christ" he muttered and turned off the music, replacing it with the weather forecast. Liz noticed the tiny note of discomfort in his voice.

"Are we okay, baby?" she asked.

"Of course" Mike scoffed. "These guys always play it safe" he said as Liz scanned the horizon uneasily. "Don't worry. We're only about ten miles or so out now."

"Mikey, I really want to go back, okay?"

"Ya, okay" he sulked. They were being pushed by the current down the coast from the estuary. When he rounded the boat up to a course that would take them directly home, it put them sideways to the waves. In that position, they rolled violently and the seas seemed much, much bigger. They began to understand what the forecaster had been talking about.

"Mikey…"

"Don't worry about it. When I punch it up a bit, things will smooth out. It's just that the harbor is a bit upwind now." Then, as though by magic, the bold, yellow hull rose and gained speed, dampening some of the rolling. Then the engine died. Mike had not seen the faded, oil stained line that was stretched out ahead of them on the water. Just another piece of flotsam. The oceans are filled with them. Now it was wrapped around the shafts of both propellers like bands of steel. One end trailed back from the stern. Mike saw it when he turned. "Oh, oh" was all he could manage as he pulled back the throttles and turned off the engine.

"What is it Mikey?"

"We ran over some line. It's wrapped around the props."

"Can we get it off?"

"Not in these waves."

"What do we do?"

"We get the bloody coast guard to earn their pay." As he spoke, another gust of wind caught the loose end of his life jacket strap and it whipped his face. Liz was holding on, trying to steady herself. Mike worked his way back to the driver's seat from which he had stumbled and picked up the microphone. Jackie heard the call come over Asylum's radio.

"Burnside Coastguard Radio, Burnside Coastguard Radio, Burnside Coastguard Radio." His voice was calm and measured. If he was feeling any urgency, it did not show. "This is Predator, Predator, Predator."

"Felicity" Jackie called, "I think you'll want to hear this." She came out of the engine room quickly.

"What is it?"

"Listen." Mike, though not nervous, was impatient. He changed the nature of his call to vessel in distress – no imminent risk to life.

"Pan, pan, pan...pan, pan, pan...This is the motor vessel Predator. Location – approximately ten miles southwest of Ravenshead Estuary. My propellers are fouled and I am drifting." He waited for one minute, and receiving no reply, repeated the transmission. Still, he got no reply and was about to key the microphone for another attempt.

"Predator...Burnside Coastguard Radio. Be advised, all rescue craft are involved in rescues at this time. Continue to advise position. If your condition puts you at physical risk, declare a mayday at that time. Any vessel able to render assistance to Predator switch to channel 23 and advise position and vessel type. Burnside Coastguard Radio out."

"So, what do you think?" Jackie asked Felicity.

"Rosemary...Kazuo...get down here!" she shouted up the companionway. When they arrived, she rolled a chart out on the table. "Jackie, you may as well take a look at this. Kaz?" The younger girl pulled the hair away from her face, thought for a moment, leaned over the table and drew an "x" on the chart with a pencil indicating a position close to shore and some miles down the coast. "Rose?" She took a little longer and placed her "x" a few miles to the east and more inshore. "Why?"

"Tide's turning, wind's increasing. Little plastic boat like that'll blow like a cork."

"Mmmhmmm" Felicity mumbled in agreement, leaning over the table and placing an "x" considerably closer to shore, so close the edges of the letter almost touched the coastline. "Waves are getting up now. Like you said, little plastic boat. Wind's all over the place, but the wave direction is more or less constant. However you figure it, it's going to be an absolute bitch."

"I don't get it" Jackie finally blurted out. Predator said they were fifteen miles out." The women turned and looked at him like he was a complete idiot.

"Rose?" Felicity invited and the woman turned to him.

"Jackie, we know this guy very well. He has no judgement at all on the water. He's probably closer to five miles from shore at this moment."

"Then I still don't get it. Your positions show him a lot closer to shore than that. I mean, Felicity, you almost have him on the shore.

"I know" Felicity answered grimly.

"These marks aren't where he is now, Jackie" Rosemary continued. "They're where we think he'll be when we get there...if we get there." Just then, the big brass chronometer on the bulkhead rang out 5:00 p.m.

"Call Tony again" Felicity ordered, "find out what's holding him up." Rosemary pulled out her cellphone and dialed.

"Tony...Rose. Where are you?" She spoke as she turned to the others. "He says to look out the window. How did you get here so fast?" she asked, then laughed and spoke to Felicity. "He says he knew you would have to play the Good Samaritan today."

"Tell him he's a cunning poker player."

"Oh you saucy bugger" Rose snorted. "He says to get on deck and help with the cables." Half an hour later, Asylum was lowered gently into the water.

"Lifejackets!" Felicity shouted, and everyone did as ordered, Kazuo throwing one to Jackie who tied it tightly. In the wheelhouse, Felicity set her throttles for half speed and churning mud fanned out behind the tug. Below, milk bottles left out on a table, crashed to the floor. Felicity looked aft to make sure the stern was clear and saw how the wake resembled the clouds scudding in the gathering darkness. Though it was still light enough to see without too much difficulty, she turned the vessel's navigation lights on. A quick glance around showed her that the tug had been properly set up for offshore work. Without being asked, Kazuo had even rigged safety lines fore and aft in case people had to work on deck in really rough seas. Felicity pointed to the lines when Kazuo looked over, and gave her the thumbs up. As Jackie watched, he was impressed by how quietly and methodically the women went about their work. Asylum was not fast. Her twin Caterpillar 3512TA engines driving twin propellers with a total of 2890 horsepower, could only bring her to 13.2 knots in calm water. Her strength was in towing or pushing. She sported a single drum tow winch with a 90-ton brake capacity – far more than she would need to pull Predator, or a dozen like her, if she could get to them. As they made their way toward the open sea, the vessel began to lift and settle on the rising surge coming into the mouth of the estuary. On shore, an Officer of the Day at the local yacht club was struggling to lower flags.

"Jeesus" Jackie swore as one of the club's inflatables raced across their bow, hoping to do some good for someone offshore. As the boat sped away from them, Rosemary and Kazuo, who had both crowded into the wheelhouse, watched intently.

"Oh brother" Rosemary sighed.

"Duh" Kazuo scoffed.

"This aughtta be good," Felicity added.

"What...what?" Jackie asked.

"Watch" Felicity answered. As he did, Jackie saw the inflatable roar over one wave, sending spray flying in all directions. Without slowing, it rocketed up the face of a much larger wave and went straight up in the air, the stern, weighed down by the large engine, actually leaving the water. The whole thing hanging there like a space shuttle ready for launch. The two crew members were thrown head over heels into the sea as the boat landed and ran off in a large circle. As one, the women broke into hysterical laughter.

"Yachties" Rosemary sniffed.

Felicity altered course toward them. In five minutes, they were within a hundred yards. The two men in the water were wearing only T-shirts. In the cold water, they were already developing the first symptoms of hypothermia as numbness set in, and they began to shake. Felicity called the yacht club on the radio and advised them to get ready to receive some cold members.

The course of the inflatable was hard to track in the growing waves, even though she had kept an eye on it. Asylum was close now, but a wave threw the little boat onto a new course. The men in the water were looking toward Asylum coming at them from the opposite direction and did not see the approach of the inflatable. Felicity did, and she brought the engines up to full speed. The men couldn't believe their eyes, thinking they were about to be run down by the tug towering, now, above them and carrying a ferocious, roaring wave at her bows. At the last moment, however, Felicity swung the boat hard to the right, then to the left, swerving closely around the men as the runaway inflatable slammed into its heavy steel hull on the starboard side. Jackie looked out through the open wheelhouse door in time to see Kazuo leap from Asylum's railing into the little boat. As she did, it raced off again, causing her to fall face first into the gas tank at the stern. Still, she managed to get the craft under control. Racing around Asylum's stern, she drew up to the cold, confused men and helped them out of the water. It took some doing in the growing waves and by the time they were aboard, they were barely able to help themselves.

"You okay?" Felicity called out from the wheelhouse.

"Not so good" Kazuo answered, feeling for the front teeth which had been knocked out.

"Can you take them back?"

"Yes, no problem."

"Okay, go ahead, and get your face looked at. I'll see you when we get back. Have you got the hand held radio?" Confirming that she did, Felicity resumed her original course at top speed. Kazuo surfed off down the waves with the inflatable; the two men huddled over against the wind that froze them through their waterlogged clothing.

Rosemary and Jackie stood on either side of the steering wheel, looking out at the ocean. Felicity was steering a course about twenty degrees off the waves to minimize their pounding. Still, the ride was rough and getting rougher. Like any large vessel, a tug is sluggish to steer and Jackie marveled at how she rounded up at just the right moment for the more menacing waves. He imagined Felicity thinking several waves ahead in a three dimensional, rolling chess game. With some waves canceling others and still others combining in a synergistic effect, anything could happen despite a captain's skill. A cross-wave rolled the tug hard enough sideways that the three of them had to brace quickly.

"I want you two in safety harnesses...now" Felicity ordered. Rosemary grabbed two from a locker. It was not so different from a trapeze harness, which Jackie had used in dinghy racing and he slipped into it easily. He tested the stainless steel carabiner clip at the front of it. It closed with a loud snap. With several thousand pounds breaking strength, he knew his body would break in half long before the hook would. On deck, he would attach it to the safety line so no wave could sweep him off the boat.

Aboard Predator, Liz was starting to turn green. Lashed by wind and spray, she had sought shelter in the vessel's cramped cabin. There, however, she had found the movement magnified and without a stable horizon, had quickly become nauseated. She was fast on her way to becoming what charter fishermen love to call, a Martian, due to her color. Hunched over, she groped her way back up to the cockpit.

"Mikey, I can't take much more of this. Don't you have any seasick pills or something?"

"No, I told you to stay on deck. If you're..." Before he could finish, the woman was vomiting over the side. "Just stay on deck and look at the horizon." The sight of her prompted him to make another radio call. He keyed the microphone and informed the coast guard operator that his crew was now sick. That got no response. The operator at the other end was busy with saving lives. What did get his attention was the position given at the end of Mike's call. In giving it, Mike had thought nothing of it. It was just a bunch of numbers. Latitude and Longitude. The global positioning system, which his concern now prompted him to use reluctantly, was a wonder of modern engineering. It sent a signal to satellites overhead, which sent signals back indicating his position. In fact, his rate of drift was much greater than what he could realize by looking at the surface of the water. His position now, was much closer to shore. The operator placed his coordinates on a chart and measured the distance to land. Fog had developed inshore which Mike had not noticed until the operator spoke.

"Predator...Burnside Coastguard Radio. I show you five nautical miles from shore, sir. At your present rate of drift, it would be prudent for you to deploy a sea anchor, if you have one. Anything to slow you down." A sea anchor, a proper one, also called a drogue, looks like a parachute or windsock, and, pulled along underwater, does two things. It slows a boat down and turns the point, from which it is fastened, toward the waves. Predator did not have one. Mike's anger at his helplessness was rising.

"No way, Coast Guard. No way am I that close to shore...over."

"If your GPS is accurate, sir, you are five miles off." Mike thought it over and decided there was no point in arguing.

"I'll see what I can do to make some kind of sea anchor, then. When can you get to me?"

There was a long pause at the other end. "Coast Guard?"

"You may be on your own for some time, sir. We will get to you as soon as possible. Wait one minute." There was another pause as the operator responded to another call. It was Asylum. "Predator, I am advised that a tug is working toward your position and will be approaching from the west. They should get to you within the hour. Burnside Coast Guard radio out." Just to be safe, the operator circled Predator's icon on his situation board. In little more than an hour, he knew the small boat could be on the rocks.

Mike set about trying to concoct some kind of sea anchor. He took two anchors, tied them to three extra life jackets and a collapsible bicycle that he kept below for riding around at various ports of call. By the design of the boat, it was far too slippery and dangerous to walk up the deck to the bow in the heaving waves, so he got Liz to help him take everything apart again, move it below and forward to the deck hatch. One by one, he lifted the pieces up to the deck and tied them together again with half-inch anchor line. Securing the line to the bow cleat, he pushed the whole mess over the bow into the sea. As he did, a wave smacked the boat sideways, pouring a torrent of water below. For a moment, nothing happened, then, slowly the line stretched away from the boat, straining and rising from the perpendicular to an angle of fifty degrees or so. As it did, the bow swung slowly around into the waves, the rocking and pitching reduced dramatically, and the boat slowed its drifting noticeably. Mike tried to picture the odd collection of objects being dragged along underwater. It seemed almost laughable, but it was working. After a moment, though, as if it were a fishing line attacked by some large fish, it tore off sideways for twenty feet and then stopped, the boat rounding up to the new direction and taking waves at an angle again. Then the boat swung downwind from it again and everything was fine again until the next time. Very simply, Mike was a lousy tier of knots and while some slipped, others came completely undone, changing the shape of the underwater junkpile, slewing it off on a new tangent. The net result, however, was an improvement in their situation. He watched the line a little longer, checked where it was tied off on the cleat, then worked his way back to the cockpit.

"Mikey, that's a lot better. Are we going to be okay?"

"There's a tug on the way, Liz. We'll be back in the condo laughing about all of this in a few hours. Anyway, it's not so bad. I always told you you should get some color, and baby have you got color. I've never seen anyone so green."

"I feel like hell. Anyway, maybe we can finally get off our feet for a while." They sat down on the damp vinyl cushions and looked out, their gaze quickly returning to the cockpit. Their world was now reduced to a swirling enclosure of fog out of which vicious waves lunged to pass growling down the sides. Unseen until the last second, they had Liz literally sitting on the edge of her seat, as far from the water as possible.

"Anything?" Rosemary asked as Felicity peered at the radar display.

"Thought I had a blip a few minutes ago, right about here." She pointed to a place on the screen.

"Try them again?"

"May as well."

"Predator, Predator, Predator, this is Asylum, Asylum, Asylum." There was no answer. After punching in the weather channel, Mike had forgotten to return to the calling channel. No calls could be received. Rosemary repeated the call, and having no success, called the Coast Guard to advise them of the situation. Asylum's progress was slow now. While her radar was reliable, small craft did not register well on it. The waves, now as tall and at time taller than her wheelhouse, demanded Felicity's total concentration. The most direct route to the stricken craft would put the tug sideways to the waves which presented the danger of actually rolling the vessel over. So they would instead take a course with the waves more or less on the bow, a course that would eventually take them away from Predator. Eventually, however, they would be able to turn and run down the wind and seas toward her at a safe angle.

"Do you have anyone back home, Jackie?" Felicity asked. "Someone who…needs you?"

"No, why?" he asked, steadying himself against a bulkhead.

"This is going to be a closer thing than I thought. I hadn't counted on this damn fog."

"What's going to happen?"

"It depends."

"On?"

"On whether or not they clear Ram's Head. It's a rocky headland that sticks a way out into the sea. If they run aground there, we will be too late. That's the bad news. The good news is, there are a couple of small beaches. They might make it out alive on their own."

"And if they don't run aground there?"

"Then that'll give us another half hour. After that, it's all bad – rocks as big as small islands, current in all directions, nowhere to land. It's called the Dragon's Teeth and for good reason. The place will chew you up and spit you out."

"Why are you doing this? He wouldn't cross the street to help you or me or the others."

"Oh, he's not so bad, really. He's just a big dumb jerk like all the rest of the big dumb jerks. If we don't look after them, who else will? Know what I mean?"

"No, why look after them at all?"

"Because we can. What are you going to do, let them drown?" Jackie did not answer and Felicity was in no mood to be bogged down in an ethical debate. "You two get some heaving lines ready on deck and keep a sharp lookout. Use safety lines."

"Jackie, let's go" Rosemary said, and the two of them snugged their foul weather jackets around their necks then disappeared through the door. It was the roughest water Jackie had ever seen. At the top of the stairs, he clung to the railing and looked out over the few clear pockets afforded by the fog. Waves that charged past and started to break had their frothy crests blown off by the wind. Black, gusting, cat's paws ripped across the seascape at odd angles. Rosemary had given him a black baseball cap with ASYLUM emblazoned across the front in pink letters. His hair was the same color as hers and with his long ponytail secured through the back of the cap, like hers, they were difficult to tell apart from the back, bundled as they were in yellow jackets.

Felicity knew every part of Rosemary's body though, the smoothest and softest, the callused and the scarred. She knew where their bodies fit, the space between breast and shoulder where she could rest her head, the fine, soft hairs at the nape of her neck that she could caress with her lips, the triceps and biceps that rivaled her own, the open grave tattoo on her left buttock to which she verbally consigned any thing or thought that caused her pain. Felicity always wondered when she kissed it, if Rosemary would one day visualize her there. Love was such a dangerous thing, the best lovers – savage in their honesty. How beautiful she was in a strong sort of way. Her tentativeness now, as she worked her way forward along the safety line, all the more appealing. Felicity hungered for her then and there, wanted to leave the wheelhouse and the vessel to the mercies of the Goddess and take her there on the deck, on the hard, salty steel, tossed like a plaything among the murderous odds of the confused seas. Jesus.

It took a moment to register. First she felt violated. As the figure turned to signal the attaching of the heaving lines, the face that looked up at her was not the rounded features of Rosemary, but Jackie, his narrower, oblong contours peering up. But had she not felt a twinge of excitement, just for an instant after he turned…that was it…that was it…it had seemed as though she had seen her woman in a new way. After so long together, what was it now, ten years? It was good, necessary to find new things to love. But it was Jackie. She couldn't take her eyes off him. Out of the periphery of her vision, there was something else. She felt it more than saw it. The other figure, Rosemary this time, was gesturing wildly. Felicity saw it too late. Moving her eyes from Jackie to her, she did catch a glimpse of it. A huge wave, roaring down at them out of the fog directly ahead. *Oh God*, she thought, as it lifted Asylum high then dropped them like a rock, the two yellow figures on the foredeck flying through the air like cartoon characters or kites. They came down hard, Rosemary breaking her knee on a large cleat. Jackie piling neck – first into the safety line. After a moment, he was able to scramble to his feet. Checking for blood, he found none. Rosemary was toughing it out as best she could, but a series of expletives filled the foredeck.

With Jackie's help, she made it back to the cabin and fell into her bunk. Returning to the wheelhouse, Jackie delivered the bad news.

"Good thing you came along. Thanks" Felicity said, "I can't leave the wheel in these conditions. This changes things. It's you and me now. What do you say, are you game to save this jerk's ass or not?"

"We've come this far" Jackie offered lamely, "Sure, why not?" Felicity was unconvinced and studied him intently.

"What, what is it? Is there a problem here?"

"No problem."

"Be sure, because in a very short while, you are going to be very busy down there, on your own, with lives depending on you." Jackie looked out the window she had pointed to. It offered a view onto the stern deck. Rosemary had also strung a safety line out there but it was hard to imagine how anyone could stand, let alone work out there. Vast waves, rolling, churning solidities marched past, foam streaked and relentless. He was glad for the fog that mercifully kept the larger seascape from view. His neck, burned from the rope, made him wince as he absently touched it. "That's a bad burn. It must hurt like a bitch in the spray."

"I didn't notice, to tell you the truth. How long 'till we get to Predator?"

"Too late if they don't clear Ram's Head, and I would think, with only minutes to spare, if they do."

"The Dragon's Teeth?"

"That's right."

"So, how long?"

"Fifteen minutes. I'm starting my run in now. Hold on." She turned on the internal intercom. "Rose, I'm turning." But it wasn't easy. If she changed course and put the tug broadside to the wrong wave, they could get rolled. So she scanned the wave sets ahead of her, what she could see of them in the shifting fog, and finding a small break in the pattern, spun the wheel while bringing the engines to full speed. Everything looked fine, but then another nasty roller came at them out of the grey and caught their starboard quarter, trying to spin the boat while lifting the stern. This would broach the vessel, knock her on her side and Felicity fought for control. Slowly, Asylum left the perpendicular, pitching slowly down and tilting over, all the while gently corkscrewing to the right.

"Oh shit," said Jackie, moving closer to the doorway.

"Rose" Felicity said over the intercom.

"I know" came the tight reply.

"Stand by."

The vessel reached a point at which Jackie thought it must be impossible not to go over. His life completely beyond his control, he found himself oddly at peace. In moments, perhaps, the Creator would be explaining to him why his life had been such a painful engma. Then they just seemed to hang there. Another wave, Felicity knew, would turn them over.

"Now, Rose!" As she spoke, Felicity looked out the back window. Jackie followed her gaze. It might have been his imagination, but he thought he felt a surge of heat in the wheelhouse descend from the ceiling. Then the window cracked in an odd geometric pattern of concentric circles and astern of them the same pattern bubbled in the mass of the next rising sea 'till the thing collapsed into a harmless froth. As it did, Asylum settled back to an upright position and Felicity turned back to the wheel. In that moment, she had seemed to experience a huge fatigue. Shoulders slumped and head bowed, Jackie watched her regroup then bring the engines down from full speed.

"That was interesting," he said.

"Ya, we almost lost it."

"No, I mean what you and Rose did with the wave."

"Yes...well...thanks. Do you think you can handle the helm?"

"I don't know."

"Try, I'll watch you."

He picked up her motion on the wheel and took over without any interruption to the vessel's course.

"Good, Jackie...good...good...good. Port. Faster...feel it coming. Now back...back. Quick! Faster! Not too far...not too far. Hold it...hold it...feel it, feel it. Now turn to meet the wave. Turn...turn...NO.NO. Not that way. Here, let me." She took the helm just before he allowed it to slew off into another broach. Under her touch, Asylum lined up with the waves and proceeded steadily downwind. "It takes some getting used to, I guess." To change the subject, she adjusted the resolution on the radar screen, setting it to read to a narrow radius. "We're close now Jackie. See? Here's what's within three miles." When she threw the switch, he was astonished to see how close they had passed to Ram's Head and how fast they were closing on the coast and the Dragon's Teeth themselves. "We'll make one, maybe two passes about five hundred yards off the Teeth – run the full length of them. Maybe we'll get lucky. One of three things is going to happen. We don't find anything and go home. Or, we find them on the boat and get them aboard somehow. Or we fish them out of the water, alive or dead."

She spoke calmly, matter of factly. "I can get us there, but if we find them, you're on your own. I'll have to stay at the wheel. I can talk to you through the speaker on the foredeck, but you won't be able to talk to me. Stay alert. I may have to maneuver suddenly." She then gave him some hand signals to use to call for faster and slower speeds, forward and reverse. After wishing each other luck, he made his way down to the stern deck and threw boarding nets over each side. These could be used by a person in the water to climb up the steep sides of the vessel. He also clipped onto the safety line. Then he went as far forward as he could get and wedged himself into the bow. He strained his ears and eyes to the maximum.

Felicity was trying her best to match the speed of the waves, but Asylum was going a little faster and the roar of the bow wave drowned out all other sound. This was replaced by the rumble of the engines when the vessel slowed and the bow wave subsided again and again.

"Fool", Jackie thought, "how did I get myself into this? This is the kind of guy who bashes people like me." Then, from another part of his mind, came an old familiar idea. "Everyone is made by God. Everyone. We screw things up. We fail to understand who we are, but we're made by God." He clung to this thought like a life ring in a vicious sea. It gave him hope. At the same time, it was a torment, a mirage, which when he reached out to it, disappeared and disappeared and disappeared. Still, no matter what, he would imagine all creatures made by a loving Creator. Not imagine…no…it was more than that…know. He knew without doubt that people were made by a Source that would reveal itself and its master plan when the time was right. Illusions and misfortunes of all kinds were merely tests to be encountered and learned from, tests which worked in us necessary revisions. Still, to save a bigot, someone who denied even his right to exist. He didn't know whether to laugh or cry. No matter. Jackie was good at deferring fear or confusion. When and if the moment arrived, he would know what to do. How he wished he was dressed in something feminine. A cocktail dress, long ruby red nails, matching lipstick, and if the bastard so much as smirked as she leaned over to pluck him from the sea, she'd let him make a hole in the water. Let him take his hate and fear and judgment down, down, down to where the waste of modern society was disintegrating in the depths. Whatever. He and she would know what to do. A brief electronic crackle, and the speaker came to life.

"I'm starting my turn to run parallel to the shore. Keep your eyes open" Felicity called out. He waved back. Soon, they were sideways to the waves and it was all Jackie could do to keep his feet under him. Stare as he might, he saw nothing. Then Asylum turned up into the waves, the engine noise muffled down an instant and Jackie thought that he heard something. A moan, a cry...something. Then the engine rumble increased again and there was nothing but the crashing of the seas against the bow and spray flying everywhere. Conditions were still deteriorating and Felicity had decided it was too dangerous to continue.

The storm aside, if anything went wrong with Asylum's engines or steering, they would be on the rocks in a very short time. Out through the fog, lay the jagged, rocky shorelines of the Teeth. Local fishermen called them simply the Mangle. She knew that if the engines were shut off, you would hear the surf breaking wildly against them. The fog was a blessing, she thought. At least Jackie wouldn't see how closely they were threading the needle by coming in so close. But this was where logic said Predator should be. Simple physics. Felicity, too, wondered why she was there risking her own and the others' lives over a man who was, despite his big mouth, a complete unknown. But wasn't he, like she, only ever just finding his way over the rolling immensity, trying to find a part of himself and liking the way of things...there.

That was how she thought about it. She experienced him more as a rebellious sibling, one who just did not have it in him to be nice to people like her. Strangely though, as a fellow sailor, she had a bond with him. The sea is an implacable killer as well as an impartial bestower of gifts. Those who sail upon her, all humans,

Splicing the Light   213

owed it to one another, to render assistance when she got like this. Any saving hand, she knew, in a time of need, is a welcome hand. Still, enough is enough, she thought, some things are meant to be.

The vessel pounded into another wave, sending sheets of spray in all directions and Felicity decreased power. Quieter now, the eerie wailing again asserted itself in the whistling wind. Not just a wailing. *"Yes,"* Jackie thought…*"there…there…notes…some kind of melody…Jesus Christ…music."* Out there in the swirling mountains of white. He turned to the wheelhouse and cupped his ear. After a moment of confusion, Felicity opened the door, leaned out for a moment, and just as quickly, regained the wheel. She shrugged, having heard nothing over the engine, but Jackie turned again to the bow and tried to understand where the sound was coming from. It grew louder and quieter, came from the right, then the left. He closed his eyes and listened, tried to see in his imagination the source of it. What he saw was 338. Suspended in the colorless geography of his mind…338, but it kept moving and higher and lower numbers spun into view. He had psychic premonitions all the time. They were wrong more often than they were right and even if they were frequently right, they made him suspicious of his own imaginings. A bit of detail came into the frame of his vision. It was as though he was looking at the rotating numerals of a hand-bearing compass. *"That's it,"* he thought, *"a course to steer to Predator!"* He turned and started to hold his hands up to Felicity, intending to signal the course, but stopped in mid motion. If Asylum continued on, they would go right past. Anyway, course 338 would take them directly toward the rocks. *"Fuck it,"* he thought, but the number burned in his imagination.

He had always sensed great danger in turning his back on psychic gifts and vision. Life always went bad afterwards, very bad. He turned to the wheelhouse. Felicity was looking past him. He made the witch's sign, then held three fingers up, then three, then eight and pointed off in the rough direction.

"That will put us on the rocks" came the stern voice over the loudspeaker. Jackie just shrugged his shoulders, pointed half heartedly in the same direction and leaned against the bow rail with his back to her. "Are you sure?" crackled the loudspeaker. Jackie motioned that his certainty was only so-so. Felicity checked the radar. They were less than half a mile from the Dragon's Teeth. If there was any doubt, the waves heaping up in the shoaling waters confirmed it.

"Felicity? Rose. Just a hunch, nothing really clear, but if it's safe, you might think about going just a bit to port." With a great effort, she hobbled back to her bunk.

"It most certainly is not safe, but for your information, Jackie just said the same thing." Felicity turned off the internal intercom and brought the engine rpm's up, steering hard to port then easing off the power when they were once again going with the waves. Jackie motioned for her to slow down, and as she did, he heard the sound again, only much louder and closer. It was a song he hated, the rough lyrics now partly audible over the surge of waves. "Bitch...nobody's

...gonna...take what's mine." Then it stopped abruptly amid a thunderous cracking sound. Now there was a new sound. A background roar like the sound of a stadium full of people cheering. An amorphous rushing tumult like the command to "hush" that you can hear where seas explode on shores, and power, compressed, explodes in light and thunder. Asylum was beginning to be rocked by waves rebounding off the Teeth. *"We're too close,"* Jackie thought, afraid for the first time. There was one small blessing though. As the wind approached the shore and its small cliffs, it rose up to follow the contours of the land and carried up with it the dense fog. As though a curtain was being lifted on a stage, first twenty – five, then fifty feet of ocean came clearly into view ahead of them and then, what remained of the yellow racing boat, broken in half, the bow section tossed about in the waves. *"Well, that's it,"* Jackie thought as he turned to signal Felicity, but as his gaze swept aft, he saw Mike, barely able to keep head above water, off the beam. Felicity saw him, too, and keyed the microphone.

"Pick him up on the starboard quarter."

There, Asylum's sides were lower and Jackie's chances of getting him aboard were increased.

"Son of a bitch" Jackie said and worked his way toward the stern, clipping and unclipping his hook to the different sections of safety line along the way. The after deck of the tug was broad and flat. There were few things to brace against as she rolled in the seaway. Mike kept disappearing in the troughs, and reappearing, to Jackie's mind, like a bad vision, on the crests. Clearly, he wouldn't last much longer. There was something wrong with his life jacket and one arm was actually out of it. He clung to the thing with both hands and vomited twice in the brief glimpses Jackie had of him. Somehow Felicity had managed to maneuver close to him and Jackie threw a cargo net over the side. He looked around for whatever else might be of use and saw a long red pole with three hooks on the end lying along the deck on the port side. Unsnapping his safety hook, he timed a lunge across the deck to Asylum's arrival at the top of a crest and grabbed the thing with both hands, wrenching it from its clips and rehooking to the safety line before the tug dropped into the trough and rolled heavily. He had seen such things on other workboats. They were used to snag and remove garbage from harbors, from the corners where wind and current always drove it.

"*How perfect,*" he thought. Asylum was close now, so close that he lost sight of Mike under the side railing. However, when Jackie tried to lean over with the pole, the safety line prevented him. To get in position to reach the man, he would have to unclip from it. "*Let me get this right,*" he thought, as a wave threw him off his feet. "*I'm supposed to save the life of a guy who wants people like me dead.*"

"What are you waiting for?" boomed Felicity's voice. Jackie looked up at her and the pain in his face was real, the eyes hard and hopeless. "Get on with it, Jackie. I can't hold this position."

"They hate us" he roared.

"Get the man out of the water, Jackie."

"They hate us."

"*He's losing it,*" she thought. She knew she should have expected something like this. She cursed herself for her stupidity.

"Yes, they hate us" she responded, "Now get the fucking garbage out of our ocean." Jackie, who had been staring at the pole, looked up at her and unclipped from the safety line. He leaned against the side and bent over, holding the pole in both hands. There below him was Mike, but not the Mike he expected. This face was broken in spirit. In it, there was only terror and helplessness. A gash ran from his forehead down through his nose and across his cheek.

"Hey!" Jackie yelled. "Grab the cargo net, you dumb shit!" But the man was almost unresponsive, though he did manage to look up. Then the backwash from Asylum coming down a wave washed over him knocking him completely out of his lifejacket and about ten feet from the boat. There was something perverse about the whole thing to Jackie. He had prepared himself to see a man leering up at him, rolling his eyes when he realized he was about to be rescued by what he took for a queer. But there wasn't even that, just a frail lump of flesh, near death, human flotsam tossed by great powers of wind and wave.

"*Shit*," he thought, and he screamed "Do you know what you fucking people have cost me?" and he leaned as far over the side as he could, lashing out with the pole, but it came down just inches short. Collapsing back into the boat, he tied the loose end of his safety tether around the ankle of his right leg, leaned over the railing again while flailing out once more in a huge arc with the pole, at the same time, letting his feet come up off the deck 'till he lay balanced over the railing like a teeter totter. The hook came down just behind Mike who was staring uncomprehendingly at him, and Jackie pulled with all the strength he could muster. One of the hooks buried deeply under his left shoulder blade and Mike suddenly came to life in a howl of pain.

"Jesus Christ" Felicity whistled, as she watched Jackie poised over the railing, unable to get back into the boat. Then there was other movement on the deck. Rosemary had crawled out onto the deck and was struggling to make her way to Jackie. When she arrived below him, she braced her one good leg against the side of the boat, put a bear hug around Jackie's legs and pressed back with all her might. She pressed so hard that she came up off the deck but that was all it took for Jackie to wiggle himself back into the boat and get his feet on the deck. Still, it took all of his strength to hold onto the pole.

"Rosemary, untie the rope around my leg" he ordered.

Hand over hand, he pulled the pole in until Mike was banging against the side of the boat, blood pouring from the puncture in his back. This time, however, his brain clearing from a mixture of pain and adrenaline, he managed to grab on weakly to the cargo net. Jackie straddled the railing, leaned over, and one rung at a time, pulling for all he was worth, finally got the man up to where he could collapse over the railing.

"The woman?" Jackie shouted at him as Felicity swung Asylum offshore, "Where's the woman?" Mike mumbled something about her jumping off the boat in a panicked attempt to swim to shore as they passed Ram's Head. So, Felicity broke off the search and headed back to the estuary. Looking down at the man, Jackie was filled with loathing and turned to help Rosemary below.

"Take him below. Warm him up" Felicity ordered over the speaker.

"The hell I will" Jackie shouted back, making ready to pull Rosemary off the deck, but she refused.

"Do what the skipper says."

"But it's not right."

"No, it's orders...just orders."

So, Jackie got the man below, wrapped him in a warm blanket and stuck a cup of hot tea in his hands. Mike, however, just stared off blankly into space.

"How is he?" Felicity asked as Jackie entered the wheelhouse. In a hoarse whisper, he answered.

"As you ordered. He's below. He's warm." Jackie drew himself up in a fetal position on the floor behind her.

"And how are you? That was the most bizarre bit of seamanship I have ever seen!"

"I wanted him dead."

"I know, but you saved him."

"For all the wrong reasons."

Chapter Eighteen
Coven

When Asylum returned to port and was squared away at the dock, Mike and Rosemary were carried off to hospital. Felicity reminded Jackie of Sybil's order. He wearily protested. She insisted.

"You said you came to Europe for adventure. Well? Gathering in the forest with the world's most famous coven isn't an opportunity that comes to just anyone."

"What would I have to do?" Felicity answered nonchalantly with the witch's credo.

"An thou harme none, do what thou wilt. Take your cues from Sybil and only speak when someone speaks to you. I think she just has some questions about your doodling, you know, Sybil's Circle."

"Oh, that thing. Look, we just went through hell out there." He motioned energetically toward the sea where spectacular waves were exploding over the breakwalls. "Can't this wait? I think I've had enough adventure for one day."

"Jackie, things are happening around here. I can't go into it. Sybil can if she wants, but time is a factor here. Just a few hours more and then you can sleep as long as you want and after that, we'll have some serious partying to do. What do you say?"

"But what the hell do I have to do with any of this?"

"Hey, I just drive the boat."

"Like hell." He was giddy from exhaustion, his mind and emotions a maelstrom. Storms usually made him euphoric. Saving a jock in the midst of one seemed, somehow, obscene – the calm he had always found at the center, in this case, rotten and fraught with conflict. His breath was shallow, his muscles tight. This he noticed and when he noticed and breathed deeply, relaxing everything all at once, it was as though he fell a great distance. He brushed his hand over his face. Stubble, He would take care of that one day, he thought. Laser hair removal. What he wanted right now was a shave, a hot bubble bath and to change into something soft and feminine. He wanted several very strong drinks and he wanted to cry. Then he would reach that emotional bedrock from which he could once again collect his bearings. Right now he was as lost as he had ever been. Simply, events had just gotten more exotic all around him. He was still the same. Life had evolved around him in its endlessly varied profusion. Despite everything that had happened on his journey, he felt locked in a conundrum.

"I don't like the person who saved the jock" he said in a monotone.

"That's a scary thing to say" Felicity replied.

"It wasn't me."

"What do you mean?"

"It took too much strength."

"And you're not strong?"

"I don't want to be – not that strong."

"I could have pulled him from the water with one arm. Are you saying there is something wrong with me?"

"No...no....I..."

"Why are you so afraid of being a man?"

"You can't understand."

"Try me."

"I can do man things, but I'm not a man. Every time I do a man thing, something inside me screams that I'm betraying...betraying...betraying..."

"Betraying what?"

"The woman I am inside. You can laugh now."

"I'm not going to laugh. Why the hell don't you just take the pills, get the operation and have done with it, instead of tearing up yourself and everyone around you?"

"Because there are times when I do feel like a man. Christ, I'm a man and I'm not a man. I'm a woman, and I'm not a woman. I'm both. I'm neither. I'm a mistake, and I hurt and I hate everything. I'm apart from everything, and I'm afraid that I always was, and I'm afraid that I always will be, and I think I'm sick, and I just wish I wasn't so afraid to die, because then I could end this nightmare. I thought travelling might provide some answers. I don't know why. I guess I was just dumb. I thought I might find people like me. I'm so alone. And now I'm saving the fucking bastards who want me dead. Ha, ha, ha. Well if you can't kill yourself, I guess you do the next best thing. So sure, let's go to the big secret coven in the forest and talk about the fucking spiritual graffiti." Jackie felt squeezed out of his life onto another plane of existence. It was where he always ended up in his depression – a small world with safe boundaries that seemed to pulsate with pain. It was a kind of sanctuary, a holy place where he spoke with a new voice...like the time he tried to kill himself. The one place where he seemed real to himself.

The meeting did not go well. Jackie walked into the forest clearing with Felicity ambling along behind, grinning hugely.

"It was the only way he would agree to come," she said as Sybil Crowleigh, hands on hips in displeasure, made to say something.

"There goes the energy" someone chimed in peevishly from the circle.

"You know the rule," Crowleigh added caustically.

"You said bring him. Okay, I brought...her. It was this or nothing."

"Womyn, born of womyn, Felicity, with a 'y', remember?" another voice cut through. The light of several torches, revealed a circle of naked, "sky clad" as they called it, dancers – six men and six women, plus Crowleigh, the High Priestess.

"Has he been drinking, too?" the old witch continued.

"Yes, she's had a snootfull. I wouldn't provoke her." Jackie nodded approvingly at her and stepped forward into the light, hair neatly ponytailed in a large, black velvet band, wearing a floor length, long sleeved, black sequined dress. It sparkled grandly in the torchlight. He stood before them, wobbly, in a pair of shiny mid-heeled Mary Janes borrowed from Rosemary.

"You wanted me here so badly. Well, here I am." Felicity tried to grab his arm, but he brushed her off and took several unsteady steps closer to the group, his head held high, his voice a defiant contralto. He drew up in front of the girl who had spoken last, assumed a relaxed plié, tossed back his head saucily, and rolled his eyes.

"Womyn with a 'y' born of womyn with a 'y'? You must be joking," he said. "At this moment, I have no more choice about being a woman than you do. What do you know about the spirit of the Goddess? The Goddess goes where she wants. She works with whomever she wants. You're so one dimensional" he said turning to the others, "the whole bunch of you. I could just toss my cookies right here in your oh so precious circle." For a second or two, he rocked unsteadily and looked as though he might do just that. Then he straightened up and spoke in a giddy, slurred voice. "Tell me, boys and girls, who at this moment is being more genuine, you in your sky clad magnificence, or me in this somewhat overdone getup? No answer? At a loss for words are we? Don't you think it's lovely? Oh my goodness, the way the fire reflects from it. The way it shimmers like a river of moonlight. I can tell you, guys, it feels just like a river of moonlight. Anyway, where was I? Oh, yes, circles. I have been dragged here after the most terrible day at the office to blab about circles. Did I tell you that today is my birthday? That's okay, I just realized it myself." The old witch rolled her eyes at Felicity who threw her hands up in bemused resignation. The old witch motioned for the group to sit. "Good idea. We're going to be here a while because I have a story to tell you. Now, I know you all have witch names and I don't know them. So what? I have a couple of names too. It's Jacqueline at the moment. So please use it." He turned to the old woman. "You too." The witch suppressed a reaction and just twitched.

"Please go on," she said, icily.

"Thank you. Well, there's good news and there's bad news. I'll give you the bad news first. You're sitting on all this crop circle activity and you think it's some big deal. You think that because I drew this thing you call Sybil's Circle, that there's some big, meaningful something going on. You've made this big thing out of nothing. You could get as much magic out of a bathroom stall because that's all it is, spiritual graffiti." He paused for a moment as the witches laughed and caught each other's eyes. "Laugh if you want, but that's all it is, a bunch of punk spirits defacing the planet where it will last for a while. Annabel was here. Baelfor rules. It's nothing personal and you're not in on any great mystery, but I can see you've gotten all twisted out of shape over all of this. You've gotten so obsessed with the things that you think you own them – like the Goddess was trying to talk to you personally or something. Ya, well maybe I'm here because I'm a world authority on obsession, so I'm going to tell you a story.

Let's call it the Clamshell Suite. Where I live, there are freshwater clams, and one day, when I was a child, my parents took me to the countryside. There was a small lake with a sandy bottom. A lot of kids were there swimming. The air was full of laughter and joy. But I didn't know how to swim, and I wanted to more than anything. Standing there up to my waist in the waves, I noticed something bright on the bottom. So, I took a breath, leaned over and grabbed the thing. As you have guessed, it was a clamshell, hard and ugly on the outside, smooth and shiny on the inside with the sun shining on it. But, I didn't stick it in my bathing trunks and go back to shore. I threw it away. Only as far as I thought I could retrieve it, mind you. I guess I just thought I would find a way. Anyway, it skittered down to the bottom about six or seven feet away and lay there glowing, though I could just barely see it. I resisted the urge to walk toward it and took a huge breath instead, then just got down in the water and clawed and pulled and kicked and flailed however I could. Eventually, I was there. It wasn't pretty, and I don't think anyone would call it swimming. It was ugly. But I had the shell. Again. The next time, as you can guess, I threw it even further and by the time I got to it, I thought my lungs were going to burst, but I got it. You get the idea. Okay, so maybe I'm drunk, and maybe I'm just fucked up, but there's a point here somewhere though I don't really remember what it was except to tell you what my spirit guide told me last night. She said –" He turned to Crowleigh "and maybe this is what you're supposed to hear from me. She said 'Go beyond.

Some dead end puzzles are put along the path just to see if you develop the wisdom to leave them alone. Not all puzzles' she said, 'are to be solved.' You see, some of them are just scratching posts of the spirit. Do you like that? I made it up. They're not an end in themselves. And we shouldn't hate them for being something that couldn't be mastered and we shouldn't hate ourselves because we couldn't master them or even understand them. Fuck, I don't have a clue of what I'm talking about and now that I've made a complete fool of myself, I think I'll just fall on my face, here in jolly old England. Sorry for ruining your dance." Then he slumped to the ground and sat there looking around the clearing.

The moon was a black crackled silver in the treetops. The air, cool and rich with dew. Whatever the place was, whatever the people were about, he liked the fact that it was not about grubbing for money and all that goes along with that. It was just a bunch of people worshipping as they felt in a place that seemed right. *"As ditzy as they are,"* Jackie thought, *"they seem to be,"* there was no other word for it, *"home."* How he wished it could be home for him. But once again, it was a time and a place that was not completely right. The symmetry of the coven circle was ruined, in his mind, by the six males and six females that made it up. Even here in the depths of a foreign forest, he felt the grip of binary human thinking. Male power balancing female power. Be one. Be the other. Take your place. Don't confuse things.

It was the same with the ceremonial tools laid out by the makeshift altar. The cauldron, moon and cup – to be filled, receptive, feminine. The sword – phallic, the sun – disseminator of heat and light, giving, male. The left side of the altar – feminine for the Goddess. The right – masculine, for the God. Wicca had, he realized, just taken the either – or mindset of the species and softened the edges a little. In his imagination, a vertical line appeared. Then it was crossed by a horizontal one. Then the tortured body of Christ manifested at the intersection of the two. *"Was it this thinking that Christ gave his life to staunch,"* he asked himself. *"Mankind's addiction to soul splitting polarities?"*

"Jackie?"

"Why did mankind think it needed that," he asked himself. *"What was the payoff? Don't people realize how little of themselves they were consigning themselves to live?"*

"Jackie? Are you okay?" It was Sybil Crowleigh.

"It's okay. I'll take care of him," said a young woman who pushed past the High Priestess and took him by the hand. "It's okay. I see this. Trust me. I know what I'm doing."

"Later" the older woman commanded, pulling her back abruptly. Undeterred, the woman shook herself free and laughing, danced under the witch's outstretched arm limbo fashion. This caused a round of giggles and mumbling in the coven. "Veronique, stop this!" the older woman ordered, and intending only to wave her off, raised her hand. She mistimed it, however, and the younger woman was knocked to the ground on her back.

"Bitch!" she rasped, slapping away the witch's hand.

The scene froze as a deathly anticipation took hold of the clearing. Eyes darted or fixed on the ground. God knows she had been warned. Of all the coven members, she was the most troublesome, the least…committed.

"I've had enough of this bullshit," she said as cheerfully as if she was saying good morning.

"I'm warning you!"

"I'm terrified" the young woman answered sarcastically. Rising, she shook the dust from her hands. Her hair was gathered in tight cornrows that trailed off into brightly beaded braids that swung and clicked as she moved. She spoke with an accent that Jackie could not place, part Caribbean, and part something else. He liked her defiance. Nearby, the dancers had neatly placed their clothing on the ground. As she dressed, it seemed as though she was melting into the night. Black body suit with a short black skirt over. A pair of black jazz pumps. She swirled a maroon sweater over her shoulder. "You really do need to come with me," she called to him and her voice was sultry, deep and refined – an educated voice, the voice of someone who has seen a lot.

"Jackie, stay where you are! Natasha – Veronique, get back here! You know you cannot leave the –"

"Your white gods have no power over me. I should have left a long time ago. Now, I am going."

"If you do this, I'll –"

"You'll what? You know better. Even in this place" she gestured grandly, fingers splayed, to the forest and the firelight, "you have no power over the Orishas." Jackie took a few steps toward her.

Chapter Nineteen
The Orishas

"You want to take off with this voodoo tramp, you go right ahead" the old witch snapped. "But don't say I didn't warn you. Only evil will come of it. Your voodoo is nothing...nothing."

"Nothing?" the woman repeated full of fury. "Then explain this." To Jackie's astonishment, she walked over to the fire and with apparent abandon, pulled out eight red coals, placing them between the fingers of each hand, brandishing them in complex, flowing movements like a flamenco dancer or a Tibetan monk. Then, just as suddenly, she flung them with disdain back into the fire. Jackie couldn't help himself.

"Jeesus Christ" he muttered.

"Come" the woman said, her voice warm as a southern breeze.

"You'll need these" Felicity said, throwing her the keys to Asylum. "Leave them in the usual place, Nat."

"Nice car," Jackie said as he slumped down into the seat of the old Jaguar Mark VI. The leather was soft and pipe tobacco in the open ashtray put out a rich aroma.

"It's daddy's." Her jasmine perfume was crisp and sensuous. When they arrived at the tug, she took his hand. "You might like to change. The bars will be closing now and the police will be all over the place. It's illegal to cross dress here, you know, and no offense, but you have a lot to learn about makeup if you want to pass as a woman.

"I'm not cross dressed." She studied him for a moment.

"No, maybe you're not, but that's what the cops will say, and they call the shots. So please, grab your things, throw on something butch and let's get out of here.

"Why do I need to come with you?"

"I don't know. I just know you do."

Jackie looked into her deep, black eyes and they seemed so familiar somehow. He wasn't attracted to her. Her fingers were long and narrow and no one would say she was beautiful, not even handsome. Not cute either. She carried herself with grace and pride, a kind of nobility. Where it came from, he could not guess. But that, together with her voice, was entirely remarkable. Her lack of surface beauty, seemed to him, completely incongruous. An unfinished work.

"What are you looking at?" she asked.

"I don't know. I'm sorry."

"Don't be sorry. It may be that we have known each other before..." she motioned to their surroundings, "...before this."

"Really?"

"Yes, this type of odd feeling comes when we run into old friends in this world. We may be old friends. Yes, I think so."

"I'll change."

Finally, in the drive to wherever the woman was taking him, Jackie passed out from exhaustion and drink. The next morning, he awoke to the drowsy smell and sounds of rain. He moved and waited for the headache he was sure would come. There wasn't one. England, yes, and he was in a bed. That much he knew. Then it all came back to him. He opened his eyes. "Voodoo tramp." That's what the old witch had called her. He could still taste the venom in her voice. Candles. He was surrounded by candles. White candles in a dark room and the rain falling. Spirit sigils – signatures—on the walls. He had seen them before in dreams – some of them, but there were extra lines and shapes here that he hadn't seen before.

"Veronique?" he called out.

"Ah...so you're awake. Good." She saw the look of apprehension in his eyes. "Not to worry. You have been attended to while you slept. Your body was so bruised and you were in a lot of pain through the night."

"I don't remember."

"No. That's good. The spirits like the candlelight. They have worked to heal you. Unfortunately, they are very literal and I don't know if they found all the right places." Jackie tried to move and winced with the pain of a contracted tendon. "Obviously not. You will have to tell them where it hurts." Jackie started to get up. The woman pushed him back down. "First, you must thank them for their efforts."

"What are their names?"

"Ah, it is very good that you ask. They will like that. Names are important. Names are power. But it is enough that you thank them all together. There will be time for names later if you like." So Jackie thanked the unseen powers that the woman had said were ministering to him even at that moment. It was true. His body was covered in cuts and bruises from his efforts aboard Asylum. In the heat of rescue and later, in his drunken state, he had not noticed. He should be hurting much more than he was.

"No, not like that" she said hurriedly as he tried to help by blowing out a candle. "That is very bad luck. Never blow out a candle. With a dead match, she gently bent the flaming wick back into the melted wax at its base. It went out without making any smoke. "Like this" she said, "and think a thank you to the spirits who attend the flame as you do it, please."

As he reached for the next candle and held it close, it suddenly flared and crackled, spitting out a shower of tiny sparks in all directions.

"Oh!" he cried and held it quickly at arm's length.

"Sometimes, they think they are very funny" she laughed.

The days passed at a pleasant pace. Jackie found it difficult to understand the relationship that had begun to draw them closer. She knew he would leave when his money ran out and still she had not objected when he bought the groceries or took her out to pubs for a night of drinking. At the rate he was going, he would have to get back to London and his flight home in a matter of weeks. One evening, he had returned from a local to find the house in darkness except for the flickering candles that she usually set out. Sandalwood incense spiced the air. She was seated at a piano. A black mini grand with the top propped open. She was wearing black leather pants and a white, lacey French peasant blouse under a black leather vest. Around her neck a dark choker with a cameo of some sort. How lucky Jackie thought himself to be in this place at this time. How far away seemed all danger, all crudeness, all of the ugliness of life amid the common herd. She paid him no notice and sat as though entranced. Then her left hand produced a rich chord far down the keyboard and her right foot pressed the sustain pedal. It was a dark sound, like the room, with just a little light. The two high notes that sounded as her right hand flew up past the octaves, unfolded like a question. A fifth in the bass – the answer.

"Do you play piano, Jackie?"

"No."

"Any musical instrument?"

"No."

"Come here…play."

"I told you, I can't play."

"I know that…play anyway…" Jackie sat down on the bench.

"Just mess around and let me know when you find some sounds that you like. Throw the clamshell."

The first notes came from deep in the bass as he walked a group of five notes up slowly, finger by finger. He started to play intervals though he didn't know what they were called. He played a second and didn't like it. A third relaxed him a little. A fourth brought no change and a fifth drew him over the keyboard. He played the fifth again with more power and sustained it as he had seen her do. Immediately, he added a note from a black key above, withdrawing his hands at the ugliness of it. Again, he played the fifth and the next white key down from the black one. The sounds merged beautifully. He played the next three notes down, then back up two. It sounded almost like he felt – said what he would never have words for. Maybe, he thought, he was reading too much into it. He stopped and found a third in the left hand that went with the fifth. Then he played the fifth while filling in notes from the right hand, then the third in the left sent things in a slightly new direction and he followed with new notes in the right that seemed to add to the effect. It sounded darkly Celtic or Gregorian, sonorous and simple yet impressive.

Natasha – Veronique poured herself a glass of Pernod and mixed in a little water, listening intently. His sense of rhythm was good, and while there was the unmistakable non-legato playing of the amateur, there was a variation of touch, an attempt to express, to articulate something.

"It's amazing" he enthused.

"Oh, it wasn't that good."

"No, no. I know it sounds like crap. It's just that I'm surprised I could get both hands to produce something together like that. I always thought that would be the worst part of learning the piano. You know, getting both hands to work together, especially when they're far apart.

"That comes with time."

"I wish I could play."

"So learn."

"You'll teach me?"

"Sure" she said in her sultry low way.

"I have to go back soon, and –"

"I'll get you started. Consider this your first lesson. You can get another teacher when you get home."

"What's in it for you?"

"Must there be something 'in it' for me?"

"Yes."

"Perhaps you are right. Maybe I wish to keep you here."

"I've already told you, I have to go back sooner or later."

"One can always find a way to do what he is intended to do."

"Am I intended to stay?"

"I do not know. Do you want to stay?"

"I don't know."

"The Orishas will decide, and as they always do, they will provide." Her faith was absolute, and Jackie was surprised to find himself touched by it.

"Tell me about your Orishas."

"Okay" she said, coming over to the piano, "May I?" Jackie got up. "You know, when I think of them and all they have done for me in this life...well, words fail. This is how I see one of them." There were large pillows on the floor covered in Persian carpet-like fabric. Jackie bunched a couple up and got comfortable.

"Ready."

Natasha-Veronique took another swallow from her Pernod and felt the cool liquid all the way down. Then her left hand described an arc in the candlelight and glided down into sound. Jackie closed his eyes. The music came in gentle, rhythmic measures, as much ebb as flow. For some reason, he saw wheat fields and wind moving through them like cat's paws on water – a golden landscape bending, flowing, brushed aside as though by unseen passers-by.

"This was Agwe, spirit of the sea." Another drink and she was off again into a light, bright, sweeping piece that made no deep statements at all. "Aida Wedo – spirit of the rainbow." The pieces that followed saturated the room in color and stripped it bare, brought Jackie's heart into his mouth, then plunged him into rapid despair. On and on she played her understanding of the spirits of her world – of Erzulie the female spirit of love – of Shango, spirit of storms – of Baron Samedi, guardian of the grave, and the gentle Osun, spirit of healing streams. More than once, Jackie rubbed his eyes as Natasha-Veronique seemed in the low light actually to change, to swell and grow until she seemed to merge with the shadows. For an instant, he thought he could see through her to the wall beyond and once he felt as though she was there beside him on the floor. The longer the music went on, the less there seemed to be a center anywhere. And then the strangest thing happened. In the midst of her improvisation, he knew what was coming next. Knew it and did not know how. A smile spread out on his face. It was all good, that sound – and fluid and sure. He felt himself lifted and compelled to dance. "Mama Loa, Papa Loa" She was chanting now in the background between notes. Then only her right hand was playing and with her left she raised her glass high and dripped the contents into another empty glass that lay on the piano. A long, slow, high trickle. Then she played the sound of the water note for note. "Yemanja"   she   intoned.   "Yemanja...Osun...Ogou Balanjo...Mawu Lisa –"

"Shango" Jackie added from across the room as he spun in a slow arc.

"Shango" Natasha-Veronique confirmed, somewhat surprised as she fixed Jackie with her eyes. "Yes...Shango – spirit of storms. You say it so gently, Jackie." From some kind of trance, Jackie spoke, half aloud, half in whisper.

"...and thunder rock the silence unaccused and rainfall hold no thing in chains as storms will do what storms must be..."

"My god, where does that come from? Stop dancing. Come here. Where does that come from?"

"I...I think I wrote it...I...oh my god, what's happening to me?" The room was melting away from him and there were rainbows around the edges of everything."

"Lie down" the woman commanded. "Your ti bon ange has decided to leave for a bit. Your little guardian angel. You also have a big one – your gros bon ange. I'm sorry. I think it is my fault. The spirit presence is very strong in this room and your ti bon ange was making room for someone else. How are you now?" Jackie let out a long breath and smiled. "Ah, your angel returns. C'est bon. Reste tranquil." She went into the kitchen and returned with a large scotch on the rocks. "You are a writer? Those words were your words, Jackie?" He nodded. "Where do you get such ideas – 'thunder rock the silence unaccused.' It's amazing. I could never do such a thing. I think now I understand why the Loas have brought us together. I give you music. You give me words. Will you teach me how to put words like that?"

"I don't know if –"

"Of course you can."

And so a kind of collaboration began. For three weeks, each one doing what could be done to help the other find expression in music and words. It was not perfect or pretty. To Natasha-Veronique's endless consternation, Jackie would stop every time he made a mistake on the keyboard, announcing summarily, "No, no, that's wrong. I'm starting again." And she commanding, "No, keep going! Don't stop. Mistakes are released into the world forever. They cannot be called back. Neither do they remain. Continue!" For her part, she had an equally difficult time just getting at what she wanted to write, let alone finding the words for it.

"I cannot tell you how to feel" Jackie would groan. "No one can. What do you think, how do you feel? Go inside. Look. Ask. Listen. Write without judging. Later you can revise. Spill it. Now! What must be said?" Often his student would throw something in frustration. Ashtrays were a favorite, pens, too. One had stuck in the wall like a dagger. They left it there as an artistic statement. In the alcoholic lucidity of the moment, it had seemed to make perfect sense.

One evening, Jackie came back from a walk to find the front door unlocked and ajar. Natasha-Veronique was usually very particular about her security. This was the first time that Jackie had found it open. He felt as though he had walked onto the set of a movie. Ahead of him, down past the end of the hallway, was a tall, dark figure of a man moving stealthily toward the woman who was reading with her back to him. The man was powerfully built. You could tell from the narrowness of his waist and the breadth of his shoulders. Slowly, he raised both arms. It was clear he intended to grab her.

"Touch her and you die, shit head!" Jackie said in the coldest voice he could muster. Then he grabbed the glass flower vase from the entryway table, smashed it against the wall where it yielded a vicious edge and brandished it at the intruder as Jackie walked briskly toward him. The man turned. "Veronique, get out of here!" Jackie ordered, then he grabbed the man's tie and pulled his face down to the glass. But there was something wrong. Jackie had seen the look in the man's eyes as he spun around. It was a look of genuine surprise and...confusion. Natasha-Veronique was on her feet. Jackie's hand came up instead and caught the man flush in the chin.

"Papa!"

"Oh shit," said Jackie, too late.

Like a sack of potatoes, Natasha-Veronique's father collapsed on the carpet. There was a rush for ice cubes, for water, for a towel. When the two agreed that the man was just knocked out, and his daughter had offered to explain everything, Jackie turned to go.

"Come back here," said the man groggily. "Anyone who would so violently protect my daughter is someone I would like to meet. Jeesus Christ-" he said with surprise, "I have a splitting headache."

"Jackie, this is my father, Antoine Laporte. Papa, this is Jackie Northam. She...he is teaching me to write. I am teaching him how to play the piano." The man extended his hand. Jackie shook with him. There was something very old in the man's eyes, the same something Jackie had seen in Sybil Crowleigh's eyes, a power, but this time more volatile, less static, more elemental. Still, it was hard to know what to make of him. He could have been anywhere from thirty to sixty years of age.

"I'm sorry, Mr. Laporte. I really thought –"

"Yes. I guess from behind, a dark shadow of a man sneaking up on a woman. You did the right thing." For a moment, Natasha-Veronique and he spoke in French. Jackie could not catch most of it. "She tells me you have some interest in...spiritual matters. Perhaps we could talk when –"

"Papa works for the Haitian embassy in London. He is also –" she lowered her voice, "a houngan, a priest."

"I just kicked a voodoo priest in the head?"

"Well...yes."

"Actually," the man said, "we do not use that word. We use Vodun."

"And the needles and the dolls?"

"Hollywood. Neither is really necessary."

"Oh shit."

"Not to worry" the man continued. If you are here, it is only because the Loa wish it."

"What does he mean?" Jackie asked, turning to Natasha-Veronique.

"Papa" she pleaded.

"Girl, you should tell people, so the proper respect can be paid. This may be an old coach house, but it is also a hounfour, a Vodun temple. Not used much, but a temple all the same." He turned to Jackie. "Sometimes, hounsis, students of Vodun, come here for ceremonies. You must behave...correctly...while you are here. Have you been behaving...correctly, Natasha-Veronique?" His big brown eyes moved from her to Jackie and back again.

"Oui, Papa."

"Vraiment?"

"Vraiment, but he stays here."

"Natasha –"

"He stays."

Clearly she had staked out some new position in some murky middle ground between them. Jackie wondered who had the momentum. Her father stalled for time.

"Let me at least get to know your...protector."

"Jackie?"

"Ya, sure. It's the least I can do."

So the two sat down and talked while Natasha-Veronique provided a steady stream of food and drink. Antoine Laporte, Jackie learned, was a press attaché, a man of words and images, whose job it was to present his Ambassador and his country in the desired light. Though it brought him no great joy or prestige, he was good at his job. His wife, however, stayed in Haiti where she was involved in many pursuits. She developed outreach programs for the poor. She was also organizing local artisans into an association that, she hoped, would effectively bring their art to the world.

"What do you do, Jackie, if you don't mind me asking?"

"Well, I guess I'm sort of on holiday right now. I've been travelling around a bit. First Greece and now here."

"Have you ever been to my part of the world?"

"Haiti? No, but I would like to go, some day."

"Oh? And why is that?" Jackie felt himself being edged into a corner. There was nothing to do.

"Actually, I wonder if Vodun might hold some answers for me."

"Well then. It looks like Haiti has come to you. Ask away. If I can't answer your questions, no one in Vodun can. I'm sorry if that sounds arrogant, but it's true. Anyway, go ahead." Jackie considered his options. How easy it had become for him to talk to near strangers about the most personal of subjects.

"It's quite personal. I wouldn't want to embarrass you."

"Jackie, Vodun followers allow spirits to take over their bodies. We liken it to being mounted...as a horse is mounted...nothing could be more personal."

"I see...okay...I guess I would like to know how transgender and transsexual people are viewed in Vodun."

"Because you are like that?"

"Yes."

"Well" He remembered how his daughter had referred to Jackie in the feminine. Earlier. "And if you find that my faith sees these things in a positive light, you would wish to become a member of that community?"

"It seems unlikely. I mean. I'm not black." The man was amused, however.

"No problem. In its origins, nothing could be blacker. Vodun was practiced originally in Dahomey, now Benin in West Africa. Yes, why indeed would a white...person embrace a black religion. It's almost as strange as a black man becoming a Christian, don't you think?"

"Touché."

"Ah, vous parlez français?"

"Très mal."

"Okay, we'll speak English. Let me see, how does Vodun view transgender and transsexual people, you ask." He paused to confirm the terms.

"Yes, that's right."

"Transsexual, I know. One wants to have surgery to change the body. Male to female and vice versa. I am less comfortable with this other term, trans-"

"Transgender. We're called TG's for short. TG's feel like they are of both genders. It's sort of an umbrella term. Some want to live as either gender when they feel like it. Some go on hormones to level out their mood changes. A lot of us just feel stuck in the middle – torn in both directions."

"And you?"

"I don't know why I am alive. My spirit is ripped in half. I tried to kill myself. Much of the time, I feel like a woman. Most of the time. At other times, I suppose I feel like some kind of a man."

"Do you mind if I smoke?" asked the man, looking past Jackie to the wall.

"No, go ahead." He pulled out a thin, gnarly cigar and lit it.

"In my home town, Port-au-Prince, such people can be found standing in two's or three's with their heads down, whispering. They are not really approved of, you see. So they keep their voices down. To be honest, we do not really know what to make of them. Most of us do not go there – to the place where male and female touch in one person. It...unsettles us. Men like to think that women need them. Women like to think men need them. Gays and lesbians do not want the landscape confused by those who change too much. Nobody does. I have heard some hounsis say that transgender people," he stumbled over the word, "are actually just mounted frequently or accompanied closely by feminine spirits, and not knowing this, waste their lives in confusion. Others say that the ti bon ange of transgender people has been brutally attacked by practitioners of black magic while the spirit has been absent from their body in dreams. Still others think you are unnatural. Some think you are shamans who do not realize the fact. They think this because you bridge two worlds and yet somehow remain whole where most people would crumble psychologically. Such people's hatred is rooted in jealousy. Does your life really have to be about this? I'm sorry, I can't believe I just said that. You tried to kill yourself over this. The pain must be unimaginable. The world, nature is so wonderful, so...it seems so...blameless."

"Even the hurricanes?"

"Yes. And I'm sometimes afraid that my whole existence is a mistake...a corruption...that I just don't get the point. It's an Old Testament thing."

"Well, I am not a psychiatrist, but if all of these things were true, what is the best thing that you could do in this life? If you were in court, accused of a crime and about to be found guilty, what would you want your attorney to do?"

"Show something good that I had done."

"Have you done anything good in this life, Jackie or have you pursued this search for yourself to the exclusion of everything else?"

"Oh fuck." Jackie wrapped his arms around his solar plexus and began rocking. "Who is supposed to do the good, the man me or the woman me?"

"Just do the good. I don't think it matters."

"You know," said Natasha-Veronique, bringing more food and drink to the two of them, "I'll bet you've done more for people than you realize."

"No, it's true. I haven't been able to think about anything else since I was a kid. Maybe I've been wrapped up in myself for my whole life. Maybe I do need to get beyond myself."

"That doesn't mean you have to stop trying to figure yourself out."

"Yes, I know, but what good has that ever done me?"

"Maybe the common herd doesn't want you to figure yourself out. Maybe if you figure yourself out, and you're not like them in the end, then that says they are doing something wrong in suppressing you."

"Please, Natasha, the young man…Jackie, has enough to think about. You have to pardon her, Jackie. She is quite the revolutionary."

"Well anyway, Jackie, if you still feel the same about this tomorrow, why don't you join me at Maximus?" Maximus was a drop in center for street people, troubled youth and others. A small two story brick building, it provided small rooms and meeting areas for outreach to a variety of groups in the community. She worked there as a Coordinator. The night had settled into a party of drink, food and music.

Chapter Twenty

Al áne

"Have you worked with any kind of outreach program before?" Natasha-Veronique asked Jackie as they rode the double decker bus to Maximum the next morning. He was flipping through a local counter culture newspaper, "dynaMO." In the classified section, there was an ad for the center.

MAXIMUS

A journey of a thousand miles begins with a single step.

Confucius

There was a cartoon style line drawing of the building striding toward a brilliant sunrise in the kind of workboots popular among teenagers. The building was androgynous. Mr. or Ms. Maximus was blowing a harmonica and winged notes flew into the air. "Bring it on!" the sun said with open arms. Further down, the various interest groups were listed. "SeCond Chance, Victims of Abuse, Gay Youth, and so on and so on.

"No." I haven't helped people like these. I've been people like these.

"Even better."

"Ya but no one was able to help me. What makes you think I will be able to help anybody else?"

"A lot of the time, all they really need is someone to listen – someone to help them find the words. Look at what you did for me with the song lyrics." It was true. Through his encouragement – harsh at times, gentle and subtle at others – she had put words to at least five songs and started work in other forms. Growing up the daughter of a Haitian Vodun priest and a Russian mother had created some unique hells for her. Like any child, she was struggling to push up through the circumstances of her birth to the sunlight of whatever individual expression was possible for her. He was helping her to find her voice although he did not see the work in such grand terms. "Can you cook?" she asked with a smile?

"Ya, I'm not bad, why?" She took the newspaper from him and with a pen she was using for crosswords, circled something. If you don't want to talk, why not cook? This group," she had circled something called Food on the Fly, "is basically street people who don't get enough to eat. We provide them with a breakfast seven days a week." I am sure they would love the help. Two of the helpers are transsexual – one male to female, the other female to male.

"Really" Jackie said, feeling a bit uneasy. So many people like him were so poor at passing as the desired gender. That was, he had always thought, the point – to blend in – to be accepted. In a way, he didn't even want to know other people like himself. And yet, he wondered, was a man who looked only partly like a woman any worse than someone with one eye or leg, than someone with no muscle control or someone confined to a wheel chair. Was a "readable" transsexual any less of a human being? He was aware of the inconsistency in his thinking and it bothered him.

"You don't seem very interested."

"I'm not."

The building was tired, but it positively radiated energy. Something deep in the old wooden walls, the threadbare carpet, the little semicircles of chairs in the middle of resonant rooms, the riot of colors on the bulletin boards.

It was still early and the caretaker had let them in. She was a sweet, grandmotherly Ukrainian woman.

"Good morning, Ms. Laporte. You are very early today. Again the Food Bank has delivered canned goods to the back door and then gone away. What do you want to do with it?"

"Oh, it will have to go into the kitchen for sorting."

"I know but I cannot lift such cases."

"It's okay," said Jackie, "I'll do it."

"Mila, this is Jackie. He's come to see what we are all about here."

"And such a gentleman. Thank you very much. This way please." Jackie made his way through the spotless kitchen with its neatly hung pots, pans and ladles. Everything had been worked hard – dents, stains, cracks and other kinds of wear marks abounded. There was a faint trace of vinegar in the air. "This way" Mila said in her sing song voice. When she rolled up a sliding door, Jackie was faced with a pallet taller than he was, loaded with cans of all sorts crammed into cardboard boxes. Tomato sauce, stew, creamed corn, vegetables. He checked a few of them. Some were near the expiry date, others were imperfect – slightly dented, labels torn, but most of them seemed perfectly fine.

"How can people give all of this away?" he asked.

"Oh, you'd be surprised. Some people really do care about their fellow humans. And we ask for help. No, no we are not too proud. Besides, we put the names of donors in our advertisements. It's good for their good will advertising. How much would they have to pay otherwise?"

"I like the way you think, Mila."

"Good. It's nice to be liked. Now unload please."

Jackie set to work stacking the cans on shelves. After a while, the kitchen door slammed open. Jackie was half way into one of the storage cupboards.

"What the hell are you doing there?" a rough male voice demanded.

"I'm with Natasha-Veronique. I'm helping out."

"Is that so" and the door slammed closed then opened quietly.

"Jackie, how are you getting on?" It was Natasha-Veronique. "I see you already met Bart."

"Is that who that was? I don't think he liked me."

"He doesn't like anyone, but he's a tireless cook. Humor him. Let's sit down and look at your options. So what can you do for us?"

"I can clean the washrooms" Jackie said matter-of-factly.

"You're kidding. Nobody wants to do that and Mila really can't keep up. But why? I mean they really do get gross."

"I used to practice at a Zen center. The washrooms were part of my practice. A selfless work for the sangha, the other Zen students.

"Okay, but this is not going to be the same thing. Anyway, if you want to, go for it. Mila will love you. There are two male and two female washrooms. Just hang a sign on the door before you start work.

Economic realities presented him with facilities very much like the austere version at the Zen center. Chipped tile floors, white porcelain, metal cubicles, painted particleboard walls. He hung the sign on the doorknob and after confirming no one was there, set to work.

"Jackie." It was Mila at the door. "People are backing up at the other washroom. Are you about finished?"

"Ya, almost, another few minutes." The woman walked in.

"Oh my goodness" she said as she ran her hands over the windowsill. No dust. The toilet paper reserve roll was in its proper place. The taps had been polished and the wastebasket emptied.

"Boy, you sure know how to clean. Even the soap trays. Boy oh boy oh boy." She walked out shaking her head. Jackie didn't know if she was approving or disapproving. Mumbling away in Ukrainian, she disappeared down the hallway. Jackie turned as he was about to leave. The room was spotless and smelled, if not fresh, at least very clean. He wondered how long the satisfaction of providing troubled people with a sanitary place to use the toilet would last. When he came back to do it all again at lunch time, there was a syringe in the garbage can, water all over the counter top, cigarettes in the urinals, the urinals unflushed and toilet paper strewn everywhere.

At the Zen center, he knew the students appreciated his efforts. No one needed to say a word. Mindfulness saw to it. This was different. There was no mindfulness here. Only sloppiness and ego. Willful neglect. He turned off the taps that had been left running.

"How do you do it, Mila?" he asked as she came past the door.

"Oh, I am paid. It's just a job, but really people are such pigs, aren't they?"

"Yes, people are pigs."

"Don't do so much – just basic cleaning or you will get frustrated" she offered cheerfully.

"You're amazing, Mila."

"Yes, this is true."

Jackie returned to the carriage house bone weary, his thighs and back aching.

'Are you okay?" Natasha-Veronique asked. "You look terrible."

"I haven't worked that hard in a long time."

"There's pasta in the fridge." After he had eaten and washed it down with some dark ale, he felt better and sat down at the piano. Tchaikovsky's "French Song", a song for children blossomed after a fashion in the silence, but beautiful and evocative in Jackie's mind. He never got tired of playing it. It sounded very Russian – sonorous and deeply atmospheric despite its simplicity. An odd thing had happened from the earliest moment of his learning it. In his imagination, a vivid scene had presented itself. A wooden table with mellowed red color to it, a crude wooden chair. He was seated there, looking out an ornately frosted window. There was a small yard with brittle, brown plant stems sticking through deep snow, a tangled low hedge and beyond the ground fell slightly away revealing a panorama of blowing and drifting. But there was a fire in the fireplace and he was writing away. It felt like Russia, and he felt completely at peace with himself. He was a man in his late 40's and alone. The image was so strong, he had to play through it, despite it. Almost like trying to focus beyond the prismatic effects of a bad migraine, yet pleasurable.

"You are dreaming," said Natasha-Veronique "and you are getting very heavy. This is a children's song. Play it lightly, like this." She moved him over and began to play. Her touch was lighter, faster, more supple. Her fluid technique transformed the piece. It was the same notes and not the same notes, as though she had taken the same clay that he had molded and formed it into something entirely new. Her touch was so...feminine, a genuine femininity that he knew he could never attain, that he would, at best, crudely approximate. "You live too much in your head, you know that" she said.

"I know it and feel it." He felt himself sinking again. "Who is my Orisha?" he asked, wondering which of the Vodun lesser gods was responsible for him. Each person, she had said, was guided and helped by one of the pantheon of Orishas.

"There is only one that is both male and female. Obatala."

"Tell me about him."

"Orishas have their favored colors – colors they recognize in ceremonies as well – Obatala's is white. White for purity. With this white, he may wear a little splash of color – blue, purple, violet, red, pink. He is the owner of all heads. I will tell you about that some day. And he is wise, one of the wisest of them all. He is also called the 'old man' because of this. He was present at creation. He knows all things. Why do you ask this?"

"Because I need help. Sometimes, I feel like my whole life has been one long, slow motion breakdown. Maybe that is why I am so tired all the time. And I'm running out of places to look for help. I mean...no offence, but look at me. Here I am in this carriage house. I've been in churches and temples, rooming houses and rooftops. I've been on beaches and boats, mountaintops and balconies. I've prayed to God, Jaweh, Allah and the Goddess. I've been poked, prodded and tested by psychiatrists and psychologists. I've had a glass thing put over my dick to test God knows what and I've tried to spill my blood all over God's creation and now here I am in a carriage house that's really a voodoo temple and if someone or something doesn't...IT MEANT NOTHING FOR ME TO BE AT THAT PLACE TODAY. I HATED IT. I DON'T CARE ABOUT THOSE PEOPLE. I HATE THEM. THEY HATE ME. I DON'T WANT TO DO GOOD FOR ANYONE. I HATE MYSELF FOR FEELING LIKE THAT. BUT THAT'S WHAT I AM. I DON'T LIKE MYSELF. I DON'T LIKE THE WORLD AND I DON'T LIKE BEING CONSCIOUS 'CAUSE I HURT WHERE I DON'T EVEN HAVE PLACES."

"Whew, I didn't realize –"

"There was a guy today, in his 40's or 50's. When I was taking a break in the reading room, he walked in. He was the worst looking queen I have ever seen. No, strike that. He was like most of the queens I've seen – trying hard to look like a woman, but obviously male. It was pathetic.

"What was he like?"

"Cheap red patent leather stiletto heels. Blue jeans. A peasant blouse. Hairy arms and legs. No makeup. Heavily boned. Male pattern baldness. It was pathetic and...and..."

"Yes?"

"He had this hopeless look in his eye. I recognized myself there. He looked how I feel – ugly and unnatural. I will never be beautiful."

"Is that what you want, to be beautiful?" she asked, moving closer and sounding genuinely curious.

"Womanly, would do. Genuinely womanly, so that when I feel that way, I can be accepted that way."

"I think a lot of that comes from inside. But do you really want to menstruate and have the pain that comes with it? Do you want the mood swings? Do you want less physical strength? Do you want the life of reduced possibilities that comes along with being a woman in this man's world? Have you really thought this through? Well, I'm sure you've been through all of this before. Anyway, there are a lot of women who aren't beautiful, not even cute, women who don't even look like women. There are all kinds of women. Believe me, Jackie you are much more feminine in some ways than many women I know – if we are talking about traditional views of womanhood."

"Such as?"

"You can't stop feeling for other people. You can't turn it off. You want not to care, but you do care even about people you don't like. And you feel betrayed by your own caring because you end up trying to do good things for people who hate you."

"Jeesus Christ!"

"Oh, does that hit a nerve?"

"You can't imagine."

"You know what I think your problem is? You keep falling into the same trap over and over again. You seem to want to be one or the other – male or female, but you keep bouncing between the two."

"No...no, that's wrong...I'm both...I think."

"You say that and you may believe it, but from what I've seen, you're not living it. Your situation looks to me like a pinball bouncing back and forth between two whatevers or something going back and forth between magnets. I don't know. It's weird. Anyway, you seem to be in some kind of vicious circle and somehow you have to break out of it."

"I know, I know."

"Music won't do that. It may provide a voice for you. We may end up hearing every exquisite note of your personal agony, but it won't free you and Obatala isn't going to come down from the sky or God or Allah and make things okay. They may reward your efforts, guide you, correct you, but they aren't going to do it for you. God, I sound like my mother, but it's true. I don't care. You have to do something to like yourself. You have to find a way."

"What if I make a big mistake?"

"Isn't there enough of you to make a few mistakes with?"

"I guess I don't think so."

"You're not serious. What do you think – that you'll just use yourself up and disappear?"

"No, but if I try everything and nothing works and there's nothing left to try…then –"

"Then Obatala will open –"

"Fuck Obatala, fuck it all. Oh Jesus Christ, have you ever been there? Have you? No. I didn't think so. Don't tell me what it's like to look everywhere for yourself and not be able to find yourself. This is not a little game. You get tired and when you get so tired that every thought hurts, you just want to stop hurting. I've been there. I've been where the only thing between a blade and these veins was fear. Can you understand that? God did nothing. Obatala did nothing. No god or goddess anywhere did anything. You know sometimes I think this whole life is a punishment for something I did in another life."

"Like what?"

"Well, there's a witch back home. I had her in an English class for a few days. Can you believe that? She took one look at me and dropped the course. She said I had been a Catholic priest during the middle ages, that I wrote the 'Malleus Maleficarum,' the 'Witches Hammer.' That was the book they used to recognize and prosecute witches. She believed I was responsible for the deaths of hundreds of thousands of witches."

"Of women."

"Yes…women."

"And you believe in a witch's ability to see things?"

"I…I…"

"You sometimes have this ability?"

"Yes…so…maybe…"

"Witches can be wrong, like anybody else. Maybe she just didn't like you. Maybe you're trying to become a woman to atone for what you believe to be true."

"No, whether or not it's true, I was like I am long before I met her."

"Have you tried just giving up? I mean just stop looking for explanations?"

"Ya, I tried Zen for that. You know – just doing spontaneously, without thinking. Didn't work. There's no me to get past my own thoughts."

"Oh brother."

"What?"

"There's no end to it is there?"

"Not that I've found. And I'm so sick of it. Of me."

"Are you ever at peace with it?"

"Only when I'm writing and the rage is howling. It's like I can almost write myself into being – see myself clear and real."

"And what are you like then?"

"I'm a diamond with all facets flashing – all the colors. The male, the female, everything between and everything beyond."

"Wow, ever had anything published?"

"No."

"Why not, it sounds so...transcendental, so spiritual...people would like to see life from that perspective. People need to see life like that. It's a good feeling, you say?"

"Yes, but maybe also I'm just really fucked up and what I write isn't nearly as good as I think it is. When I'm writing, it sounds like great stuff – true, real. Later, when the passion has passed, it reads like so much sentimental whining."

"Have you ever been possessed, Jackie?"

"What? You mean like by a demon?"

"No, I mean like by a good spirit like one of the Orishas."

"No...why?"

"You sound like a new hounsis who is afraid to be ridden because of what he might do or say. They're afraid of looking and sounding ridiculous. In fact, they should be honored when a spirit chooses them. They also honor the spirit by being willing to be ridden. It takes great faith and love. Perhaps your spirits just come and go as they please and it's hard for you to keep up, so you feel thrown around."

"I'm sorry, we are still talking about gender here aren't we?"

"I don't know about that. I'm talking about surrender. Perhaps not surrendering as you were born to do, you surrender only in little acts of softness but only when it's convenient for you. Father is conducting a ceremony downstairs tomorrow night. You would be welcome. You should come and watch. You might learn something. Less talk and more action, that's what you need."

The next day, when Jackie got home from the center, he was even more exhausted than the day before. He couldn't stop yawning, too tired even to eat. He had forgotten about the ceremony. The air was moist with dew and cool, the first undeniable touch of autumn. Someone had strung straw colored, paper lanterns up the path to the entrance. In the gathering darkness, they hung there gently rocking like fat fireflies. Something about the light and the air sent a surge of joy through him. The wind shifted and he caught the fragrance of incense. The dancing darknesses in the carriage house told him that someone had lit the main room, the temple area, with candles. As he watched, he realized that it was not people but the shadows of posts and furnishings that were moving.

"Excuse me" someone said from behind as they hurried past dressed head to toe in white clothing.

"Pardon" said another in a French accent, passing on the other side. They hurried up the old, cracked sidewalk, talking away happily into the building. Others followed.

"So, are you coming?" asked Natasha-Veronique, suddenly beside him. He protested that he had just arrived, was exhausted and didn't have the right clothes on. "Excuses, excuses. Tired is good. Maybe you won't be so tight. Anyway, do what you want. Come. Go. It is all the same. If it is for you to be there, you will be there. Nothing I can say makes any difference."

"*How at peace she seems,*" Jackie thought. "*As though everything will work out fine. How good it must feel to think like that. How restful and hopeful.*" And then he was walking with her and he felt the doorway go past him as he entered the room.

Her father seemed neither pleased nor displeased to see him. "*Odd,*" Jackie thought, "*He seems bigger.*" Everyone was standing and Jackie took a position along one wall where he would have a good view. There was an altar of sorts – a white, jeweled robe and flowers, Christian and Vodoun signs and symbols, images of saints and orishas. Bouquets of flowers, large and tiny, filled the room. A fragrance of ginger and other spices moved on the air currents. Gradually, the voices quieted and without a sign everyone turned to the houngan, the priest – Natasha-Veronique's father no more. Here stood a man beyond the place and time. He glided through his movements, motioning to the gathered faithful. At a gesture, drummers began a deep, resonant beat that seemed somehow to take the edges off the room. A slow, heartbeat of a sound. Then the houngan had a chicken by the feet and wheeled it aloft, before dispatching it so quickly Jackie could not see how it was done.

Others had filled in between him and the center of the action. A glimpse here and there was the best he could do. Words were said in French, English and a language foreign to him. Though he could not grasp all of the meaning, their musicality and trance inducing qualities were somehow familiar. He felt like he was back in the Zen temple chanting with the sangha. He could see it all so clearly, could feel the chill December wind of those days issue in through the open windows as the cadence rising to feverish intensity before ending in an impassioned whisper of the last syllables.

...the path is one
the path is one
when all is said and done and done
the path is one
...the journey ever is the guide
no demons left to tear aside
each moment glistening in the light.
each place a place to take delight

"*The rhythm,*" he thought, "*the drumming must be getting to me...and the exhaustion.*" Were people moving away from him? He thought so. For an instant, he realized he was mumbling the beautiful words from his past – yet not mumbling. In fact, he caught himself grumbling a low, quiet, unnerving growl. The ones who moved away from him seemed to do so almost as though on cue. They showed no surprise or discomfort. He wondered if they even knew they were doing it. Anyway, it improved his view of the room. Then suddenly, there in front of him, stood the Poteau Mitan, the central pillar of the ceremonies. The houngan was standing just to one side. It seemed to Jackie that the man shot a glance in his direction while turning in time to the drumbeat. Perspiration was forming into a shiny film on his forehead. He was speaking rapidly now, holding aloft object after object – fruit, flowers, a cornucopia of offerings. From his mouth, he sprayed liquid into the air and gestured with his hands. It felt something like a wiccan cone of power being raised. It felt like those special Zen moments when chanting voices made a synergetic leap onto a new dynamic and everyone felt transported. Jackie felt hot. If he could have sat down, he would have. *"Maybe,"* he thought, *"the whole obsessive travel to Europe had finally taken its toll."* Despite a background euphoria that he could not account for, he felt distinctly unwell, felt danger – all of his psychic and emotional warning bells going off at once. He felt like he was fighting, but what? Why couldn't he stop thinking? His mind – he couldn't stop the thoughts filling it. *"What the fuck am I doing here with all of these people?"* He asked himself. There was no denying it. He was the only person in the room who wasn't black, who wasn't a follower. He looked at the faces and the more intensely he looked, the less real they seemed. No one made eye contact with him. Soon he noticed that he was swaying, had been swaying for who knows how long, just like all the others. *"Hell, no one is looking at any one,"* he thought. He felt a mild sense of panic like a meditator awaking suddenly from the depths of his thought to find himself hardly breathing. But here it was different. There was no sense of rejoining the familiar, the known. This was more a recognition that one is in the midst of a lucid dream state. Everyone in the room was moving, maybe it was a dance. He thought the tempo had increased. He was getting hotter. He could not remember drinking anything and yet he knew he was not in his right mind. As much as he felt apprehensive, he felt elation. A nameless joy without reason as far as he could tell. Maybe, he thought, someone had slipped him something. A girl once had slipped a large quantity of LSD into his drink on a blind date. The only way he had gotten through it with his synapses in one piece was to yield to it completely. Lightning had flashed before his eyes right there in the her room. Moments later, they were making wild, passionate love. In the morning, while she slept, he left and cursed her, amazed to find himself still sane.

Psychics, he had learned the hard way, should never take drugs. Universes one is not prepared for come calling, open up unbidden, before one is ready to deal with the realities. Better to stay sober and make what progress is possible, one meditation at a time, then one can function in any world that opens. He felt now, like he felt then. And either the Poteau – Mitan was moving toward him or he toward it. Either way, the two of them were getting closer. Again the houngan fired a brief look in his direction, then made a gesture in the air. Instantly, two large, male helpers appeared from either side of the pole, their arms outstretched. For a moment, Jackie had the absurd thought that he was a ballet dancer and they were preparing to lift him into the air. "*It must be a hallucination,*" he thought, but then he was there and almost in their arms. Just before he reached them, however, he had an acute sensation, first of being emptied, then of being filled. Then time and space became completely meaningless and he was being lifted – and if not lifted, then he was flying. The two helpers had seen him coming, had seen the signs…the look in the eye, something odd in his movement and, as importantly, the way people moved around him. When he reached them, he collapsed completely for a moment and they held him up. Then the houngan was before him.

"Obatala, we welcome you, great Orisha."

Suddenly, rainbows were dancing along the edges of each thing in the room. Jackie's heart soared at the beauty and the majesty of it. It was the last thing he remembered.

Natasha-Veronique watched, very little surprised, as the great master of all heads rode Jackie's body. His petit bon ange, she knew had temporarily left him to make room for the great orisha, Creator of all living things. The houngan stepped aside as Obatala, now in his old man form, bent over and stiff, moved past him to the offerings table. He lifted the vessel into which the chicken's blood had been drained and drank from it. When he turned again, it was a woman moving sensuously to the drumbeat.

At the center of the room, the expressive eyes of the woman rolled back as she tilted her head to one side, a wrist posed on her hip which was seductively thrust out to the side. When her eyes rolled back and her body straightened, both legs were replanted firmly astride and both hands went to her hips in a posture of defiance. The eyes hardened and narrowed and the orisha scanned the throng of bodies. It walked against the flow of the dancers who were circling the room now even faster, singled out a female hounsis and stood directly in the terrified girl's path. The helpers appeared as though on cue. Jackie collapsed into their arms and suddenly the girl was possessed as the orisha transferred to her body. Jackie was taken off to a corner of the room and laid out on the floor to sleep until such time as he would return to his senses. At some point, an hour or so later, as Natasha-Veronique would tell it, his ti bon ange did indeed return to him as he slowly regained his wits.

"If you only knew –" she said with a broad smile and a look of wonder – "how you have been honored. Outsiders are very rarely ridden. I cannot remember the last time. Oh, Jackie, this is wonderful. I am so happy for you. How do you feel?"

"I can't make sense of it."

"What do you mean?"

"I don't know how I feel. Okay, I just need to be alone for a while."

"Jackie...what's wrong?" But he did not answer, struggling instead slowly to his feet and gesturing toward the floor as though trying to quiet a room full of voices.

"I can't," he said.

"Can't what?"

"I can't. I can't. It's too much."

"I know. Jackie, it's okay, I know" she said, moving closer.

"It's too much."

"Time will give you perspective. Give yourself time."

"I mean, what just happened? What really happened?" After some thought, Natasha-Veronique clasped her hands in front of her and tightened slightly.

"An orisha showed you something that it thought you were ready to see?"

"But I wasn't. I can't take any more. I saw so much – you wouldn't believe. Now I have more questions than I had before. I need answers, not more questions. That's why I'm here. That's why I came all the way –"

"The orishas do not make mistakes. Maybe questions are your answer."

"What does that mean?"

"I don't know. I don't know why I said it. What do you want to do?"

"I want to go...home." He said the word before he could stop himself.

"Home?"

"Upstairs. I want to get really drunk and play the piano until I pass out on it. I want to stop thinking."

"Okay. I need to sleep. If you need anything, wake me up." She took a long look at him, then turned to go but stopped at the door. "Jackie...don't do anything silly, okay?"

"Okay."

"Promise?"

"Promise. Cross my heart and..."

"Just cross your heart." Jackie slowly made the sign of the cross over his heart as she turned again for the door.

He made his way upstairs and slumped over the piano, his arms outstretched. One finger found a key way up the high notes and pressed it. Like a small bird's cry, the faint sound found the air and was gone. A finger on his other hand found a deep note on the other end. He felt it more than he heard it as the vibration carried from the soundboard through the mahogany of the piano, up through his body. It seemed to last a long time. *"Ya, deep things last the longest,"* he thought, *"nothing new here. High notes don't last."* His mind was awash in images and he felt he had no more identity than anything inundated and awash in any ocean. An ocean of questions and feelings. And no part of him any longer coherent, cohesive enough to attempt answers or process what he felt. It was beyond depression. Only his fear of death prevented him from finding a way to end the pain. If life took one beyond what could be endured, what hideous experience might the next life hold. Only the thought of an eternal hell for suicides kept him from ending it. In a way, he welcomed the thought of his body's complete self-destruction. If he could just step back from it and be patient, avoid complicity in it. Go to the next life, broken but guiltless, perhaps everything would finally be okay on some cosmic scale. But he did feel sorry for himself. He did allow himself that. He felt like life asking itself a question it could not answer and stay whole. And so, ultimately, he felt like a fool. Like the Fool of the Tarot cards. A prettily dressed young man, purse slung over his shoulder, carrying a white flower of innocence in a gently bent hand, stepping, oblivious, off a cliff.

"The rainbows around everything, what did the rainbows mean," he asked himself. And everything had looked as though he was seeing it through a blue filter after that. Faces had melted, had gone forward and backward in time. He himself had aged and

regressed, felt brittle and then young and dynamic. He had been female, had been male and all the while, conscious of an expression of self that was changeless, secure, whole. For an instant, everything had made sense and the universe had seemed to have a point. If only he could remember. But the orisha or whatever it had been, was gone now. At a loss to understand, he sunk to his knees beside the piano.

"Well, here I am Lord...more screwed up than ever and as you know, it's all too much again. We both know I don't have the guts to kill myself. Whatever." He gathered himself into a posture of serious prayer, hands clasped, head down, eyes closed. "Please put into my head the thoughts that will keep me on the path that you approve of. Please put into my heart, the feelings that you approve of. Where I've been wrong in my thinking or feeling, please show me. I always thought good was being myself. Now I don't know anymore. In the name of the mercy and love of our Lord, Jesus Christ, I pray that you will enter my life so I really know it's you, and show me your will. Otherwise, I guess I'll just have to keep on keeping on the best way I know how." Watching from the bedroom, Natasha-Veronique could only shake her head and silently close the door.

The next day, Jackie got up late and made his way to Maximus, hoping to do something physical. Stacking boxes would have been good, sweeping floors. Anything to get his mind off of the new reality the Vodoun ceremony had dropped into his life. He walked up to the door in a black tunic over black tights and a pair of black, mid-heeled sandals that he had picked up at a sale. The young woman clerk had been most helpful. The world, he realized was changing slowly after all.

"They suit you," she had said. He had wondered if she really meant it. At the door, he was met by Mila.

"Oh, Jackie, is there some theatre today? Nobody told me. Do I need to set up chairs or prepare something?"

"No, Mila. This is me."

"What do you mean this is you?"

"I'm a woman and a man, Mila. Sometimes I dress for the woman, sometimes for the man." He sounded sure of himself. But he was losing his nerve. What had possessed him to show up, en femme, he could not imagine. The leers, sneers and giggles he had passed on the way seemed so distant. He had almost felt sorrow for the people who stared at him. They were, he felt, part of a smaller reality, a tight and narrow understanding of life. The possession or the prayer had changed him. For a while, he had somehow gotten beyond registering disapproval of others. As arrogant as it seemed to him, he did feel that he had embarked almost on a kind of separate, parallel reality where people like him were normal. The caretaker was dressed in coarse, black overalls with a heavy, off white, knit sweater, her gray hair cascading down over the collar. She was, he thought, the funkiest old woman he had ever met. She was handsome, experienced, and full of life. The slight arch in her back, the callused hands attested to that.

"But you are such a nice young...I mean you were, before now, such a nice young man. Oi, oi, oi, what the world is coming to, I don't know. And your mother, what does she say?"

"My mother says she wishes she was dead, Mila."

"Oh...I see...so...there is nothing...to do. No...I guess not." Grief spread out across her face. At any other time, Jackie would have found her response turning his own gaze into his own soul. He would have felt guilty for causing someone else anguish and then resentful for having felt the guilt. Now, he felt only indifference.

"Whoa, Jackie" said the young woman at the reception desk as he entered the main hallway. "You look so...different. I mean – "

"I know. What needs to be done?"

"Well" she said, flustered, "Let me see." She checked behind her on the wall where workers who were in or out were marked on a whiteboard. "I'm not really sure. I mean you can't really work like that, can you?"

"No, I don't suppose so."

"Still, Andrea's not in yet...some kind of car trouble. She was going to look after the sitting room today. You know she has a list of street kids that she meets with – just to give them someone to check in with and keep an eye on things. I think you know a few of them. You could just do that 'till she slows up and give a brief orientation to anybody new who comes in. But –"

She continued looking him up and down, "are you going to change or what?"

"No, I'm not going to change. What you see is what you get...for now."

"Okay" she said doubtfully. "Does Veronica know...that you're here? Do you want me to tell her?" By then, two other assistants behind the counter had joined the woman and were working hard to hide their surprise at his appearance. Jackie caught every motion of their eyes and lips.

"No, I'll probably bump into her later."

"Oh my God" someone said from the reception desk as he entered the sitting room.

"Shhhhh" someone responded.

The first thing to capture his attention was a ten-foot mahogany table. A big chunk had been knocked off one of the pedestal bases recently. Its blond core contrasted sharply with the dark wood veneer. The slanted rays of the morning sun served up the table's imperfections – the stains, the scars, the uneven edges where fingernails had chipped off bits of wood. Indestructible metal auditorium chairs were stacked against a wall. Too long lace curtains trailed on the floor both sides of the large window. A too small lampshade had been fitted around the single light bulb in the ceiling. A threadbare imitation Persian carpet lay in the center of the floor. In a corner of the room, four dilapidated sofas made a small, enclosed space. Along one wall, sagging shelving held a chaotic assortment of cheap adventure novels, well thumbed comic books, support service pamphlets, serious novels and a couple of old National Geographic magazines. A door slammed somewhere, then a small, nervous boy dressed in leather and a dog collar with spikes was standing in the doorway.

"Where's Andrea?" he demanded.

"She's not in yet."

"Why not?"

"She had some car –"

"When is she going to be here?"

"I guess –"

"I'll come back." The boy turned and walked out, then turned again. "Are you...a guy or a chick or what?"

"Or what."

"Shit" the boy muttered as he left.

"Duhhhhhhh" Jackie intoned, parrying the word. He walked over to the table and placed his hand on it. It was smooth and warm. He sat down facing into the sun and closed his eyes.

"Excuse me" a voice sounded from behind him. "Excuse me. They told me I could find Andrea here. Are you Andrea?" Jackie turned to face the stranger. "Oh, I'm sorry. They said –"

"That's okay. She's not here yet. Can I help you?"

"Well, I think I'll just wait around, if you don't mind. I came by earlier in the week and they said I really should speak with her if you know what I mean."

"No, I'm afraid I don't. I don't know her. I'm just filling in."

"The world is changing so fast," said the woman. She was in her late forties. A kind face. Patient. The face of a mother who had seen the trials and tribulations of children. She had a great smile and her voice was rich and resonant. She gazed aimlessly around the room, took a couple of directionless steps. "Do you work here?"

"Yes, off and on, whenever they need me. I'm just filling in for Andrea until she gets here, so maybe you would like to —"

"Oh no, that's okay. It's not your usual problem."

"Well, if you want to talk, I'll be here." He took a book from the shelf and laid it on the table, facing again into the sun. He closed his eyes and drank in its warmth. Sensations and images from the Vodoun ceremony kept imposing themselves on his thought. He began to follow his breath.

"Kids...I don't know...you want the best for them..." The fact that his back was turned didn't seem to make any difference to the woman. Maybe, he thought, it was easier for her that way. He could hear her emotional exhaustion. "You know they're going to go their own way. I can't believe I'm here. When did you say she's going to get here?"

"I don't really know. They just said she had car trouble."

"So, she might not get here at all."

"I guess."

"Okay. I'll give it a few minutes and then I'll try again later."

"Okay." The floorboard creaked as she moved slowly about the room behind him. Jackie imagined how huge the sound would be if he had a piano to fill its spare expanse.

"I guess queers have it pretty hard eh, Jackie."

"I have no idea." She was fishing. He didn't feel like biting.

"Of course. I didn't mean...I mean they do a lot of counseling here at Maximus in that area."

"Yes. It's one of the things they do." By the sound of it, she had just sat down on one of the sofas. Five or ten minutes passed and Jackie's mind had turned to the return air ticket he had in his backpack. In a little over a week, it would be decision time. He would either be on the British Airways flight back across the Atlantic or he would not. It had been a long time since he had meditated. He felt a strong need to do so. To get beyond the many thoughts and feelings that filled him to overflowing. *"And maybe that is somehow part of it,"* he thought – being filled, just like the cup of the wiccan rites. A receptacle for life. A vessel of perception and sense. No, it was all too weird. When he meditated, he would transcend such imagery. Gone would be the names of things and all existential handholds. He would make of himself an emptiness, to be filled by the teaching that brings with it serene, detached, understanding. He believed that such rain could fall when the earth was right and ready. But time was running out. Money was running out and all his fine plans would soon be ground into nothingness by the plodding of customs officers and flight attendants with their safety instructions.

What had it all been about? Did he know himself, feel one iota better about himself than before he cast himself upon the European unknown? He was different, more confused. Nothing was resolved. Maybe it was all a big waste of time. He tried to remember exactly the thoughts and feelings that had brought him to this place and time. Fear. That was it. Fear and desperation. Fear of being alone with a self that could not be lived. But to be honest, he had not thought about ending his life since he had arrived in Greece. Why was that, he wondered. How gently, imperceptibly, the thought had left him, replaced, he supposed by the myriad distractions that present themselves to any traveler. Once the novelty was gone, once the things he was seeing, he was no longer seeing for the first time, then his old life would resurface. Once he had eased himself back into the familiar, he thought, his own strangeness would be inescapable again. A transgender in a room of straight people. He thought he might as well be on another planet.

"Do you mind if I ask you a personal question?" the woman asked.

"No, I don't mind."

"Are you a drag queen?"

"No. Drag queens are gay. I'm not gay."

"Oh, then you're a transvestite."

"No. Transvestites are straight males who get their jollies dressing and acting like women."

"Oh…" The woman paused in her confusion. "So why are you dressed that way?"

"Have I asked you why you came in here looking so frumpy?" Jackie thought.

"You're a woman. The guy who just walked out is a man. I'm a transgender."

"The last time I checked, there were only two genders," she said with mild condescension.

"Maybe you should check again" Jackie replied, echoing her tone.

"Gosh…I'm confused. I guess I really don't know what I'm talking about, do I?"

"It's a confusing subject. Is there a problem with your boy?"

"Well yes. That's why I'm here."

"Would you like to talk about it?"

"Well, yes. I guess –"

"I'll never buy another English car as long as I live!" a voice exclaimed from the entry hall. Then the door slammed. They're such absolute shit. Good morning girls!"

"Good morning, Andrea." This was followed by some loud whispers.

"Mrs. Tate?" the woman asked from the doorway, though her eyes were focussed on Jackie.

"Yes."

"Hi. I'm Andrea. I'm so sorry to be late, but I've had an absolutely beastly morning. If you'll just follow me, we can get started tout de suite." She was very shapely. About six feet tall. Fiery red hair. Tight, sleeveless leopard print dress. Four-inch heels and 1920's rhinestone sun glasses. "You're Raymond's mom?"

"Yes, that's right."

"Oh my gosh, what are you trying to do to us, Charlene?" the woman called to the reception area, "This place must be a hundred degrees? Can't you do something? Are you hot, Mrs. Tate?"

"Well, no –"

"How am I supposed to work in these conditions?" She removed her wide brimmed, white straw hat with a flourish, yellow ribbons trailing behind like the tail of a kite. Jackie recognized the voice as male. The contrived falsetto, the bigger than life intonation, the elongation of descriptive words, the catty edge to the statements. It was a stage voice, designed for effect. Same for the body language. *"Hit us over the head, why don't you,"* he thought. Mrs. Tate rose as instructed but looked, hesitatingly, to Jackie. He, however, had already decided not to get involved. He was no match, he knew for the rapier-like repartee of the average drag queen. Nor did he take pleasure in the linguistic cat and mouse games that seemed so much a part of that scene. Andrea had already noticed the woman's lack of enthusiasm. "I'm so sorry," she said. Did I interrupt something?"

"No" Jackie replied, playing with one of his earrings, "we were just chatting." In a state of obvious alarm, Mrs. Tate followed Andrea out of the room to discuss Raymond's problem. Jackie felt the room return to itself – silence creeping outward from the last place of sound, the energy smoothing, easing to a calm evenness. <u>Diamonds of the World</u> read the title of the book he had taken from the shelf. On the cover, an exquisite, brilliant-cut gem sparkled against a black velvet background. *"As black,"* he thought *"as the hearts of people who disapprove of people like me."* As black as God's silence.

It seemed pretentious to think of himself as a diamond, something so precious and rare, but he couldn't help himself. Was he, he wondered, also formed the way he was as a result of great forces. Carbon subjected to forces so intense that he became a kind of clarity that could split light into rainbows. *"Am I a prism of some kind? Is that why I'm constantly feeling, constantly changing?"* He didn't even understand what he was asking himself, but he did feel an immediate affinity for the image that lay in his lap. Diamonds were few and far between. Some people, he knew, think that to be part of a small group, a different group, is to be, somehow, less. The majority is the majority precisely because a greater number of people agreed on some facet of reality. But diamonds, he knew, were no less in meaning or value than the expanses of undifferentiated rock in which they occurred just because they were fewer and occupied space differently. *"Obviously,"* he thought, *"you can't have diamonds without having a lot of less spectacular stuff in which to find them."* Then he remembered how many times he had wished he could be like the majority. Suddenly, the absurdity of a diamond wishing it could be like the crud surrounding it occurred to him. He began reading.

Diamonds, it said, were only found in certain deposits, which amounted to different kinds of rock. Reading on, he realized that the diamond owed its existence in part to the very mass that had enclosed it and exerted such pressure on it. The very unspectacular mass had created something infinitely harder and clearer, and in the right light, more brilliant, than itself – a splitter of light, an enduring rainbow maker. The irony hit him like a clap of thunder. And the need to live his life in some kind of light seemed suddenly important and urgent. The notion of the rock mass accepting or rejecting the diamond seemed ridiculous. He waited for some flaw to appear in the analogy. Diamonds, he knew, had flaws. Diamonds also got released from the ground, got cut and polished. He would deal with the last part of the analogy later and scribbled some notes about it in his book. Suddenly, the book that he had absent-mindedly taken from the shelf seemed like a blessing, a gift. Spirits, he knew, did that kind of thing from time to time. Humans took it for coincidence or synchronicity. So, for a moment, he felt himself to be part of some context that made sense, something he could feel a part of, however abstract the concept. A diamond in the fertile landscape of straight culture. In the fertile landscape of gay culture. *"Who would have thought it,"* he mused. Diamonds don't make diamonds. They just make life richer for everyone else by doing pleasant things with the light – God's light, and by being hard enough to stay genuine in the face of the world's disapproval. If only, he thought, he could maintain the ideas that were in his mind, keep the confidence and sense of worth he now had. How to do pleasant things with God's light. That was the question.

"How's it going? They told me you had come in. That's a nice look." It was Natasha-Veronique coming into the room as Jackie turned. "Oh, why so serious?"

"I've got a lot on my mind as usual."

"And you're thinking about leaving?"

"Time is getting short. Ya, I guess that's been in the background for a while now. To be honest, I'm dreading going back and my flight is in a few days."

"Is it really so bad in America?"

"America, the America I know is a gray stoneland of the spirit. A bunch of tight, money grubbing people who judge everything. And they're all ethical anarchists."

"Maybe you can change some of them."

"I came here to change myself."

"And have you?"

"I...don't know. I'm...still alive. I can dress and act as I feel here, but it's not real. Let's face it, I'm on holiday...kind of. I can do what I want. When I go back, I'll have to get another job, and I'm afraid the magic will just evaporate. Things are so exotic and interesting and...old here. Back home, there's no depth. Everything is new. I mean c'mon, you have street lamps here older than my country."

"Does that matter?"

"Ya, it does somehow. It's like...no, this is too corny."

"Go on."

"Well it's like you aren't a part of anything deep, anything old."

"Oh boy, I really cannot believe you. You inspired the lyrics to 'Child of the Universe.' Do you remember working on that with me? Am I talking to the same person?" It was true. It was a brave and inclusive song celebrating man's spiritual nature and rooting his being in the heavens. It was a positive song. A song of hope, celebration and deep conviction that spoke of flying and dreaming and breaking through the chains that bind, of opening eyes that could no longer see.

"And now you're going to stand here and tell me you don't want to go home. Do you just do this for kicks? Is it some kind of game to you?"

"I –"

"If you're a child of the universe, what the hell does it matter where you fucking live? I'm sorry, but you're really pissing me off."

"I –"

"You know bloody well who you are. You've always known. You knew it so clearly you almost killed yourself. And why would you do that?" She was shouting at him. "Tell me that. No answer? Then I'll tell you. You're afraid of your birthright. You're scared shitless. You think if you let go, even for a moment, something terrible is going to happen to you. That you'll fly out the window, fly straight out of your body and never get back in. And the longer you stay with your trembling feet holding tight to the perch, the more something inside you is grieving. God, no wonder you're so bloody depressed all the time. And if you go crazy in the process, so fucking what? I mean look where you are for God's sake."

She motioned passionately around the empty room, her eyes on fire. Jackie couldn't get the point.

"This is a place for hurting people, hurting, desperate people. And how do most of them get that way – it's called life on planet earth. People who don't know their source making life miserable for everyone else. And people like you who have some vague inkling. You see enough about how people turn their backs on the…Creator to be outraged and you don't have enough faith to protect yourself. God, you're like a fledgling eagle that's too afraid of the fall to flap your wings." She was almost screaming at him, poking at him with each phrase until he was backed into the sunshine near the table again. "Who are you?" she yelled.

"Duh."

"You know what I mean, who are you?"

"Natasha, would you please –"

"Come on girl. Humor me. Don't think about it. Say it! Who are you? Say it!"

At that moment, something snapped and Jackie's heart rate shot up. He wanted to smack her. He wanted to be anywhere but there. He felt like something was shifting within him.

"Back off. You don't know –"

"What is it Jackie? It's okay in a song. It's okay in your notebook. Questions and metaphors, doodles and poems. Pithy little aphorisms. All nice and safe. Who are you Jackie, at source?"

"*The journey has been a fraud,*" he thought. He felt it now. It had been an escape. He could see now he had not the slightest possibility of setting himself on any kind of path to anywhere. "*What does any of it matter,*" he wondered. "*Does anyone else on the planet really know any more about himself than I do? Maybe they're just satisfied with surface effects. All the psychiatrists, the counselors, the religious zealots – aren't they all, at core, safe, middle class citizens leading safe, middle class lives, all the time judging the rest of us who are out here on the edge asking real, dangerous questions? And I've been looking to them for acceptance? Oh shit, what have I been doing? Maybe there is no real loneliness when the only other choice is acceptance by those who deny life."* A breakthrough of some kind felt imminent.

"I'm a spirit." Natasha-Veronique's body relaxed and her tone became softer but clever. She sat on the table and ran her hand over its warm surface.

"How do you explain your body?"

"It's...it's a thing I live in to experience this world for a time."

"Why would you want to do that?"

"I have something to learn?"

"A spirit" she said with derision. Was it sincere or faked? "that can fly around the universe, needs to go into a mortal, human body to learn a lesson? Please."

"How should I know? Maybe, spirits don't know who they are either. Maybe we're all working it out."

"Not all."

"No. That's the problem. If we were all working it out, it wouldn't be a problem."

"They can't."

"I know."

"It's too much for most of them."

"It's too much for me."

"So stop, Jackie."

"I can't."

"Can't or don't want to?"

"Nothing else seems as important."

"I know what you mean, girl."

"We're the death of the party."

"The rain on the parade."

"The Grinch that stole Christmas."

"The wet blanket."

"The bores."

"The basket cases."

"Yah."

"Yah...So where does that leave you, Jackie?"

"Alone. Just like anybody else who is trying to work the big stuff out."

"Do you know where the word comes from?"

"What word?"

"Alone."

"No idea."

"In Old English, around 900 A.D., when a Viking could come around the next corner without warning, to be "al áne" – all one, alone, was to be whole, self-sufficient, able to exist on one's own. Only today, does it mean isolated, lonely."

"Alone was a good thing?"

"It beat, as you say, a kick in the pants."

"Like a diamond."

"What's that?"

"Nothing, just a book I was reading."

"I think your god wants you to learn a delicate thing, something to do with being alone. I think that's why your god doesn't talk to you. The silence is necessary."

"Like the space between the notes?"

"Like the space between the notes."

"Are you telling me it was this simple all along. I can't –"

"Imagine a music where there was never any space between the notes. The problem with the world is it has forgotten to play legato or plays legato too damn much – I don't know which." Jackie struggled to understand, but could not. Veronica smiled sadly at his anguish. "So," she said taking his hand and lifting it, "this is meant to make some kind of music." With her thumb, she stroked the underside of his forearm, "even when they are telling you to carve it." Only then did he glimpse the pale slash marks on her own slender wrist.

ISBN 142512546-8